P9-CSC-213

Essentials of
Accounting

Sixth Edition

Robert N. Anthony

Harvard Business School

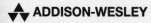 **ADDISON-WESLEY**

An imprint of Addison Wesley Longman, Inc.

Reading, Massachusetts • Harlow, England • Menlo Park, California
Berkeley, California • Don Mills, Ontario • Sydney
Bonn • Amsterdam • Tokyo • Mexico City

for Katherine

Publishing Partner: Michael Roche
Sponsoring Editor: Kate Morgan
Production Supervisor: Patricia A. Oduor
Composition: Jacqueline Davies
Text Design: Marie E. McAdam
Cover Designer: Trudi Gershenov
Illustrators: ST Associates/George Nichols
Supervisor of Manufacturing: Hugh Crawford

The Coca-Cola® logo appearing on page 21 is a registered trademark of the Coca-Cola Company. Used with permission of the Coca-Cola Company.

The 7•UP® logo appearing on page 21 is a registered trademark of the Seven-Up Company. Used with permission of the Seven-Up Company.

Library of Congress Cataloging-in-Publication Data

Anthony, Robert Newton, 1916–
    Essentials of accounting / Robert N. Anthony.—6th ed.
      p. cm.
    ISBN 0-201-84866-X (pbk.)
    1. Accounting.   I. Title
HF5635.A6879   1996
657—dc20   96-34147
                                        CIP

Reprinted with corrections, June 1999

Copyright © 1997, 1993, 1988, 1983, 1976, 1964 by Addison-Wesley Publishing Company, Inc.
All rights reserved. No part of this publication may be reproduced, stored in a retrieval system, or transmitted, in any form or by any means, electronic, mechanical, photocopying, recording, or otherwise, without the prior written permission of the publisher. Printed in the United States of America.

5 6 7 8 9 10-CRS-01 00 99

YOU MAY BE INTERESTED IN . . .

A Review of
Essentials of Accounting, 6th Edition

This handy 6" × 9" paperback volume contains the complete text and examples in *Essentials of Accounting, 6th Edition*, but without the programmed questions and responses. It features:

- An expanded accounting glossary with over 500 terms
- A summary of financial accounting concepts
- An explanation of financial statements
- An introduction to the preparation and use of financial accounting information

Two ways to order!

To order by phone, call 1-800-822-6339. Outside the U.S., please call 617-944-3700 ext. 5190

To order by mail, please complete and mail the handy coupon below!

-- *cut here* --

	Price	**Quantity**	**Subtotal**
A Review of Essentials of Accounting ISBN 0-201-44278-7	$21.45 ×	_____ =	_____
		plus Local Sales Tax	_____
		Total	_____

Name _____

Address _____

City/State _____ Zip _____

Phone Number _____

Addison-Wesley's Guarantee of Satisfaction: If you are not satisfied with any title, return it within 30 days and we'll refund the full amount paid. Price subject to change without notice. Price good in U.S. only.

❑ Yes, I want to save! My check or money order for the total order (including local sales tax) is enclosed with this form. Addison-Wesley will pay the postage and handling, and I'll get the same return privileges outlined in the Guarantee of Satisfaction.

❑ Please charge my order to my credit card. I understand that I'll be charged for local sales tax, plus shipping and handling. If I'm not completely satisfied with any book, I can return it within 30 days for a full credit to my account.

❑ VISA   ❑ MasterCard   ❑ American Express

Acct. #_____ Exp. date _____

Signature _____
Please Sign Here (Offer invalid unless signed)

Please ship via ❑ U.S. Mail   ❑ U.P.S. ground

Place this form in an envelope and mail it to Addison-Wesley Publishing Company, 1 Jacob Way, Reading, MA 01867. Attn. Order Department.

Contents

The following is in a separate booklet attached to the back of the book.

Introduction

This book will help you teach yourself the essential ideas of accounting. You will learn what accounting information can—and cannot—tell you about an organization.

Accounting is the principal way of organizing and reporting financial information. Although there are differences in detail, the general structure and rules are similar in most countries and in most types of organizations.

Accounting has been called the language of business. Learning this language is complicated by the fact that many words used in accounting do not mean quite the same thing as they mean in everyday life. When using accounting words, it is important that you understand their accounting meaning.

As in any language, some accounting rules and terms have a single correct meaning, and others are like dialects in that their meaning varies with different users. You will learn to understand and allow for these differences.

HOW TO USE THIS PROGRAM

This program consists of "frames." Each frame asks you to DO something: answer a question, make a calculation, fill in blanks. But these frames are NOT tests. As in most learning experiences, you learn by doing. You should be able to complete most frames without difficulty.

Procedures

- Read each frame in the left-hand column, while covering the right-hand column with the mask provided.

- *Write* your response in the space provided. Experience has shown that if you don't write your response, you will not retain nearly as much information.

- Check your response by moving the mask so as to uncover the correct response in the right-hand column.

- If your response is correct, go to the next frame. Otherwise, study the frame again and try to understand why you were wrong.

- Some frames refer you to *Exhibits*. These are in a separate booklet. Remove it and use it when you are asked to do so.

- At the end of each part, there is a post test; you will find it in the separate booklet. When you have completed a part, complete the post test. If you have difficulty with it, review the frames on this topic.

- Do not skip frames. If you have difficulty with a particular point, go back to the frame in which it was first mentioned and review from there.

- NOTE: Halfway through the book, the pages reverse so that the response column will always be on the right-hand side of the page.

Technical Conventions

_____ = Fill in the one word that is missing.

.... = Fill in the one *or more* words that are missing.

— — — — — = Fill in the letters that are missing, one to each underline.

... [Yes / No] = Underline or circle the correct alternative.

INSTRUCTOR'S GUIDE

An Instructor's Guide is available for the Sixth Edition. The Instructor's Guide contains an overview of the text, instructions on how to use *Essentials of Accounting*, and quiz and examination material. This manual is provided free upon adoption.

The Instructor's Guide may be obtained by contacting your local Addison Wesley Longman sales representative, by calling 1-800-552-2499, or by writing to:

Business and Economics Marketing
Higher Education Publishing Group
Addison Wesley Longman
1 Jacob Way
Reading, MA 01867

Part 1

Basic Concepts and the Balance Sheet

Learning Objectives

In this part you will learn:

• The nature of the balance sheet.

• The accounting meaning of assets, liabilities, and equity.

• The first three of the nine concepts that govern all accounting:

    • The dual-aspect concept.

    • The money-measurement concept.

    • The entity concept.

1-1. Accounting is a language. The purpose of any language is to convey information. Accounting information is provided by reports called **financial statements**. This program helps you understand what the numbers in the financial statements mean and how they can be used. Please tear out Exhibit 1 (in the separate booklet) to see one of these financial statements. As indicated by the title at the top of the page, this report is called a _ _ _ _ _ _ _ **sheet**.

Balance

On an item like this, fill in one letter for each underline and then compare it with the correct answer, found here.

NOTE: Be sure to cover up the answers with the mask provided.

CONCLUDING NOTE

You now know the *essentials* of accounting. There is, of course, much more to the subject. Nevertheless, you now have a basic framework into which you can fit many other transactions when you encounter them. Moreover, notes are added to the financial statements which help explain them and give more detail than the statements themselves. You should always read these notes carefully.

We have used a common set of terms throughout this program. Unfortunately, there is no standard set of terms. Companies can use other terminology. Nevertheless, from your knowledge of the nature of the balance sheet and the income statement, you can usually figure out what is meant by a term that is not used in this program.

Some transactions are governed by specific rules that are not described in this introductory treatment. For further study, see Robert N. Anthony and James S. Reece, *Accounting Principles*, 7th ed. (Homewood, Illinois: Richard D. Irwin, Inc., 1995).

ACKNOWLEDGMENTS

Dr. Matthew Israel developed the program for the First Edition.

Dr. Philip E. Meyers, Boston University, developed the original Glossary.

Prof. David L. Schwarzkopf, Bentley College, revised the Glossary and post tests for the Fifth Edition. He also made many helpful suggestions for the text.

Illustrations were developed by C. Stewart Anthony, Phil Carver, Jerrold E. Moore, and Carol Flaherty. Illustrations in the Sixth Edition were revised by George Nichols.

Student testing for the Fifth Edition was conducted by Prof. Joseph Hilmy, George Washington University.

The following made suggestions that were helpful in preparing this program: Patricia P. Douglas, University of Montana; Philip G. Edwards; Adolf Enthoven, University of Texas at Dallas; Michelle H. Hamar, University of Massachusetts at Boston; Julie H. Hertenstein, Harvard Business School; David L. Johnson, University of St. Thomas; Donald E. Keller, California State University, Long Beach; Steven Lilien, Baruch College; James L. McKenney, Harvard Business School; Owen D. Murray, Arthur D. Little School of Management; Leslie Pearlman, Boston University; Suresh Radhakrishnan, Rutgers University; Claudia Raynal, State National Bank; Robert Riccio, The World Bank; Jonathan B. Schiff, Fairleigh Dickinson University; David L. Schwarzkopf, Bentley College; Carol Steen, Carnegie Mellon University; and Fred Wehrhahn, Marshall & Isley Corporation.

Betty Cloud was my efficient, hard-working secretary.

I appreciate the advice and help of all these persons.

ELEMENTS OF THE BALANCE SHEET

1-2. A balance sheet gives financial information about an **entity**. The name of the entity that this balance sheet refers to is ___ ___ ___ ___ ___ ___ ___ ___ ___ ___ ___ ___ ___.

Garsden
Company

1-3. An entity is any organization for which financial statements are prepared. A business is an ___ ___ ___ ___ ___ ___; a college, a government, a church, and a synagogue are also ___ ___ ___ ___ ___ ___ ___ ___.

entity
entities

1-4. The balance sheet is a snapshot of the financial position of the entity as of one moment in time. As indicated by the heading in Exhibit 1, the balance sheet for Garsden Company reports its financial position as of December 31, ___ ___ ___ ___.

1995

1-5. The date December 31, 1995, means [circle A or B]:
   A. it was prepared on December 31, 1995.
   B. it reports the entity's financial position as of December 31, 1995.

B
(Probably, it was prepared early in 1996.)

1-6. Thus, the heading tells three things: (1) the fact that the report is a b___ ___ ___ ___ ___ ___ ___   s___ ___ ___ ___, (2) the name of the ___ ___ ___ ___ ___ ___, and (3) the "as of " date.

balance sheet
entity

1-7. The Garsden Company balance sheet has two sides. The heading of the left side is A___ ___ ___ ___ ___, and the heading of the right side is L___ ___ ___ ___ ___ ___ ___ ___ ___ ___ ___ and E___ ___ ___ ___ ___ ___. We shall describe the meaning of each side.

Assets
Liabilities   Equity

ASSETS

1-8. Assets are valuable resources owned by the entity. An entity needs cash, equipment, and other resources in order to operate. These resources are its a___ ___ ___ ___ ___. The balance sheet shows the amounts of each of these assets as of a certain date.

assets

KEY POINTS TO REMEMBER

• The financial statements do not tell the whole story about an entity because they report only past events, do not report market values, and are based on judgments and estimates. Nevertheless, they provide important information.

• Financial statements are analyzed by using ratios, rather than absolute dollar amounts. These ratios are compared with those for the same entity in the past, with those for similar entities, or with standards based on judgment.

• An overall measure of performance is Return on Equity (ROE). It takes into account both profitability and the capital used in generating profits. Another overall measure is Return on Permanent Capital, or Return on Investment, which is the ratio of profits (adjusted for interest and taxes) to total permanent capital.

• An entity with a low profit margin can provide a good return on equity investment if it has a sufficiently high capital turnover.

• In addition to information about profitability, financial statements provide information about the entity's liquidity and solvency.

You have completed Part 11 of this program. If you think you understand the material in this part, you should now take Post Test 11, which is in the separate booklet. If you are uncertain about your understanding, you should review Part 11.

The post test will serve both to test your comprehension and to review the highlights of Part 11. After taking the post test, you may find that you are unsure about certain points. You should review these points.

1-9. For example, the amount of Cash that Garsden Company owned on December 31, 1995 was $__,__ __ __,000.

$1,449,000
(Note that numbers on the Exhibit 1 balance sheet omit 000.)

1-10. Assets are resources **owned** by Garsden Company. Its employees, although usually its most valuable resource, . . . [are / are not] accounting assets.

are not
(No one owns humans since the abolition of slavery.)

On an item like this, circle the answer of your choice.

LIABILITIES AND EQUITY

1-11. The right side of the balance sheet shows the sources that provided the entity's assets. As the heading indicates, there are two general types of sources, L__ __ __ __ __ __ __ __ __ __ and E__ __ __ __ __.

Liabilities   Equity

1-12. Liabilities are the entity's obligations to outside parties who have furnished resources. These parties are generally called **creditors** because they have extended credit to the entity. As Exhibit 1 indicates, suppliers have extended credit in the amount of $5,602,000 as indicated by the item A__ __ __ __ __ __ __ p__ __ __ __ __ __.

Accounts payable

1-13. Creditors have a **claim** against the assets in the amount shown as the liability. For example, a bank has loaned $1,000,000 to Garsden Company, and therefore has a claim of this amount, as indicated by the item, __ __ __ __ __   __ __ __ __   __ __ __ __ __ __ __.

Bank loan payable

1-14. Because an entity will use its assets to pay its claims, the claims are claims against __ __ __ __ __ __. They are claims against all the assets, not any particular asset.

assets

TESTS OF FINANCIAL CONDITION

> **NOTE:** A business must be concerned with more than profitability. It must also maintain a sound financial condition. This means that it must be able to pay its debts when they come due.

11-74. Ability to meet current obligations is called **liquidity**. The ratio of current assets to current liabilities, called the _____ ratio, is a widely used measure of liquidity.

current

11-75. Ability to meet long-term obligations is called **solvency**. If a high proportion of permanent capital is obtained from debt, rather than from equity, this increases the danger of insolvency. The proportion of debt is indicated by the d__ __ __   r__ __ __ __ .

debt ratio

> **NOTE:** Any of dozens of other ratios may be used for various purposes in analyzing the profitability and financial condition of a business. Those described here are the ones in most general use. Others give a more detailed picture of the important relationships.

11-76. Financial analysts form their opinions about a company partly by studying ratios such as those we have presented. They also study the details of the financial statements, including the notes that accompany these statements. They obtain additional information by conversations and visits because they realize that the financial statements tell . . . [only part of the / the whole] story about the company.

only part of the

1-15. The other source of the funds that an entity uses to acquire its assets is called **Equity**. In Garsden Company, equity investors provided funds for which they received common stock. The total amount supplied by equity investors is called **Total paid-in capital**. In Garsden Company, it was $__ __,__ __ __,000. (We shall describe the details in a later part.)

$12,256,000

> **NOTE:** The name is Equity (singular) not Equities (plural) even though there are several sources of equity.

1-16. Equity funds also come from a second source, the profits or **earnings** generated by the entity. The amount of these earnings that has not been paid to equity investors in the form of dividends is retained in the entity, and therefore is called __ __ __ __ __ __ __ __ __ earnings. In Garsden Company, the amount was $__ __,__ __ __,000.

Retained
$13,640,000

1-17. Thus, there are two sources of equity funds: (1) the amount provided directly by equity investors, which is called __ __ __ __ __-__ __ __ __ __ __ __ __ __ __ , and (2) the amount retained from profits (or earnings), which is called __ __ __ __ __ __ __ __ __ __ __ __ __ __ __ __ __ .

Paid-in
capital
Retained earnings

1-18. Creditors can sue the entity if the amounts due them are not paid. Equity investors have only a *residual claim*; if the entity is dissolved, they get whatever is left after the liabilities have been paid, which may be nothing. Liabilities therefore are a . . . [stronger / weaker] claim against the assets, and equity is a . . . [stronger / weaker] claim.

stronger
weaker

1-19. Thus, the right-hand side of the balance sheet reports two types of claims: (1) the claims of creditors, which are __ __ __ __ __ __ __ __ __ __ __ __ __ , and (2) the residual claim of equity investors, which is __ __ __ __ __ __ __ __ .

liabilities
equity

> **NOTE:** We have described the right-hand side of the balance sheet in two somewhat different ways: (1) as the amount of funds supplied by creditors and equity investors, and (2) as the claims of these parties against the assets. Both are correct.

11-71. For example, consider the following results for a supermarket and a department store, each with $10 million of sales revenue.

	Supermarket	Department store
	(000 omitted)	
Sales revenue	$10,000	$10,000
EBIT	400	2,000
Permanent capital	1,000	5,000

The EBIT margin for the supermarket is only

$$\frac{\$\boxed{}}{\$\boxed{}} = \underline{}\%$$

$$\frac{\$400}{\$10,000} = 4\%$$

and for the department store, it is

$$\frac{\$\boxed{}}{\$\boxed{}} = \underline{}\%.$$

$$\frac{\$2,000}{\$10,000} = 20\%$$

The ratio for the department store is much . . . [lower / higher].

higher

11-72. However, the department store has more expensive fixtures, a larger inventory, and a lower inventory turnover than the supermarket, so its capital turnover is lower. Calculate the capital turnover of each.

	Sales	÷ Permanent Capital	= Capital turnover
Supermarket	$_____	÷ $_____	= _____ times
Department store	$_____	÷ $_____	= _____ times

$10,000 ÷ $1,000 = 10 times

$10,000 ÷ $5,000 = 2 times

11-73. The return on permanent capital is the same in both companies, as you can see for yourself in the following calculation.

	EBIT margin	* Capital turnover	= Return on permanent capital
Supermarket	0._____	* _____ times	= _____ %
Department store	0._____	* _____ times	= _____ %

0.04 * 10 = 40%

0.20 * 2 = 40%

DUAL-ASPECT CONCEPT

1-20. Whatever assets remain after the liabilities are taken into account will be claimed by the equity investors. Consider the case of an entity whose assets total $10,000, and whose liabilities total $4,000. Its equity must be $_____ .

$6,000 (= $10,000 – $4,000)

> *A single blank indicates that the answer is one word or, when preceded by the dollar sign as it is here, one amount.*

1-21. (1) Any assets not claimed by creditors will be claimed by equity investors, and (2) the total amount of claims (liabilities + equity) cannot exceed what there is to be claimed. Therefore, the total amount of assets will always be . . . [greater than / equal to / less than] the total amount of liabilities plus equity.

equal to

1-22. Here is the balance sheet of Garsden Company, greatly condensed so as to focus on the main elements, and disregarding the thousands:

GARSDEN COMPANY
Balance Sheet as of December 31, 1995
(000 omitted)

Assets		Liabilities & Equity	
Cash	$ 1,449	Liabilities	$12,343
Other assets	36,790	Equity	25,896
Total	$38,239	Total	$38,239

The total of the left side is $__ __,__ __ __,000, and the total of the right side is $__ __,__ __ __,000.

38,239,000

38,239,000

11-66. American manufacturing companies have a capital turnover ratio of roughly two times on average. A company that has a large capital investment in relation to its sales revenue is called a **capital-intensive** company. A capital-intensive company, such as a steel manufacturing company or a public utility, has a relatively . . . [high / low] capital turnover.

low

11-67. Another way of finding the return on permanent capital is to multiply the EBIT margin ratio by the capital turnover. Calculate this relationship.

EBIT margin (Frame 11-62)	*	Capital turnover (Frame 11-65)	=	Return on permanent capital
☐ %	*	☐	=	☐ %

14% * 1.8 = 25%

11-68. This formula suggests two fundamental ways in which the profitability of a business can be improved:

1. . . . [increase / decrease] the EBIT margin ratio.
2. . . . [increase / decrease] the capital turnover.

increase

increase
(If you had difficulty in following these relationships, try some numbers of your own.)

COMMENTS ON PROFITABILITY MEASUREMENT

11-69. In the analysis above, we used ratios because absolute dollar amounts are . . . [rarely / often] useful in understanding what has happened in a business.

rarely

11-70. Also, we focused on *both* income and the capital used in earning that income. Focusing on just one of these elements can be . . . [just as good / misleading].

misleading

1-23. As shown by the Garsden Company balance sheet given in frame 1-22:

1. $38,239 of these funds were supplied to the entity from sources listed on the . . . [left / right] side.

   right

2. They are invested in assets listed on the . . . [left / right] side.

   left

3. The total amount of assets must be the same as the amount of the sources of these assets. The amount of these assets therefore must be $__ __,__ __ __,000.

   38,239,000

1-24. This is another way of saying that total assets must always equal total __ __ __ __ __ __ __ __ __ __ __ __ plus __ __ __ __ __ __.

liabilities   equity

1-25. If the total assets are less than the total liabilities plus equity, the reason may be (circle one):

A. Assets have been lost or stolen.

B. The accountant has made an error.

B
(When correctly done, the two sides are always equal.)

1-26. The fact that total assets must equal, or **balance**, total liabilities plus equity is why the statement is called a __ __ __ __ __ __ __ __ __ __ __ __. This equality tells nothing about the entity's financial condition; it always exists unless the accountant has made a mistake.

balance
sheet

1-27. This equality leads to what is called the **dual-aspect concept**. The two aspects to which this concept refers are (1) _____ and (2) _____ plus _____, and the concept states that these two aspects are always _____. (In what relation to each other?)

assets
liabilities   equity
equal

1-28. This equality exists even if liabilities are greater than assets. For example, if in an unprofitable business assets were $100,000 and liabilities were $120,000, equity would be a [positive / negative] amount of $_____.

negative
$20,000

11-61. The return used in this calculation is **Earnings Before** the deduction of **Interest** and **Taxes** on income. It is abbreviated by the first letters of the words in boldface, or ___ ___ ___ ___ .

EBIT

11-62. As with other income statement numbers, Earnings Before Interest and Taxes (EBIT) is expressed as the percentage of sales revenue. This gives the **EBIT margin**. Calculate it for Arlen Company.

$$\frac{\text{EBIT}}{\text{Sales revenue}} = \frac{\boxed{\$}}{\boxed{\$}} = \boxed{}\% \quad \text{EBIT margin}$$

$$\frac{\$42}{\$300} = 14\%$$

Enter the numerator and denominator of the EBIT margin ratio on Line 7 of Exhibit 14.

Numerator: EBIT
Denominator: Sales revenue

11-63. The permanent capital as of December 31, 19x2, is the debt capital (i.e., noncurrent liabilities) of $_____,000 plus the equity capital of $_____,000, a total of $_____,000. The return on permanent capital is found by dividing EBIT by this total. Calculate the return on permanent capital.

$40

$130 $170 (= $40 + $130)

$$\frac{\boxed{}}{\boxed{}\boxed{}} = \frac{\boxed{\$}}{\boxed{\$}} = \boxed{}\%$$

$$\frac{\text{EBIT}}{\text{Permanent capital}} = \frac{\$42}{\$170} = 25\%$$

11-64. Copy the numerator and denominator of the return on permanent capital on Line 4 of Exhibit 14.

Numerator: EBIT (Earnings before interest and taxes)
Denominator: Permanent capital

11-65. Another ratio shows how much sales revenue was generated by each dollar of permanent capital. This ratio is called the **capital turnover** ratio. Calculate it for Arlen Company.

$$\text{Capital turnover} = \frac{\text{Sales revenue}}{\text{Permanent capital}} = \frac{\boxed{\$}}{\boxed{\$}} = \boxed{} \quad \text{times}$$

$$\frac{\$300}{\$170} = 1.8 \text{ times}$$

Copy the numerator and denominator of this ratio on Line 13 of Exhibit 14.

Numerator: Sales revenue
Denominator: Permanent capital

1-29. The dual-aspect concept is the first of nine fundamental accounting concepts we shall describe in this program. The concept can be written as an equation; that is, a statement that something is equal to something else. Write this equation, using the words assets, liabilities, and equity:

_____ = _____ + _____

Assets = Liabilities + Equity

1-30. This equation is fundamental. It governs all accounting. Write a similar equation in a form that emphasizes the fact that equity is a residual interest:

_____ – _____ = Equity

Assets – Liabilities

1-31. The liabilities of Violet Company total $3,000. Its equity totals $16,000. The company must have assets that total $_____.

$19,000 (= $3,000 + $16,000)

1-32. Suppose a business had assets totaling $20,000 and liabilities totaling $18,000. Evidently, its equity was $_____.

$2,000 = ($20,000 – $18,000)

Always equal!
The two sides **balance**.

1-33. Suppose a business has $30,000 in assets. Between the claims of the creditors (the _____) and those of equity investors, which have the first, or priority, claim? _____.

liabilities
Creditors (liabilities)

11-55. On line 2 of Exhibit 14 enter the numerator and denominator of the earnings-per-share ratio.

Numerator: Net income
Denominator: Number of shares outstanding

11-56. Earnings per share is used in calculating another ratio—the **price-earnings ratio**. It is obtained by dividing the average market price of the stock by the earnings per share. If the average market price for Arlen Company stock during 19x2 was $35, then the price-earnings ratio is the ratio of $35 to $5 or _____ to 1.

7 (= $35 ÷ $5)

11-57. On line 3 of Exhibit 14, enter the numerator and denominator of the price-earnings ratio.

Numerator: Average market price
Denominator: Earnings per share

11-58. Price-earnings ratios of many companies are published daily in the financial pages of newspapers. Often, the ratio is roughly 8 to 1, but it varies greatly depending on market conditions. If investors think that earnings per share will increase, this ratio could be much higher—perhaps 15 to 1. Apparently, investors are willing to pay . . . [more / less] per dollar of earnings in a growing company.

more

11-59. We have focused on return on equity (ROE) as an overall measure of performance. Another useful measure is the **return on permanent capital**. This shows how well the entity used its capital, without considering how much of its permanent capital came from each of the two sources: d___ ___ ___ and e___ ___ ___ ___ ___ . This ratio is also called **return on investment (ROI)**.

debt   equity

11-60. The *return* portion of this ratio is *not* net income. Net income includes a deduction for interest expense, but interest expense *is* the return on debt capital. Therefore, net income . . . [understates / overstates] the return earned on all permanent capital. Also, income tax expense often is disregarded so as to focus on purely operating activities.

understates

1-34. As a review of terms we have discussed so far, here is a list of ordinary terms. In the right-hand column, write the accounting term for each.

Ordinary Term	Accounting Term	
things of value	_____	assets
one who lends money	_____	creditor
creditors' claims	_____	liabilities
investors' claims	_____	equity

1-35. Because a balance sheet reports amounts for a point in time, the balance sheet must be dated. From here on we shall use the term "19x1" to refer to the first year, "19x2" for the next year, and so on. Thus, a balance sheet as of December 31 of the first year is dated "as of December 31, ___ __ __ __."

19x1

1-36. At the close of business on December 31, 19x1, Dowling Company had $2,000 in its bank account. It owned other assets totaling $24,000. The company owed $10,000 to creditors. Its equity was $16,000. Complete the balance sheet for Dowling Company:

DOWLING COMPANY

Balance Sheet as of _____   December 31, 19x1

Assets		Liabilities and Equity			
Cash	$	Liabilities	$	$ 2,000	$10,000
Other assets		Equity		24,000	16,000
Total	$	Total	$	$26,000	$26,000

1-37. One year later, on December 31, 19x2, Dowling Company owed $8,000 to creditors and had $3,000 in its bank account. Other assets totaled $25,000.

One item is missing. Calculate the amount of this item so that the balance sheet will balance. Prepare a balance sheet as of December 31, 19x2, on a separate piece of paper.

DOWLING COMPANY
Balance Sheet as of December 31, 19x2

Assets		Liabilities & Equity	
Cash	$ 3,000	Liabilities	$ 8,000
Other assets ...	25,000	Equity	20,000
Total	$28,000	Total	$28,000

11-49. The larger the proportion of permanent capital that is obtained from debt, the smaller is the amount of equity capital that is needed. If Arlen had obtained $85,000 of its $170,000 permanent capital from debt, its debt ratio would have been _____%, and its ROE would have been . . . [higher / lower] than the 18.5% shown in Exhibit 13.

50%
higher

11-50. However, as you learned in Part 9, a high debt ratio results in a . . . [more / less] risky capital structure than does a low debt ratio.

more

11-51. In several of the calculations above, we used balance sheet amounts taken from the ending balance sheet. For some purposes, it is more informative to use an **average** of beginning and ending balance sheet amounts. Arlen Company had $130,000 of equity at the end of 19x2. If it had $116,000 at the beginning of 19x2, its *average* equity during 19x2 was $_____. Since its net income in 19x2 was $24,000, its return on *average* equity investment was _____%.*

$123,000
19.5% (= $24,000 ÷ $123,000)

_____
* one decimal place.

11-52. The return on equity (ROE) in typical American corporations is roughly 15%. Arlen Company's performance in 19x2 was . . . [above average / below average].

above average

OTHER MEASURES OF PERFORMANCE

11-53. Another measure of performance is **earnings per share**. As the name suggests, the ratio is simply the total _____ for a given period, divided by the number of _____ of common stock outstanding.

earnings (*or* net income)
shares

11-54. Exhibit 10 shows that the earnings (i.e., net income) of Arlen Company in 19x2 was $_____, and that the number of shares outstanding during 19x2 was _____. Therefore, earnings per share was $_____.

$24,000
4,800
$5 (= $24,000 ÷ 4,800)

1-38. If Dowling Company prepared a balance sheet as of the beginning of business the next day, January 1, 19x3, would it be different from the one you prepared above? . . . [Yes / No]

No (*because nothing changes between the close of business on one day and the beginning of business on the next day*)

1-39. The term "Net assets" is sometimes used instead of "equity." It refers to the fact that equity is always the difference between A_____ and L_____.

Assets

Liabilities

MONEY–MEASUREMENT CONCEPT

1-40. If a fruit store owned $200 in cash, 100 dozen oranges, and 200 apples, could you add up its total assets from this information? . . . [Yes / No]

No (*because you can't add apples and oranges*)

Cash	$200
	100 dozen
	200
	_____
	Can't add

1-41. If you knew that the 100 dozen oranges cost $5 a dozen and the 200 apples cost $0.40 each, you could then add these amounts to the $200 cash, and find the total assets to be $_____.

$780

Cash	$200	$200
	500	(= 5 * 100)
	80	(= 0.40 * 200)
	_____	_____
	$780	$780

NOTE: We use "*" to mean "multiply by." Some people use "×."

1-42. To add together objects as different as apples, oranges, automobiles, shoes, cash, supplies, etc., they must be stated in . . . [different / similar] units.

similar

1-43. Can you add the amounts of apples and oranges if they are stated in terms of money? . . . [Yes / No]

Yes (*You could also add them to get "pieces of fruit" but this is not a useful number.*)

NOTE: The numbers used here to calculate the current ratio are amounts as of the end of the year. Seasonal factors may greatly affect the current ratio during the year. For example, a department store increases its inventory in the fall in anticipation of Christmas business, and its current ratio therefore decreases. Similar limitations affect the other measures discussed in this part.

11-45. A variation of the current ratio is the **quick ratio** (also called the **acid-test ratio**). In this ratio, inventory is excluded from the current assets, and the remainder is divided by current liabilities. This is a more stringent measure of bill-paying ability than the current ratio. Calculate this ratio for Arlen Company:

$$\frac{\text{Current assets} - \text{inventory}}{\text{Current liabilities}} = \frac{\$ \quad - }{\$ \quad} = \boxed{\quad} \text{ times}$$

$$\frac{\$140 - \$60}{\$60} = 1.3$$

11-46. Copy the numerator and the denominator of the quick ratio on Line 11 of Exhibit 14.

Numerator: Current assets – Inventory
Denominator: Current liabilities

11-47. The final ratio we shall use in examining capitalization is the **debt ratio**. As explained in Part 9, this is the ratio of debt capital to total permanent capital. Noncurrent liabilities are d_ _ _ capital, and noncurrent liabilities plus equity is t_ _ _ _ p_ _ _ _ _ _ _ _ capital. Calculate the debt ratio for Arlen Company.

debt
total
permanent

$$\frac{\boxed{\qquad}}{\boxed{\quad + \quad}} = \frac{\$ \quad}{\$ \quad} = \boxed{\quad} \%$$

$$\frac{\text{Noncurrent liabilities}}{\text{Noncurrent liabilities} + \text{equity}} = \frac{\$40}{\$40 + \$130} = 24\%$$

11-48. Copy the numerator and denominator of the debt ratio on Line 12 of Exhibit 14.

Numerator: Noncurrent liabilities
Denominator: Noncurrent liabilities + equity

1-44. The facts that appear in an accounting report are stated in units of money; that is, dollars and cents. This is the **money-measurement concept**. By converting different facts to monetary amounts, we can deal with them . . . [verbally / arithmetically]; that is, we can add one item to another, or we can _____ one item from another.

arithmetically

subtract

1-45. The money-measurement concept states that accounting reports only those facts that can be stated as m__ __ __ __ __ __ __ a__ __ __ __ __ __.

monetary amounts

1-46. If facts cannot be expressed in monetary terms, they cannot be reported on a balance sheet. Which of the following facts could be learned by reading a balance sheet of Able Company?

    A. How much cash Able Company has.
    B. The health of the president of Able Company.
    C. How much money Able Company owes.
    D. A strike is beginning at Able Company.
    E. How many automobiles Able Company owns.

A and C
(Not E because the number of automobiles is not a monetary amount.)

1-47. Because accounting reports include only facts that can be stated in monetary amounts, accounting is necessarily a(n) . . . [complete / incomplete] record of the status of a business and . . . [does / does not] always give the most important facts about a business.

incomplete

does not

1-48. Some people believe that accounting reports tell everything important that one needs to know about a business. Such a belief is . . . [correct / wrong].

wrong

1-49. The **money-measurement concept** is the second of the nine major accounting concepts to be explained in this program. The first one was the **dual-aspect concept**. What is the meaning of each of these concepts? (Write your answer on a separate piece of paper.)

Dual-aspect concept:
    Assets = Liabilities + Equity
Money-measurement concept:
    Accounting reports show only facts that can be expressed in monetary amounts.

11-39. Copy the numerator and the denominator of the inventory turnover ratio on Line 9 of Exhibit 14.

Numerator: Cost of sales
Denominator: Inventory

11-40. If Arlen Company had maintained an inventory of $90,000 to support $180,000 cost of sales, its inventory turnover would have been _____ (how many?) times, rather than 3 times. With this change, its ROE would have been . . . [higher / lower] than the 18.5% shown in Exhibit 13.

2

lower

11-41. The **current ratio** is another way of examining the current section of the balance sheet. In an earlier part we pointed out that if the ratio of current assets to current liabilities is too low, the company might not be able to pay its bills. However, if the current ratio is too high, the company would not be taking advantage of the opportunity to finance current assets with current l__ __ __ __ __ __ __ __ __ s. Additional current liabilities would . . . [increase / decrease] its ROE. Equity inevitably would be lower; otherwise, the balance sheet would not balance.

liabilities
increase

11-42. Calculate the current ratio for Arlen Company.

$$\frac{\underline{\quad\quad\quad}\ \ \underline{\quad\quad\quad}}{\underline{\quad\quad\quad}\ \ \underline{\quad\quad\quad}} = \frac{\$\ \boxed{}}{\$\ \boxed{}} = \boxed{}$$

$$\frac{\text{Current assets}}{\text{Current liabilities}} = \frac{\$140}{\$60} = 2.3$$

Numerator: Current assets
Denominator: Current liabilities

11-43. Copy the numerator and the denominator of the current ratio on Line 10 of Exhibit 14.

increase
increase

11-44. If Arlen Company decreased its current ratio to 1.5 by increasing its current liabilities, this would . . . [increase / decrease] its ROE. However, such a low current ratio would . . .[increase / decrease] the possibility that Arlen would be unable to pay its current liabilities when they come due.

ENTITY CONCEPT

1-50. Accounts are kept for **entities**, rather than for the persons who own, operate, or otherwise are associated with those entities. For example, suppose Green Company is a business entity, and Sue Smith is its owner. Sue Smith withdraws $100 from the business. In preparing financial accounts for Green Company, we should record the effect of this withdrawal on the accounts of . . . [Sue Smith / the entity].

the entity

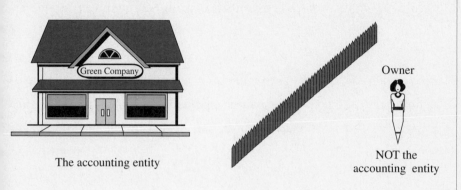

The accounting entity

Owner

NOT the accounting entity

1-51. Sue Smith withdraws $100 from Green Company, of which she is the sole owner. Smith now has $100 more cash, but she has $100 less equity in Green Company. Smith is . . . [better off / worse off / no better or worse off] than she was before.

no better or worse off

1-52. If Smith withdraws $100 from Green Company, of which she is the sole owner, she is just as well off after this withdrawal as before. What about Green Company? It now has . . . [$100 more / the same amount / $100 less] in assets.

$100 less

1-53. Evidently, an event can affect the owner in one way and the entity in another way. Financial statements of Green Company report the effect that the event has:

   A. only on the owner.

   B. only on the entity.

   C. on both the owner and the entity.

B
(Sue Smith can, of course, have her own personal financial statements.)

11-34. Thus, in examining how well an entity used its capital, we need to ask two questions:

1. Were assets kept reasonably . . . [high / low]?

2. Were liabilities kept reasonably . . . [high / low]?

low

high

11-35. Let's start with the current assets. If current assets are reasonably low in relation to sales volume, this has a(n) . . . [favorable / unfavorable] effect on ROE.

favorable

11-36. In earlier parts, two ratios for measuring current assets were described. One related to accounts receivable and was called the **days' sales uncollected**. It shows how many days of sales revenue are tied up in accounts receivable.

Calculate days' sales uncollected for Arlen Company.

$$\frac{\text{Accounts Receivable}}{\text{Sales Revenue} \div 365} = \frac{\$\boxed{}}{\$\boxed{} \div 365} = \boxed{} \text{ days' sales uncollected}$$

$$\frac{\text{Accounts receivable}}{\text{Sales revenue} \div 365} = \frac{\$40}{\$300 \div 365} = 49 \text{ days}$$

11-37. Copy the numerator and the denominator of the days' sales uncollected on Line 8 of Exhibit 14.

Numerator: Accounts receivable
Denominator: Sales revenue ÷ 365

11-38. The amount of capital tied up in inventory can be examined by calculating the **inventory turnover ratio**. Since inventory is recorded at cost, this ratio is calculated in relation to cost of sales, rather than to sales revenue.

Calculate the inventory turnover ratio for Arlen Company (refer to Exhibit 13 if necessary).

$$\frac{\text{Cost of Sales}}{\text{Inventory}} = \frac{\$\boxed{}}{\$\boxed{}} = \boxed{} \text{ times}$$

$$\frac{\text{Cost of sales}}{\text{Inventory}} = \frac{\$180}{\$60} = 3 \text{ times}$$

1-54. The fact that accounts are kept for entities as distinguished from the persons associated with those entities is called the e __ __ __ __ __ concept.

entity

1-55. Owners of some small retail stores (called "mom and pop" stores) may not identify the cost of merchandise they withdraw for personal use, personal telephone calls, and the like. If this is so, then they do not apply the _____ concept. Consequently, the financial statements of these stores are inaccurate.

entity

> **NOTE:** A business may be organized under any one of several legal forms: a corporation, a partnership (two or more owners), or a proprietorship (a single owner). The entity concept applies regardless of the legal status.

1-56. John and Ellen own the John and Ellen Laundry, a partnership. Each takes $1,000 cash from the partnership entity and deposits it into a personal bank account. An accounting report of the financial position of the John and Ellen Laundry would show that:

A. the change in the entity's equity is zero.
B. the entity has $2,000 less cash.
C. the entity has $2,000 less equity.
D. John and Ellen each have $1,000 more cash.

B and C
(John's and Ellen's personal statements would show that each had $1,000 more cash.)

> **NOTE:** Municipalities, hospitals, religious organizations, colleges, and other nonbusiness organizations are also accounting entities. Although in this program we focus on businesses, the accounting for nonbusiness entities is similar.

11-30. As background for this analysis, let's examine some relationships in Camden Company, which has the following condensed balance sheet:

Assets	Liabilities and Equity	
	Total liabilities	$400,000
	Total equity	600,000
Total $1,000,000	Total	$1,000,000

If net income was $60,000, Camden Company's return on equity (ROE) was Net income ÷ Equity, or _____%.

10% (= $60,000 ÷ $600,000)

11-31. If Camden Company could reduce its equity to $500,000, while still maintaining its net income of $60,000, its ROE would become _____%. Evidently, with net income held constant, Camden Company can increase its ROE by . . . [increasing / decreasing] its equity.

12% (= $60,000 ÷ $500,000)
decreasing

11-32. Since total assets always equal liabilities plus equity, equity can be decreased only if (1) assets are . . . [increased / decreased], (2) liabilities are . . . [increased / decreased], or (3) there is some combination of these two types of changes.

decreased
increased

11-33. For example, Camden Company's equity would be decreased by $100,000 (to $500,000) if assets were decreased by $40,000 (to $960,000) and liabilities were . . . [increased / decreased] by $_____ (to $_____). If equity was $500,000 and net income was $60,000, ROE would be

increased
$60,000 $460,000

$$\frac{\$60,000}{\$500,000} = 12\%$$

$$\frac{\boxed{\$}}{\boxed{\$}} = \boxed{\%}$$

REVIEW OF ACCOUNTING CONCEPTS

1-57. The entity concept is the third of the nine fundamental accounting concepts. The three are:

1. The dual-aspect concept is:

   $$\underline{\quad\quad\quad} = $$

   $$\underline{\quad\quad\quad\quad\quad} + \underline{\quad\quad\quad}.$$

   Assets =

   Liabilities + Equity

2. The money-measurement concept is:
   Accounting reports only facts that can be expressed in m__ __ __ __ __ __ __ a__ __ __ __ __ __.

   monetary amounts

3. The entity concept is:
   Accounts are kept for e__ __ __ __ __ __ __ __ as distinguished from the p__ __ __ __ __ __ who own those entities.

   entities

   persons

KEY POINTS TO REMEMBER

• The assets of an entity are the things of value that it owns.

• The sources of funds used to acquire assets are:

  1. liabilities and
  2. equity.

• Liabilities are sources from creditors.

• Equity consists of (1) funds obtained from equity investors, who are owners; and (2) retained earnings, which result from the entity's profitable operation.

• Creditors have a strong claim on the assets. They can sue if the amounts due them are not paid. Equity investors have only a residual claim.

• Total assets equal the total of liabilities plus equity. This is the dual-aspect concept.

• The amounts of assets, liabilities, and equity as of one point in time are reported on the entity's balance sheet.

• Accounting reports only those facts that can be stated in monetary amounts. This is the money-measurement concept.

• Business accounts are kept for entities, rather than for the persons who own, operate, or otherwise are associated with those entities. This is the entity concept.

11-25. A high gross margin does not necessarily lead to a high net income. Net income is what remains after expenses have been deducted from the gross margin, and the higher the expenses, the . . . [higher / lower] the net income.

lower

11-26. The **profit margin percentage** is a useful number for analyzing net income. You calculated it in an earlier part. Calculate it for Arlen Company.

$$\frac{\text{Net Income}\quad \boxed{\$\qquad}}{\text{Sales Revenue}\quad \boxed{\$\qquad}} = \boxed{\qquad \%^*}\ \text{profit margin}$$

$$\frac{\text{Net income}}{\text{Sales revenue}} = \frac{\$\ 24}{\$300} = 8\%$$

11-27. Copy the numerator and denominator of the profit margin percentage on Line 6 of Exhibit 14.

Numerator: Net income
Denominator: Sales revenue

11-28. Statistics on the average profit margin percentage in various industries are published and can be used by Arlen Company as a basis for comparison. Statistics on the average *dollar* amount of net income are not published. Such statistics . . . [are / are not] useful because sheer size is not a good indication of profitability.

are not

TESTS OF CAPITAL UTILIZATION

11-29. The bottom section of the diagram in Exhibit 13 shows the main components of Arlen Company's capital. The information is taken from its . . . [income statement / balance sheet]. We shall examine ratios useful in understanding these components.

balance sheet

You have completed Part 1 of this program. If you think you understand the material in this Part, you should now take Post Test 1, which is in the separate booklet. If you are uncertain about your understanding, you should review Part 1.

The post test will serve both to test your comprehension and to review the highlights of Part 1. After taking the post test, you may find that you are unsure about certain points. You should review these points before continuing with Part 2.

FACTORS AFFECTING RETURN ON EQUITY

11-21. Ratios help explain the factors that influenced return on equity.

> **NOTE:** Some ratios were explained in earlier parts. We shall review these ratios and introduce others, using the financial statements of Arlen Company in Exhibit 10 and the diagram of these factors in Exhibit 13. These ratios are to be summarized in Exhibit 14.

We have already described the Return on Equity ratio, which is:

$$\frac{\text{(numerator) Net income}}{\text{(denominator) Equity}} = \text{Return on Equity}$$

Copy the numerator and denominator of this ratio on Line 1 of Exhibit 14.

Numerator: Net income
Denominator: Equity

11-22. One factor that affects net income is gross margin. In an earlier part, you calculated the **gross margin percentage**. Calculate it for Arlen Company.

$$\frac{\text{Gross Margin}}{\text{Sales Revenue}} = \frac{\$ \qquad *}{\$ \qquad} = \boxed{\quad \%*} \text{ gross margin}$$

$$\frac{\text{Gross margin}}{\text{Sales revenue}} = \frac{\$120}{\$300} = 40\%$$

*From here on, when calculating these ratios, omit the three zeros to reduce pencil work; that is, write 120 instead of 120,000.

> **NOTE:** If you have difficulty with this or other calculations, refer to Exhibit 13, where the amounts are calculated.

11-23. On Line 5 of Exhibit 14, write the name of the numerator and of the denominator of the gross margin percentage.

Numerator: Gross margin
Denominator: Sales revenue

11-24. Gross margin percentages vary widely. A profitable supermarket may have a gross margin of only 15%. Many manufacturing companies have gross margins of about 35%. Compared with these numbers, the gross margin of Arlen Company is . . . [low / high].

Part 2

More About the Balance Sheet

Learning Objectives

In this part you will learn:

• Two more of the nine basic accounting concepts:

    • The going-concern concept.

    • The cost concept.

• The meaning of the principal items reported on a balance sheet.

GOING-CONCERN CONCEPT

2-1. Every year some entities go bankrupt or cease to operate. Most entities, however, keep on going from one year to the next. Accounting must assume either that (a) entities are about to cease operations, or (b) they are likely to keep on going. The more realistic assumption for most entities is . . . [(a) / (b)].

(b)

2-2. Accounting assumes that an entity, or **concern**, normally will keep on **going** from one year to the next. This assumption is therefore called the **g__ __ __ __ -concern concept**.

going

2-3. Specifically, the g__ __ __ __ __ -c__ __ __ __ __ __ __ concept states that accounting assumes that an entity will continue to operate indefinitely unless there is evidence to the contrary.

going-concern

11-17. Most comparisons are made in one or more of the three ways described above. Give the meaning of each.

1. **Historical**: comparing the entity with . . . .
   . . . .

   its own performance in the past

2. **External**: comparing the entity with . . . .
   . . . .

   another entity's performance or industry averages

3. **Judgmental**: comparing the entity with . . . .
   . . . .

   a standard based on our judgment

11-18. Arlen Company's net income in 19x2 was $24,000. Baker Company's net income in 19x2 was $50,000. From this information we cannot tell which company performed better. Why not? . . . .
. . . .

Because we do not know Baker Company's equity.

11-19. Baker Company's equity was $1,000,000. Its net income in 19x2 was $50,000. Its ROE was therefore

$$\frac{\boxed{\$}}{\boxed{\$}} = \underline{}\%.$$

$$\frac{\$50,000}{\$1,000,000} = 5\%$$

Arlen Company with an ROE of 18.5% performed . . . [better / worse] than Baker Company.

better

11-20. The comparison of Arlen Company's dollar amount of net income with Baker's dollar amount . . . [did / did not] provide useful information. The comparison of their **ratios** or **percentages** was . . . [useful / not useful]. Useful comparisons involve r_____s or p_____s.

did not

useful   ratios

percentages

NOTE: If the entity is not a going concern, special accounting rules apply; they are not discussed in this introductory program.

2-4. Because of the going-concern concept, accounting . . . [does / does not] report what the assets could be sold for if the entity ceases to exist.

does not

2-5. On December 31, 19x1, the balance sheet of Hamel Company reported total assets of $500,000. If Hamel Company ceases to operate,

    A. its assets could be sold for $500,000.

    B. its assets could be sold for approximately $500,000.

    C. its assets could be sold for at least $500,000.

    D. we do not know what its assets could be sold for.

D

COST CONCEPT

2-6. When an entity buys an asset, it records the amount of the asset at its cost. Thus, if Mondale Company bought a plot of land for $10,000 in 19x1, it would report on its December 31, 19x1, balance sheet the item: Land, $_____. This amount was the c___ ___ ___ of the land.

$10,000   cost

2-7. The amount for which an asset can be sold in the marketplace is called its market value. If you bought a pair of shoes a year ago for $75 and find that today you can sell them for $15, their cost was $_____, and their ___ ___ ___ ___ ___ ___ value is $_____.

$75

market $15

2-8. Some assets wear out. Inflation affects the value of some assets. For these and other reasons, the market value of assets . . . [remains the same / changes] as time goes on. Therefore, on December 31, 19x6, the market value of Mondale Company's land was probably . . . [$10,000 / less than $10,000 / different from $10,000].

changes

different from $10,000

11-12. The accounting name for the profit or return earned in a year is

n___ ___ i___ ___ ___ ___ ___ ___ .

net income

Return on equity is the percentage obtained by dividing n___ ___

i___ ___ ___ ___ ___ by e___ ___ ___ ___ ___ ___ .

net
income   equity

11-13. In 19x2 Arlen Company had net income of $24,000, and its equity on December 31, 19x2, was $130,000. Calculate its ROE for 19x2.

N_____ I_____

———————————————————— =

E_____

_____

* one decimal place

$$\frac{\text{Net Income}}{\text{Equity}} = \frac{\$\,24{,}000}{\$130{,}000} = 18.5\% \text{ ROE}$$

11-14. In order to judge how well Arlen Company performed, its 18.5% ROE must be compared with something. If in 19x1 Arlen Company had an ROE of 20%, we can say that its performance in 19x2 was . . . [better / worse] than in 19x1. This is the **historical** basis of comparison.

worse

11-15. If in 19x2 another company had an ROE of 15%, Arlen's ROE was . . . [better / worse] than the other company's. Or if in 19x2 the average ROE of companies in the same industry as Arlen was 15%, Arlen's ROE was . . . [better / worse] than the industry average. This is the **external** basis of comparison. If the other company is thought to be the best managed company in the industry, this comparison is called **benchmarking**.

better

better

11-16. Finally, if from our experience we *judge* that a company like Arlen should have earned an ROE of 20% in 19x2, we conclude that Arlen's ROE was . . . [better / worse] than this **judgmental standard**.

worse

2-9. Accounting, however, does not attempt to trace changes in the market value of most assets. Instead, accounting focuses on their cost. Thus, on its December 31, 19x6, balance sheet, Mondale Company would report the land at its c__ __ __ of $_____.

cost $10,000

2-10. The cost concept states that accounting focuses on the . . . [cost / market value] of assets, rather than on their . . . [cost / market value].

cost
market value

> **NOTE:** The cost concept is often called the "historical cost" concept. This emphasizes the fact that the numbers report what the entity *did* pay for the asset.

2-11. Many people think that the balance sheet shows what assets are *worth*, that is, their market value. This belief is . . . [true / false].

false

2-12. One reason why accounting is based on the cost concept is that it is difficult to estimate the market value of many assets. If you bought a pair of shoes for $75, the cost was clearly $_____. However, if a few months later you asked two friends to tell you the market value of these used shoes, they probably would . . . [agree / disagree] as to the amount.

$75

disagree

Cost $75
Market value???

2-13. Estimating the market value of each asset every time a balance sheet is prepared would be . . . [difficult / easy]. Furthermore, the estimates would be a matter of opinion and therefore . . . [objective / subjective]. People would disagree as to their market value.

difficult
subjective
(that is, affected by personal feelings, rather than by facts)

2-14. A second reason for using the cost concept is that the entity will not sell many of its assets immediately. Instead, it will keep them to use in its operations. The entity therefore . . . [does / does not] need to know their market value. This reason stems from the previous concept, the g__ __ __ __ -c__ __ __ __ __ __ concept.

does not

going-concern

11-7. After completing their examination, the __ __ __ __ __ __ __ s write a report giving their opinion. This o__ __ __ __ __ __ __ is reproduced in the company's annual report. A typical opinion is shown in Exhibit 12.

auditors

opinion

11-8. The opinion says that the auditors . . . [prepared / audited] the financial statements, and that these statements are the responsibility of . . . [the auditors / management].

audited

management

11-9. The opinion further states that the financial statements . . . [accurately / fairly] present the financial results.

fairly
(Because judgments and estimates are involved, no one can say that the financial statements are entirely accurate.)

11-10. In the last paragraph of the opinion, the auditors assure the reader that the statements were prepared in conformity with g_____ a_____ a_____ p_____.

generally
accepted accounting principles

NOTE: Exhibit 12 is an example of a **clean** or **unqualified** opinion. If any of the above statements cannot be made, the auditors call attention to the exceptions in what is called a **qualified** opinion. A qualified opinion can be a serious matter. If the qualification is significant, securities exchanges will suspend trading in the company's stock.

OVERALL MEASURES OF PERFORMANCE

NOTE: Although they have limitations, financial statements usually are the most useful source of information about an entity. We shall focus first on what they tell about its overall **performance**.

11-11. Equity investors (i.e., shareholders) invest money in a business in order to earn a profit, or **return**, on that equity. Thus, from the viewpoint of the shareholders, the best overall measure of the entity's performance is the r__ __ __ __ __ that was earned *on* the entity's e__ __ __ __ __ __. (This is abbreviated as ROE.)

return   equity

2-15. To summarize, the two reasons why accounting focuses on costs, rather than on market values, are that:

1. market values are difficult to estimate, that is, they are . . . [objective/ subjective], whereas costs are . . . [objective / subjective]; and

2. the _____-_____ concept makes it unnecessary to know the market value of many assets; the assets will be used in future operations rather than being sold immediately.

subjective

objective

going-concern

2-16. Accounting does not report what many of the individual assets are worth, that is, their m__ __ __ __ __ v__ __ __ __ . Accounting therefore . . . [does / does not] report what the whole entity is worth. Those who criticize accounting for its failure to report an entity's "worth" do not appreciate that this task would be difficult, subjective, and unnecessary.

market value

does not

2-17. Some assets are recorded at what they are worth. If an entity has $1,000 cash, this asset is obviously worth $_____.

$1,000

2-18. The market value of cash today is its monetary amount today. Cash is an example of a m__ __ __ __ __ __ __ asset. As we shall see in later parts, many monetary assets are measured at current monetary amounts, rather than at their c__ __ __.

monetary

cost

2-19. An entity bought land in 19x1 for $10,000. On December 31, 19x6, the entity received an offer of $20,000 for the land. This meant that the _____ _____ of the land was $20,000. At what amount should this land be reported on the balance sheet of December 31, 19x6? $_____

market value

$10,000 *(This is its historical cost.)*

2-20. A shoe store purchased shoes for $1,000. It expected to sell these shoes to customers for at least $1,500. At what amount should these shoes be reported on the balance sheet? $_____

$1,000

11-2. A second limitation is that financial statements are historical; that is, they report only events that . . . [have happened / will happen], whereas we are also interested in estimating events that . . . [have happened / will happen]. The fact that an entity earned $1 million last year . . . [definitely predicts / is not necessarily an indication of] what it will earn next year.

have happened

will happen

is not necessarily an indication of

11-3. Third, the balance sheet does not show the . . . [cost / market value] of nonmonetary assets. In accordance with the c___ __ __ concept, plant assets are reported at their . . . [unexpired cost / market value].

market value

cost

unexpired cost

Also, depreciation is a writeoff of . . . [cost / market value]. It is NOT an indication of changes in the real value of plant assets. The balance sheet . . . [does / does not] show the entity's "net worth."

cost

does not

11-4. Fourth, the accountant and management have some latitude in choosing among alternative ways of recording an event in the accounts. An example of flexibility in accounting is that in determining inventory values and cost of sales, the entity may use the L__ __ __ , F__ __ __ , or average cost method.

LIFO   FIFO

11-5. Fifth, many accounting amounts are estimates. In calculating the depreciation expense of a plant asset, for example, one must estimate its s__ __ __ __ __ __ __ l__ __ __ and its r__ __ __ __ __ __ __ v__ __ __ __ __.

service life   residual value

AUDITING

11-6. All large companies and many small ones have their accounting records examined by independent, certified public accountants. This process is called **auditing**, and the independent accountants are called __ __ __ __ __ tors.

auditors

REVIEW OF ACCOUNTING CONCEPTS

2-21. The cost concept is the fifth of the nine fundamental accounting concepts. The first five are:

1. Dual-aspect concept
2. Money-measurement concept
3. Entity concept
4. Going-concern concept
5. Cost concept

The dual-aspect concept is:

_ _ _ _ _ _ _ =

_ _ _ _ _ _ _ _ _ _ _ _ _ + _ _ _ _ _ _ _.

Assets =
Liabilities + Equity

The money-measurement concept is:

Accounting reports only facts that can be expressed in m_ _ _ _ _ _ _ _ _ _

a_ _ _ _ _ _ _.

monetary
amounts

The entity concept is:

Accounts are kept for e_ _ _ _ _ _ _ _ as distinguished from the

p_ _ _ _ _ _ _ who own those entities.

entities
persons

The going-concern concept is:

Accounting assumes that an e_ _ _ _ _ _ will continue to operate

i_ _ _ _ _ _ _ _ _ _ _ _ _.

entity
indefinitely

The cost concept is:

Accounting focuses on the _ _ _ _ _ _ of assets, rather than on their

_ _ _ _ _ _ _ _ _ _ _ _ _.

cost
market value

BALANCE SHEET ITEMS

2-22. Refer to Exhibit 1 in your booklet. This is the balance sheet we introduced in Part 1. It reports the amounts of a_ _ _ _ _ _ _,

l_ _ _ _ _ _ _ _ _ _ _ _ _, and e_ _ _ _ _ _ of Garsden

Company as of _____.

assets
liabilities   equity
December 31, 1995

Part 11

Analysis of Financial Statements

Learning Objectives

In this part you will learn:

- The limitations of financial statement analysis.
- The nature and limitations of auditing.
- An approach to analyzing financial statements.
- Overall measures of performance.
- Other ratios used in financial statement analysis.

LIMITATIONS OF FINANCIAL STATEMENT ANALYSIS

> **NOTE:** In this part, we shall describe how information in financial statements is used. Before doing this, let's review the reasons why accounting cannot provide a complete picture of the status or performance of an entity.

11-1. One limitation is suggested by the word **financial**; that is, financial statements report only events that can be measured in m__ __ __ __ ary amounts.

monetary

2-23. Remember that the note "(000 omitted)" means that the numbers are reported in thousands of dollars. For example, the number reported for Cash, $1,449, means that the amount of cash was $_____. This is common practice. It is done to make the numbers easier to read; users are not interested in the details of the last three digits.

$1,449,000

2-24. Recall also that the total of the assets always equals the total of the liabilities plus equity. Total assets were $_____, and total liabilities plus equity were $_____.

$38,239,000

$38,239,000

2-25. Most items on a balance sheet are summaries of more detailed accounts. For example, the cash is probably located in a number of separate bank accounts, in cash registers, and in petty cash boxes. The total of all the cash is $_____, rounded to the nearest thousand dollars.

$1,449,000 (NOT $1,449)

> **NOTE:** In the remainder of this part, we explain the meaning of some of the items on this balance sheet. Those not described here will be explained in later parts.

ASSETS

2-26. In Part 1 we referred to assets as val__ __ __ __ __ res__ __ __ __ __ __. Let's make this idea more specific. In order to count as an asset in accounting, an item must pass three tests.

valuable

resources

2-27. The first requirement is that the item must be **controlled** by the entity. Usually this means that the entity must **own** the item. If Able Company rents a building owned by Baker Company, this building . . . [is / is not] an asset of Able Company. The building . . . [is / is not] an asset of Baker Company.

is not

is

> **NOTE:** Certain leased items, called capital leases, are assets and are an exception to this rule. They are described in Part 8.

An asset   Not an asset

- GAAP has specific requirements for determining which cash flows are classified as investing activities and which are classified as financing activities, but statement users need not memorize these rules because they are evident from the statement itself.

- When a company is growing or when it is experiencing financial crisis, it may pay more attention to the statement of cash flows than to the income statement.

You have completed Part 10 of this program. If you think you understand the material in this part, you should now take Post Test 10, which is in the separate booklet. If you are uncertain about your understanding, you should review Part 10.

The post test will serve both to test your comprehension and to review the highlights of Part 10. After taking the post test, you may find that you are unsure about certain points. You should review these points before continuing with Part 11.

2-28. In accounting, the employees of an entity are *not* assets because the entity does not _____ them. However, if a baseball club owns a contract in which a player agrees to provide his services, the contract . . . [is / is not] an asset.

own

is *(The asset is the contract, not the player, and it is an asset only if it passes the third test, in Frame 2-30.)*

2-29. The second requirement is that the item must be **valuable** to the entity. Which of these would qualify as assets of a company that sells dresses?

    A. The company's right to collect amounts owed by customers.

    B. Regular dresses held for sale.

    C. Dresses that no one wants because they have gone out of style.

    D. A cash register in working condition.

    E. A cash register that doesn't work and can't be repaired.

A, B, and D

2-30. The third requirement is that the item must have been acquired at a **measurable cost**. Jones Company bought a trademark from another company for $1 million; this trademark . . . [is / is not] an asset of Jones Company.

is

2-31. By contrast, if Jones Company has built up an excellent reputation because of the consistently high quality of its products, this reputation . . . [is / is not] an asset in accounting, even though it may be worth many millions of dollars.

is not

2-32. "Coca-Cola" and "7•Up" are well known and valuable trademarks for soft drinks. The Coca-Cola Company developed the value of its trademark through its own efforts over many years. "Coca-Cola" . . . [is / is not] an asset in accounting. Philip Morris, Inc. purchased the Seven-Up Company. Included in the purchase was an item called "Trademarks, patents, and goodwill," valued at $390 million. In accounting, "7•Up" . . . [is / is not] an asset of Philip Morris, Inc.

is not

is

10-65. When a company is in financial difficulty, it may pay . . . [more / less] attention to its cash flow statement than to its income statement. It pays bills with cash—not net income!

more

10-66. Lenders want to know if cash flows are adequate to pay i_____t on debt and to repay the p_____ when it becomes due.

interest   principal

10-67. Similarly, shareholders want to know about the adequacy of cash flow to pay d_____s.

dividends

> **NOTE:** A number that is useful for these purposes is called **Free Cash Flow**. It is calculated by subtracting from the cash flow expected from operating activities: (1) the cash needed to purchase normal fixed asset replacements; (2) the cash required to pay long-term debt that is coming due; and (3) normal dividend payments. The difference indicates the amount, if any, that the company is likely to have available (1) to provide a cushion against unforeseen cash outflows, and (2) to provide for other spending that it might like to undertake.

KEY POINTS TO REMEMBER

- A required financial statement, the Statement of Cash Flows, reports the inflows and outflows of cash during the accounting period.

- The statement has three sections: cash flow from operating activities, cash flow from investing activities, and cash flow from financing activities.

- The cash flow from operating activities is found by adjusting net income for (1) changes in current assets and current liabilities, and (2) depreciation expense.

- Depreciation expense is not a cash flow. Because it decreases net income, it is added back to net income in order to arrive at the operating cash flow.

- In general, investing activities include the acquisition of new fixed assets and the proceeds of selling fixed assets.

- In general, financing activities include obtaining funds from long term borrowing, repayment of these borrowings, and obtaining funds from issuance of additional stock.

2-33. To summarize, for an item to be listed as an asset, it must meet three requirements:

1. It must be _ _ _ _ ed or c_ _ _ _ _ _ _ _ _ ed by the entity;

   owned   controlled

2. It must be v_ _ _ _ _ _ _ _ to the entity; and

   valuable

3. It must have been acquired at a m_ _ _ _ _ _ _ _ _ _ c_ _ _.

   measurable

   cost

2-34. Which of the following items of Homes Incorporated, a builder of houses, are its assets?

A. Its rented office, said to be worth $200,000.

B. Telephones it rents from the telephone company, worth $5,000.

C. Lumber in good condition purchased for $50,000.

D. Scrap lumber purchased for $2,000, but now worthless.

E. Its reputation for building fine houses, said to be worth $100,000.

F. Its truck, in good condition, purchased for $30,000 five years ago.

C and F
   Not A or B: not owned
   Not D: not valuable
   *Not E: not acquired at a measurable
   cost*

> **NOTE:** Assets are divided into two main categories and noncurrent liabilities also are divided into these categories. They are explained in the following section.

CURRENT ASSETS

2-35. Current assets are cash and assets that are expected to be converted into cash or used up in the near future, usually within one year. Groceries on the shelves of a grocery store . . . [are / are not] current assets. The store building . . . [is / is not] a c_ _ _ _ _ _ a_ _ _ _ _. On the balance sheet, current assets are usually reported separately from other assets.

are

is not   current

asset

> ***PLEASE DON'T PEEK:*** *If you look at the answer before writing your response, you will lose much of the educational value.*

> **NOTE:** Generally Accepted Accounting Principles (GAAP) classify other types of cash flows as either investing or financing. The investing category includes both making investments and disposition of investments; for example, sale of an item of plant is classified as an investing activity, as is the acquisition of an item of plant. Similarly, the financing category includes the repayment of borrowings as well as cash received from loans. Because the statement of cash flows shows how each item is classified, users do not need to memorize these GAAP rules.

10-61. An investing activity . . . [is / is not] always a cash outflow, and a financing activity . . . [is / is not] always a cash inflow.

is not

is not

COMPLETING THE STATEMENT OF CASH FLOWS

10-62. Calculate the increase in cash by summing the three categories in Exhibit 11, and enter this total. Note that the $_____,000 net increase in cash . . . [equals / does not equal] the change in the Cash balance as reported on the two balance sheets.

13

equals

10-63. The cash flow statement shows that although net income was $_____,000 in 19x2, Cash increased by only $_____,000. Operating activities generated $_____,000 in cash. $_____,000 of this cash was used to pay dividends. The remaining additional cash inflow was used to acquire new Plant. The cost of the new assets was $_____,000. $_____,000 of this cost was financed by additional borrowing, and cash was used for the remainder. From the cash inflows, $_____,000 remained in the Cash account.

24   13

29   10

12

6

13

USES OF THE STATEMENT OF CASH FLOWS

10-64. A forecast of cash flows helps management and other users of financial information to estimate future needs for cash. For example, when a company is growing, the increase in its accounts receivables, inventory, and fixed assets may require . . . [more / less] cash. Therefore, although growth may result in additional profits, it may . . . [generate the need for / provide] additional cash.

more

generate the need for

2-36. Cash is money on hand and money in bank accounts that can be withdrawn at any time. On January 8, Jones Company had $843 in its cash register and $12,012 in its checking account at the bank. Its cash was $_____ .

$12,855 (= $12,012 + $843)

2-37. On the evening of January 8, Jones Company deposited in its checking account $743 of the money in the cash register. After it had done this, its cash totaled $_____ .

$12,855

> **NOTE:** When an entity writes a check, the amount of its cash is not actually reduced until the check has been cashed. Nevertheless, the usual practice is to record a decrease in cash on the day the check is mailed.

2-38. Securities are stocks and bonds. They give valuable rights to the entity that owns them. The U.S. Treasury promises to pay stated amounts of money to entities that own treasury bonds. Therefore, U.S. Treasury Bonds owned by Garsden Company . . . [are / are not] assets of Garsden Company.

are

2-39. Marketable securities are securities that are expected to be converted into cash within a year. An entity owns these securities so as to earn a return on funds that otherwise would be idle. Marketable Securities are . . . [current / noncurrent] assets.

current

> **NOTE:** Investments in safe, very short-term funds, such as money market funds are often included in the cash item, rather than in marketable securities. The item is then called **cash and cash equivalents**.

2-40. An **account receivable** is an amount that is owed to the business, usually by one of its customers, as a result of the ordinary extension of credit. A customer's monthly bill from the electric company would be an a__ __ __ __ __ __   r__ __ __ __ __ __ __ __ __ of the electric company until the customer paid the bill.

account receivable

10-57. As shown in Exhibit 10, Arlen Company had a liability, mortgage bonds. The amount was $_____,000 at the beginning of 19x2 and $_____,000 at the end of 19x2. The increase of $_____,000 showed that Arlen Company issued bonds of this amount. This was a(n) . . . [investing / financing] activity. It represented a(n) . . . [increase / decrease] in cash. Enter this amount in Exhibit 11.

34

40 6

financing

increase

> NOTE: Similar to the transaction in Frame 10-54, the amount of new bonds issued may have been more than $6,000. Part of the new issue may have been used to pay off existing bonds. The issuance of, and redemption of, bonds are financing activities.

10-58. The borrowings reported in the financing section are long-term borrowings. Short-term borrowings are current liabilities, and changes in them are reported in the section on Cash Flow from O_____ A_____ .

Operating Activities

> NOTE: There is one exception to the above rule. The current portion of long-term debt is a current liability. However, for the purpose of cash flow analysis, it is reported as a financing activity.

10-59. Issuance of additional shares of a company's stock is also a financing activity. Exhibit 10 shows that Arlen Company's Paid-In Capital was $_____ at the beginning of 19x2 and $_____ at the end of 19x2. Evidently, the company . . . [did / did not] issue additional stock in 19x2.

$60,000 $60,000

did not

10-60. Dividends paid are classified as a financing activity. Exhibit 10 shows that Arlen Company paid $_____,000 of dividends in 19x2. Enter this amount in Exhibit 11. Then enter the total of the financing activities in Exhibit 11.

10

> **NOTE:** The word "net" on the Accounts Receivable line means that the amount is less than the amount that customers actually owe. The reason for this is given in Part 5.

2-41. If a customer signs a written **promissory note** agreeing to pay what is owed, the amount would be listed as a **N__ __ __ Receivable**, rather than as an _____ Receivable. An example is given below. Evidently, Garsden Company (Exhibit 1) . . . [did / did not] have any Notes Receivable.

Note

Account

did not

CONSUMER NOTE

$ *400 XX*   *July 1,* 19 *96*

FOR VALUE RECEIVED, ... *I, Fred Cochran,* ....

promise to pay to........ *Ryan Lougee* ....or order

the sum of...... *Four hundred* _____ .Dollars

in...... *one year* ....from this date with interest to be paid

...... *monthly* ....at the rate of..... *12* ....per centum per.... *annum* ....during said term, and for such further time as the said principal sum, or any part thereof shall remain unpaid.

Witness

Michael P. Vetere } *Fred Cochran*

(vertical text, left margin:)
REVISED 1961 – CHAPTER 598
FORM 306 REVISED 1959 HOBBS & WARREN, INC. PUBLISHERS, BOSTON

Secured by a Security Agreement (Chattel Mortgage) and a Financing Statement to be recorded in the Recording Office of the or County
☐☐☐ Secretary of State
☐☐ City or Town Clerk of
☐☐ Register of Deeds in the County of

2-42. Inventories are goods being held for sale, as well as supplies, raw materials, and partially finished products that will be sold upon completion. For example, a truck owned by an automobile dealer for resale to its customers . . . [is / is not] inventory. A truck owned by an entity and used to transport its own goods . . . [is / is not] inventory.

is

is not

2-43. In Exhibit 1 the inventories of Garsden Company are reported as $_____ .

$10,623,000

INVESTING AND FINANCING FLOWS

10-52. Exhibit 11 shows that in addition to cash flows from operating activities, there are two other categories on a statement of cash flows: cash flows from _____ activities and cash flows from _____ activities.

investing

financing

10-53. When a company invests in additional property or plant, the amount involved is a cash . . . [inflow to / outflow from] the company.

outflow from

> **NOTE:** The amount may not be an immediate decrease in cash because the payment of cash may have been offset by borrowing an equal amount. Nevertheless, it is recorded as a cash outflow, and the amount of the borrowing is recorded separately as a financing activity.

10-54. As shown in Exhibit 10, Arlen Company had Plant at the beginning of 19x2 that had cost $_____,000. It had $_____,000 of Plant at the end of 19x2. The increase of $_____,000 was a(n) . . . [investing / financing] activity in 19x2. Enter this amount in Exhibit 11. (The parentheses indicate that this was a cash outflow.)

108   120

12   investing

> **NOTE:** The amount of *new* plant acquired may have been more than $12,000, say $15,000; the difference of $3,000 would represent cash obtained from the sale of existing plant. Both transactions are investing activities. However, we cannot obtain a breakdown of the amount from the available information.

10-55. Similarly, if the Plant account decreased, representing the sale of plant assets, there would have been an . . . [inflow / outflow] of cash.

inflow

10-56. Companies may obtain cash by issuing debt securities, such as bonds. Issuing debt securities is a(n) . . . [investing / financing] activity.

financing

2-44. An entity's burglar alarm system is valuable because it provides protection against loss. The burglar alarm system is an asset. Would a fire insurance policy that protects the entity against losses caused by fire damage also be an asset? . . . [Yes / No]

Yes

2-45. Entities buy fire insurance protection ahead of the period that the insurance policy covers. When they buy the insurance policy, they have acquired an a __ __ __ __. Because the policy covers only a short period of time, the asset is a . . . [current / noncurrent] asset. Insurance protection can't be touched. It is an **intangible** asset.

asset

current

NOTE: Some insurance policies provide protection for more than one year; even so, they are often listed as current assets.

2-46. An intangible asset is an asset that can't be t__ __ __ __ __ __. It has no physical substance.

touched

2-47. Prepaid Expenses is the name for intangible assets that will be used up in the near future; that is, they are intangible . . . [current / noncurrent] assets. (The reason for using the word "expense" will be explained in Part 6.) Exhibit 1 shows that Garsden Company had $_____ of Prepaid Expenses on December 31, 1995.

current

$389,000

2-48. In summary, current assets consist of c_____ and of assets that are expected to be converted into c_____ or used up within a short period, usually within _____ _____ (how long?).

cash

cash

one year

NONCURRENT ASSETS

2-49. As the name suggests, assets that are expected to be useful for longer than one future year are called . . . [current / noncurrent] assets.

noncurrent

10-45. Complete the "Cash Flows from Operating Activities" section of Exhibit 11. (Remember that numbers in parentheses are subtracted.) The cash flow from operating activities was $_____,000.

29

10-46. Note that the $_____,000 adjustment for Depreciation Expense is . . . [larger than / smaller than / about the same as] the net amount of all the working capital adjustments. This is the case in many companies, especially manufacturing companies that have relatively large amounts of fixed assets.

6
larger than

10-47. As a shortcut, therefore, some analysts arrive at the operating cash flow simply by adding Depreciation Expense to Net Income. They disregard changes in working capital on the assumption that these changes net out to a minor amount. This shortcut may give the impression that depreciation is a cash flow. Such an impression is . . . [approximately correct / dead wrong].

dead wrong

SUMMARY OF OPERATING ADJUSTMENTS

10-48. If the total amount of working capital (excluding cash) did not change, and if there are no non-cash expenses, such as depreciation, cash flow from operations will be . . . [lower than / the same as / higher than] net income.

the same as

10-49. If working capital decreased, cash flow from operations will be . . . [lower than / higher than] net income.

higher than

10-50. If working capital increased, cash flow from operations will be . . . [lower than / higher than] net income.

lower than

10-51. If there was depreciation expense, cash flow from operations will be . . . [lower than / the same as / higher than] net income.

higher than

2-50. Tangible assets are assets that can be touched; they have physical substance. Buildings, trucks, and machines are t__ __ __ __ __ __ __ assets. They are also . . . [current / noncurrent] assets.

tangible

noncurrent

2-51. As indicated by the first item listed under noncurrent assets in Exhibit 1, the usual name for tangible, noncurrent assets is _____, _____, and _____. Because they are noncurrent, we know that these assets are expected to be used in the entity for more than _____ _____ (how long?).

Property

Plant   Equipment

one

year

2-52. Exhibit 1 shows the . . . [cost / market value] of property, plant, and equipment to be $26,946,000. It shows that a portion of the cost of this asset has been subtracted from the original cost because it has been "used up." This "used-up" portion is called _____ _____ and totals $_____.

cost

accumulated

depreciation $13,534,000

2-53. After this amount is subtracted, the asset amount is shown as $_____. This is the amount of cost that . . . [has / has not] been used up. (In Part 8, we shall explain this amount further.)

$13,412,000   has not

2-54. The other noncurrent asset items are **intangible assets**; that is, they have no physical substance, except as pieces of paper. The Investments item consists of securities, such as bonds. Evidently Garsden Company does not intend to turn these investments into cash within ____ _____ (how long?). If these securities were expected to be turned into cash within that period, they would be listed as a current asset, M__ __ __ __ __ __ __ __ __ S__ __ __ __ __ __ __ __ __.

one year

Marketable Securities

NET EFFECT OF WORKING CAPITAL CHANGES

10-41. Using Exhibit 11, we can find the net effect of these four adjustments. There was a net . . . [increase / decrease] of $_____,000. Changes in these items resulted in an increase in Cash that was . . . [less than / more than] net income by this amount. Enter this amount in Exhibit 11.

decrease   1

less than

10-42. In summary, an increase in current assets means that . . . [more / less] of the cash inflow was tied up in accounts receivable, inventory, and/or other current assets, with a corresponding . . . [increase / decrease] in Cash. This is why, in times when cash is low, a business tries to keep the other current assets as . . . [high / low] as feasible.

more

decrease

low

10-43. An increase in current liabilities means that . . . [more / less] cash was freed up. The cash not paid to suppliers is still in the C_____ account. This is why, in times when cash is low, a business tries to keep current liabilities as . . . [high / low] as feasible.

more

Cash

high

10-44. Users of financial statements need to understand these relationships, but there is no need to memorize them. The cash flow statement gives the net effect of each of the four types of adjustments in working capital items. Complete the following summary of them:

Change	Adjustment to Net Income	
Decrease in a current asset	add	
Increase in a current asset	[add / subtract]	subtract
Increase in a current liability	[add / subtract]	add
Decrease in a current liability	[add / subtract]	subtract

> **NOTE:** Remember that these adjustments are made to convert the net income number to a cash basis. The net income number, as reported on the income statement, is not changed.

2-55. The next noncurrent asset reported is **Patents and Trademarks**. These are rights to use patents and rights to valuable brand names or logos (such as "7•Up"). Because they are assets, we know that

   1.   they are v_ _ _ _ _ _ _ ,   valuable

   2.   they are o_ _ _ _ by Garsden Company, and   owned

   3.   they were acquired at a measurable c_ _ _.   cost

2-56. Goodwill, the final item on the asset side, has a special meaning in accounting. It arises when one company buys another company and pays more than the value of its net identifiable assets. Grady Company bought Baker Company, paying $1,400,000 cash. Baker Company's identifiable assets were judged to be worth $1,500,000, and Grady became responsible for Baker's liabilities, which totaled $500,000. Complete the following calculation:

Baker's identifiable assets	$ _____	$1,500,000
less liabilities	_____	$500,000
Net identifiable assets	_____	$1,000,000
Grady paid Baker	$1,400,000	
Therefore, goodwill was	_____	$400,000

2-57. Remember that some assets, such as automobiles, are a **property**, which is . . . [tangible / intangible] and others, such as insurance protection, are a **property right**, which is . . . [tangible / intangible].

tangible

intangible

CURRENT LIABILITIES

2-58. The right-hand side of the Garsden Company balance sheet lists the company's liabilities and equity. As explained in Part 1, these can be regarded either as c_ _ _ _ _ _ against the assets or as the s_ _ _ _ _ _ _ from which the assets were acquired. The claims of creditors and other outside parties are called l_ _ _ _ _ _ _ _ _ _.

claims

sources

liabilities

10-36. An easy way to remember whether the impact on Cash (and hence the adjustment to net income) is an addition or a subtraction is to pretend that only that account and Cash exist. For example, if Cash and Accounts Receivable were the only accounts, a decrease in Accounts Receivable would have to mean a(n) . . . [increase / decrease] in Cash.

increase

10-37. This follows from the fundamental accounting equation: _____ = _____ + _____ . To keep this equation in balance, a decrease in Accounts Receivable would necessarily mean an equal . . . [increase / decrease] in Cash, if these were the only two accounts involved.

Assets = Liabilities + Equity

increase

> **NOTE:** A change in a current asset may not have an immediate effect on Cash. For example, an increase in Inventory may be accompanied by an increase in Accounts Payable. However, the ultimate effect on Cash is as described, and the effect on other accounts will be considered when we analyze these accounts.

CHANGES IN CURRENT LIABILITIES

10-38. Changes in current liabilities have the opposite effect on Cash from changes in current assets. An increase in a current liability requires that the net income amount be adjusted to a cash basis by . . . [adding to it / subtracting from it]. A decrease in a current liability requires that the adjustment be a(n) . . . [addition / subtraction].

adding to it

subtraction

10-39. Exhibit 10 shows that Accounts Payable . . . [increased / decreased] by $_____,000. Therefore, net income is adjusted to a cash basis by . . . [adding / subtracting] this amount. Enter this change in Exhibit 11.

decreased
3
subtracting

10-40. Exhibit 10 shows that Accrued Wages . . . [increased / decreased] by $_____,000. Therefore, net income is adjusted to a cash basis by . . . [adding / subtracting] it by this amount. Enter this change in Exhibit 11.

increased
4
adding

2-59. In Exhibit 1, the first category of liabilities is _____ li-abilities. As you might expect from the discussion of current assets, current liabilities are claims that become due within a . . . [short / long] time, usually within _____ _____ (how long?).

current

short
one year

2-60. The first current liability listed in Exhibit 1 is _____ _____. These are the opposite of Accounts Receivable; that is, they are amounts that . . . [the company owes to its suppliers / are owed to the company by its customers].

Accounts
Payable
the company owes its suppliers

2-61. In December 19x1, Smith Company sold a personal computer to Brown Company for $3,000. Brown Company agreed to pay for it within 60 days. On their December 31, 19x1, balance sheets, Smith Company would report the $3,000 as Accounts . . . [Receivable / Payable] and Brown Company would report the $3,000 as Accounts . . . [Receivable / Payable].

Receivable
Payable

2-62. The next item, **Bank Loan Payable**, corresponds to the asset, Notes Receivable. It is reported separately from Accounts Payable be-cause the debt is evidenced by a promissory n__ __ __. Which statement is true?

A. Garsden owes the bank $1,000,000.
B. Garsden will pay the bank $1,000,000.
C. Both A and B are true.

note

A *(Although most liabilities will be paid, the balance sheet does not promise this.)*

> **NOTE:** Amounts owed to employees and others for services they have pro-vided but for which they have not been paid are listed as **Accrued Liabilities**. They will be described in Part 6.

10-33. Thus, if the ending balance in Accounts Receivable is less than the beginning balance, the flow to Cash is . . . [more than / less than] the amount of revenue, and the adjustment to net income must be a(n) . . . [addition / subtraction] to show the effect on Cash.

more than

addition

10-34. Finally, consider the situation in which the ending balance in Accounts Receivable was greater than the beginning balance, as illustrated in the following diagram:

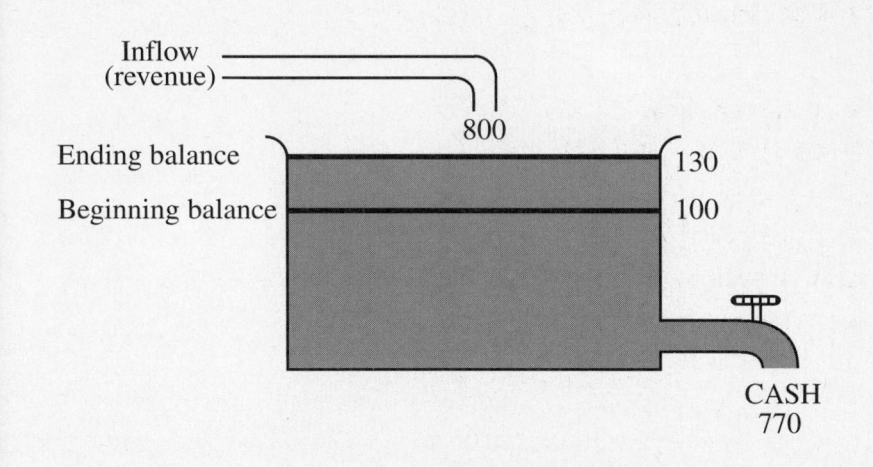

Calculate the flow to Cash by completing the following:

Beginning balance	$100
Ending balance	– _____
Change	– _____
Revenue	800
Flow to Cash	_____

130

30

770

10-35. Thus, if the ending balance in Accounts Receivable is greater than the beginning balance, the flow to Cash is . . . [more than / less than] the amount of revenue, and the adjustment to net income must be a(n) . . . [addition / subtraction] to show the effect on Cash.

less than

subtraction

2-63. Estimated Tax Liability is the amount owed to the government for taxes. It is shown separately from other liabilities, both because the amount is large and also because the exact amount owed may not be known as of the date of the balance sheet. In Exhibit 1 this amount is shown as $_____. It is a current liability because the amount is due within ____ _____ (how long?).

$1,541,000

one year

2-64. Two items of **Long-term Debt** are shown as liabilities. One, labelled "current portion," amounts to $_____. The other, listed under noncurrent liabilities, amounts to $_____. Evidently, the total amount of long-term debt is $_____.

$500,000

$2,000,000

$2,500,000

2-65. The $500,000 is shown separately as a current liability because it is due within ____ _____ (how soon?), that is, before December 31, 199__. The remaining $2,000,000 does not become due until after December 31, 199__.

one year

1996

1996

CURRENT RATIO

2-66. The current assets and current liabilities indicate the entity's ability to meet its current obligations. A measure of this ability is the **current ratio**, which is the ratio of current assets to current liabilities. For Garsden Company, the current ratio is:

$$\frac{\text{current assets}}{\text{current liabilities}} = \frac{\$ \rule{2cm}{0.4pt}}{\$ \rule{2cm}{0.4pt}} = \boxed{}^* \text{ to 1}$$

$$\frac{\$22,651,000}{\$\ 9,519,000} = 2.4 \text{ to 1}$$

_____

* Carry this amount to one decimal place.

2-67. In Garsden's industry, a current ratio of at least 2 to 1 is desirable. Garsden Company . . . [does / does not] pass this test.

does

Calculate the flow from Accounts Receivable to Cash by completing the following:

Beginning balance	$100	
Ending balance	– _____	100
Change	_____	0
Revenue	+ 800	
Flow to Cash	_____	800

10-31. Thus, if the balance in Accounts Receivable is unchanged, the inflow to Cash . . . [is / is not] the same amount as revenue, and an adjustment . . . [is / is not] necessary.

is

is not

10-32. Next, consider the situation in which the ending balance in Accounts Receivable was less than the beginning balance, as illustrated in the following diagram:

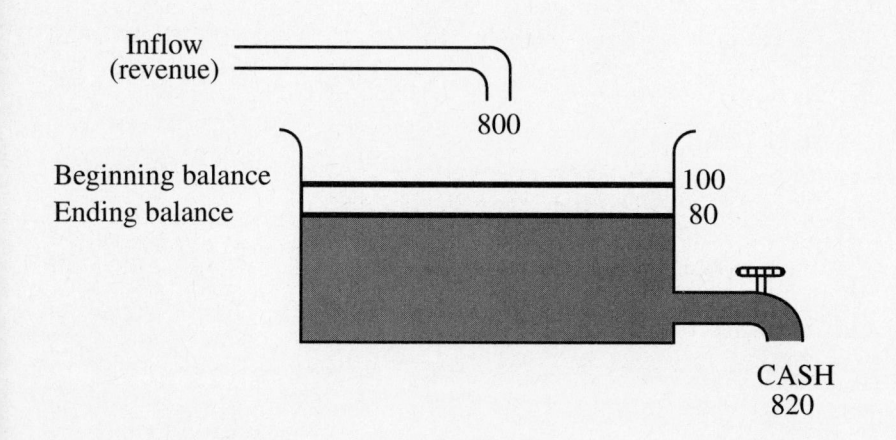

Calculate the outflow to Cash by completing the following:

Beginning balance	$100	
Ending balance	– _____	80
Change	+ _____	20
Revenue	+ 800	
Flow to Cash	_____	820

NONCURRENT LIABILITIES

2-68. As we have seen, Garsden Company has obtained funds by borrowing, and $_____ of this debt is not due to be repaid until after December 31, 199___. This amount is therefore a . . . [current / noncurrent] liability.

$2,000,000

1996   noncurrent

2-69. Suppose the $500,000 current portion was paid in 1996, and an additional $600,000 of debt became due in 1997. On the balance sheet as of December 31, 1996, the current portion of long-term debt would be reported as $_____, and the noncurrent liability would be reduced to $_____.

$600,000

$1,400,000

> **NOTE:** Although a single **liability** may have both a current portion and a noncurrent portion, a single **asset** is not always so divided. Prepaid Insurance of $2,000 covering protection for two future years is usually reported as a current asset of $2,000.

> **NOTE:** The other noncurrent liability, Deferred Income Taxes, will be described in Part 8.

2-70. Liabilities are claims against all the assets. The $5,602,000 of accounts payable on the Garsden Company balance sheet is a claim against . . . [the current assets of $22,651,000 / the total assets of $38,239,000].

the total assets of $38,239,000

EQUITY

2-71. Equity consists of capital obtained from sources that are not liabilities. As Exhibit 1 indicates, there are two sources of equity capital: (1) $12,256,000, which is labelled Total _____-__ _____ and (2) $13,640,000, which is labelled _____ _____.

Paid-in Capital

Retained Earnings

10-27. Because the increase in Cash was . . . [more than / less than] the amount of Revenues, we must . . . [add to / subtract from] net income the amount that Cash was greater than Revenues. As shown above, this was $_____,000. Enter this amount in Exhibit 11.

more than
add to

2

10-28. If Accounts Receivable had increased during the period, the adjustment of net income would be the opposite; that is, an increase in a non-cash current asset leads to an adjustment that . . . [adds to / subtracts from] net income in order to find the cash flow from operations.

subtracts from

10-29. As shown in Exhibit 10, the beginning balance in Inventory was $_____,000, and the ending balance was $_____,000, which shows that this asset . . . [increased / decreased] by $_____,000 during the year. This change had the opposite effect on Cash from the change in Accounts Receivable. Therefore, we must . . . [add to / subtract from] net income to arrive at the change in cash. Enter the $4,000 in Exhibit 11.

56   60

increased   4

subtract from

NOTE: If you are comfortable with this treatment of changes in Accounts Receivable, go to Frame 10-34. Frames 10-30 to 10-34 repeat this analysis, using diagrams. In these diagrams, the beginning balance of Accounts Receivable was $100,000 and additions during the year from sales to customers (revenues) were $800,000.

10-30. The following diagram shows the situation in which the ending balance in Accounts Receivable was the same as the balance at the beginning of the year.

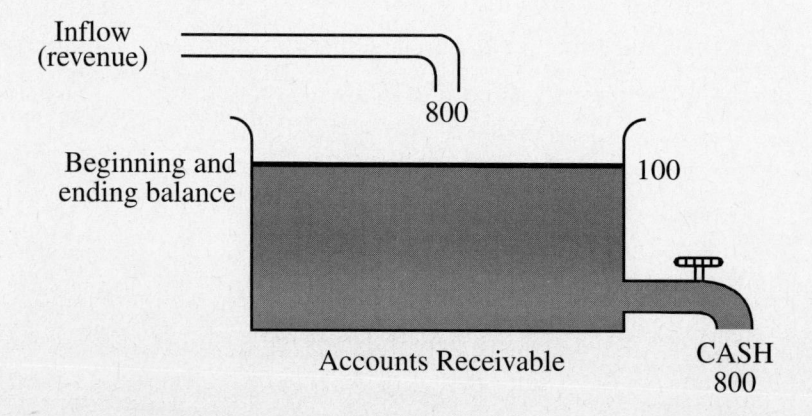

2-72. Paid-in Capital is the amount of capital supplied by equity investors. They own the entity. The details of how this item is reported depends on the type of organization. Garsden Company is a corporation, and its owners receive *shares* of common _____ as evidence of their ownership. They are therefore called s__ __ __ __ holders. Other forms of ownership will be described in Part 9.

stock

shareholders (or stockholders)

2-73. The Paid-in Capital is reported as two separate amounts: $1,000,000, which is labelled _____ _____ , and $11,256,000, labelled Additional _____-__ _____. The reasons for this distinction are described in Part 9. The important number is the total amount paid in by the shareholders, which is $_____ .

Common Stock

Paid-in Capital

$12,256,000

2-74. Thus, one type of equity in a corporation is the amount that was originally contributed by the s_____ .

shareholders (or stockholders)

2-75. Individual shareholders may sell their stock to someone else, but this has no effect on the balance sheet of the corporation. The market price of shares of General Motors Corporation stock changes practically every day; the amount of Paid-in Capital reported on the General Motors balance sheet . . . [does / does not] reflect these changes. This is consistent with the e_____ concept; transactions between individual shareholders do not affect the entity.

does not

entity

2-76. The other equity item, $13,640,000, shows the amount of equity that has been *earned* by the profitable operations of the company and that has been *retained* in the entity; hence the name, R__ __ __ __ __ __ __ __ E__ __ __ __ __ __ __ __ .

Retained

Earnings

2-77. Retained Earnings represents those amounts that have been retained in the entity after part of the company's earnings (i.e., profits) have been paid to shareholders in the form of dividends. Complete the following equation:

Retained Earnings = [_____] − [_____] .

Earnings – Dividends

10-24. Consider what the account balances would have been if Arlen Company had revenue of $300,000 but had received $302,000 cash from customers. Enter the $302,000 in the T accounts shown below and find the account balances.

Cash

Beg. bal.	7		
From customer	☐		
End. bal.	☐		

302

309

Accounts Receivable

Beg. bal.	42	From customer	☐
Sale	300		
End. bal.	☐		

302

40

Revenues

		Sale	300

10-25. The above accounts show that in this situation, the ending balance of Cash would have been . . . [$2,000 larger than / $2,000 smaller than / the same as] the Cash balance when cash receipts equaled sales revenues, as shown in Frame 10-22. The Accounts Receivable balance would have been . . . [$2,000 larger than / $2,000 smaller than / the same as] the balance when cash receipts equaled sales revenues. Revenues in 19x2 would still have been $300,000.

$2,000 larger than

$2,000 smaller than

10-26. This example shows that if the ending balance in Accounts Receivable was *less* than its beginning balance, the increase in Cash would be . . . [more than / less than / the same as] the amount of Revenues. Part of the increase in Cash would be the result of decreasing Accounts Receivable. Put another way, Cash increased partly because more old customers paid their bills and partly because of sales to new customers. This is what happened in Arlen Company.

more than

2-78. Retained Earnings are additions to equity that have accumulated since the entity began, not those of a single year. Therefore, unless Garsden Company has been in business only one year, the $13,640,000 shown as Retained Earnings as of December 31, 1995, reflects . . . [one / all previous] year(s) of operations.

all previous

2-79. The amount of Retained Earnings shows the amount of capital generated by operating activities. It is **not** cash. Cash is an asset. On December 31, 1995, the amount of Cash was $_____ . The amount of Retained Earnings was $_____ .

$1,449,000
$13,640,000

2-80. In summary, the equity section of the balance sheet reports the amount of capital obtained from two sources:

1. The amount provided directly by equity investors (i.e., shareholders in a corporation), which is called _____ - _____ _____ .

    Paid-in
    Capital

2. The amount generated by profitable operations and retained in the entity, which is called _____ _____ .

    Retained Earnings

> **NOTE:** The Equity section is often labelled "Shareholders' Equity" or "Owners' Equity."

2-81. Keep in mind the fundamental accounting equation:

[_____] = [_____] + [_____] .

Assets = Liabilities + Equity

The right-hand side of the balance sheet shows the *sources* of capital. The capital itself exists in the form of __ __ __ __ __ __ , which are reported on the left-hand side.

assets

10-21. If, in 19x2, Arlen Company received $300,000 cash from credit customers, Cash would increase and Accounts Receivable would decrease, as summarized in the following journal entry:

Dr. _____ 300

Cr. _____ _____ 300

Cash

Accounts Receivable

10-22. The above two entries have been posted to the accounts as shown below:

Cash			Accounts Receivable		
Beg. bal.	7		Beg. bal.	42	From customer 300
From customer 300			Sale	300	
End. bal.	307		End. bal.	42	

Revenues	
	Sale 300

As these accounts show, when the balance in Accounts Receivable does not change, the increase in cash is . . . [more than / less than / the same as] the sales revenue.

the same as

10-23. This is the case with all working capital accounts. If the beginning balance is the same as the ending balance, an adjustment from the accrual basis to the cash basis . . . [is / is not] necessary.

is not

KEY POINTS TO REMEMBER

The following diagram summarizes how assets are reported. (It antici-pates some details described in later Parts.)

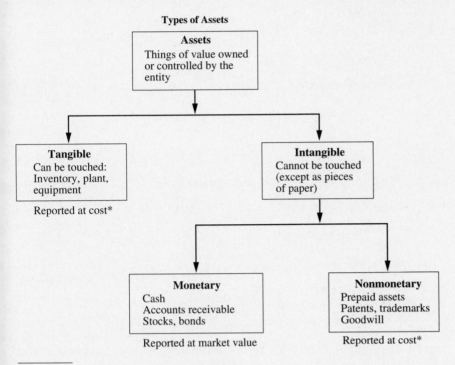

Types of Assets

Assets
Things of value owned
or controlled by the
entity

Tangible
Can be touched:
Inventory, plant,
equipment

Reported at cost*

Intangible
Cannot be touched
(except as pieces
of paper)

Monetary
Cash
Accounts receivable
Stocks, bonds

Reported at market value

Nonmonetary
Prepaid assets
Patents, trademarks
Goodwill

Reported at cost*

*Historical cost less depreciation or amortization

- The going-concern concept: Accounting assumes that an entity will continue to operate indefinitely.

- The cost concept: Accounting focuses on the cost of assets, rather than on their market value.

- Assets are valuable items that are owned or controlled by the entity and that were acquired at a measurable cost. Goodwill is not an asset unless it was purchased.

- Current assets are cash and assets that are expected to be converted into cash or used up in the near future, usually within one year.

- Current liabilities are obligations due in the near future, usually within one year.

- The current ratio is the ratio of current assets to current liabilities.

- Marketable securities are current assets; investments are noncurrent assets.

- A single liability may have both a current portion and a noncurrent portion.

- Equity consists of paid-in capital (which in a corporation is represented by shares of stock) plus earnings retained since the entity began. It does not report the market value of the stock. Retained earnings is not cash; it is part of the owners' claim on the assets.

ADJUSTMENTS FOR CHANGES IN WORKING CAPITAL ACCOUNTS

10-17. Cash, inventory, accounts receivable, and similar items that will be converted into cash in the near future are c_____ assets. Wages payable, accounts payable, and similar obligations that are due in the near future are c_____ liabilities. The difference between current assets and current liabilities is called **working capital**. Operating activities—such as making sales, purchasing materials for inventory, and incurring production, selling, and administrative expenses—are the principal causes of changes in working capital items. We shall analyze the asset and liability categories separately.

current

current

NOTE: Although cash is, of course, an item of working capital, we exclude it here because we want to analyze the impact of changes in the other working capital accounts on cash.

ADJUSTMENTS TO CURRENT ASSETS

10-18. If all revenues in 19x2 were from cash sales, cash inflows . . . [would / would not] be the same amount as revenues; that is, if sales revenues were $300,000, cash inflows would be $_____,000. However, in most companies, some sales are made to credit customers. These sales are first reported as the current asset, A__ __ __ __ __ __ __ R__ __ __ __ __ __ __ __ __ . The company will receive cash later on, when customers pay their bills.

would

300

Accounts

Receivable

10-19. In Arlen Company, all sales were credit sales. If sales in 19x2 were $300,000, Revenues would be $_____,000, and Accounts Receivable would increase by $_____,000 when these sales were made.

300

300

10-20. The journal entry summarizing the above transaction would be (omitting 000):

Dr. A_____ R_____ 300

    Cr. R_____ 300

Accounts Receivable

Revenues

You have completed Part 2 of this program. If you think you understand the material in this part, you should now take Post Test 2, which is in the separate booklet. If you are uncertain about your understanding, you should review Part 2.

The post test will serve both to test your comprehension and to review the highlights of Part 2. After taking the post test, you may find that you are unsure about certain points. You should review these points before continuing with Part 3.

10-13. If Depreciation Expense was $4,000 higher than the amount reported in Exhibit 10, Net Income would be $4,000 . . . [higher than / lower than / the same as] the amount reported. The $4,000 increase in Depreciation Expense would offset exactly the $4,000 decrease in Net Income. Cash flow would be . . . [higher than / lower than / the same as] the amount reported in Exhibit 11.

lower than

the same as

10-14. To reinforce this point, recall the journal entry that records depreciation expense:

Dr. D_____ E_____

    Cr. A_____ D_____

Depreciation Expense

    Accumulated Depreciation

The Cash account . . . [was / was not] changed by this entry.

was not

10-15. To repeat, the cash for fixed assets was paid out when the fixed assets were purchased (or when borrowings made in connection with such a purchase were paid off). Cash . . . [is / is not] affected by the depreciation charge; to do so would be double counting.

is not

> **NOTE:** Amortization of intangible assets, write-off of losses, and other non-cash expenses also are added to net income to convert net income to cash flow from operating activities.

10-16. Thus, depreciation . . . [is / is not] a source of cash! (This is a common misconception.)

is not

Part 3

Balance Sheet Changes

Learning Objectives

In this part you will learn:

* How several types of transactions change the amounts reported on the balance sheet.
* The nature of income and the income statement.

3-1. The amounts of assets, liabilities, and equity of an entity . . . [remain constant / change from day to day]. Therefore the amounts shown on its balance sheet also . . . [remain constant / change].

change from day to day

change

3-2. Although a balance sheet must be prepared at the end of each year, it can be prepared more often. In this part, you will be asked to prepare a balance sheet at the end of each day. We shall consider a business named Glendale Market owned by a proprietor, John Smith. The **entity** here is . . . [John Smith / Glendale Market].

Glendale Market

10-8. Net income is the difference between r_ _ _ _ _ _ es and e_ _ _ _ _ _ es. "Cash flow from operating activities" is the difference between operating cash inflows and operating cash outflows. To find the amount of cash flow from operating activities, we make two types of adjustments to net income: (1) for depreciation and other expenses that will not *ever* require an outflow of c_ _ _ _ , and (2) for changes in working capital accounts.

revenues

expenses

cash

ADJUSTMENT FOR DEPRECIATION EXPENSE

10-9. According to its balance sheet (Exhibit 10), Arlen Company owned Plant most of which it had acquired . . . [prior to / in] 19x2 at a cost of $_____,000. The cash outflow for these assets occurred . . . [prior to 19x2 / in 19x2].

prior to

108

prior to 19x2

10-10. According to its income statement, Arlen Company had Depreciation Expense of $_____,000 in 19x2. Depreciation writes off a portion of the cost of fixed assets. The cash outflow for the assets on hand at the beginning of 19x2 occurred in earlier years; this Depreciation Expense therefore . . . [was / was not] a cash outflow in 19x2.

6

was not

10-11. Although Depreciation Expense is subtracted from Revenue in arriving at Net Income, it is not a cash outflow. Net Income is $6,000 less than it would have been with no Depreciation Expense. Therefore, Net Income is adjusted to a cash basis by . . . [adding $6,000 to / subtracting $6,000 from] Net Income. Enter this adjustment in Exhibit 11.

adding $6,000 to

10-12. Suppose that Arlen Company had decided to charge Depreciation Expense of $10,000, rather than $6,000, in 19x2, but made no other changes in the accounts. The cash flow from operating activities would then be . . . [higher than / lower than / the same as] the amount reported in Exhibit 11.

the same as

> **NOTE:** If you answered Frame 10–12 correctly, go to Frame 10–14.

3-3. On January 2, Smith started Glendale Market by opening a bank account in its name and depositing $10,000 of his money in it. In the assets column of the following balance, enter the amount of the asset Cash that Glendale Market owned at the close of business on January 2.

GLENDALE MARKET
Balance Sheet as of January 2

Assets   Liabilities & Equity

Cash . . . . $

$10,000

3-4. Recall that a name for equity capital is "Paid-in Capital." In the space below, record the amount of paid-in capital as of the close of business on January 2.

GLENDALE MARKET
Balance Sheet as of January 2

Assets   Liabilities & Equity

Cash . . . . $10,000   . . $

Paid-in Capital $10,000

3-5. This balance sheet tells us how much cash . . . [Glendale Market / John Smith] had on January 2. The separation of Glendale Market from John Smith, the person, is an illustration of the e__ __ __ __ __ concept.

Glendale Market

entity

NOTE: An entity owned by one person, such as Glendale Market, is called a **proprietorship**. In some proprietorships, the equity item is labelled with the proprietor's name: "John Smith, Capital." This is simply a variation in terminology, not a difference in concepts.

3-6. On January 2, Glendale Market received $10,000 cash from John Smith. To record the effect of this event on the financial condition of the entity, you made _____ (how many?) changes in the balance sheet. After you made these changes, the balance sheet . . . [did / did not] balance. This is an illustration of the d__ __ __ __ -a__ __ __ __ __ concept.

two

did

dual-aspect

10-6. The indirect method analyzes income statement and balance sheet items to determine whether the offsetting entries to the debits and credits to these accounts involved credits or debits to Cash. If there was a credit to Cash, there was an . . . [inflow / outflow] of cash; the offsetting debit was an increase in an asset or a decrease in a liability account. If there was a debit to Cash, there was an . . . [inflow / outflow] of cash.

outflow

inflow

10-7. In the statement of cash flows, *cash* includes not only money, but also assets that are almost the same as money, such as certificates of deposit and money market accounts. These are equivalent to cash, and are called "cash equ__ __ __ __ ents."

equivalents

NOTE: We next develop a statement of cash flows for Arlen Company, using the indirect method and the balance sheet and income statement information in Exhibit 10.

We will work with the statement of cash flows in Exhibit 11. It consists of three sections. We will describe the first section, called "cash flow from operating activities," in some detail. We will describe the other two sections, called "cash flow from investing activities" and "cash flow from financing activities," together because the same principles apply to both. The principal purpose of this part is to show the relationship between the accrual accounting numbers and cash. The individual items on the cash flow statement are largely self explanatory.

CASH FLOW FROM OPERATING ACTIVITIES

NOTE: The first section of the statement of cash flows reports how much cash was generated by the operating activities of the period—the day-to-day activities that bring cash in from customers and pay cash out to employees and suppliers. To do this, we must first convert net income—the bottom line of the income statement—from an accrual basis to a cash basis.

3-7. A total should always be given for each side of the balance sheet. Complete the following balance sheet.

BROWN COMPANY
Balance Sheet as of June 30, 19x1

Assets		Liabilities & Equity	
Cash $50,000		Accounts payable $10,000	
		Paid-in capital 40,000	
	$		$

Total $50,000 Total $50,000

3-8. The totals of the above balance sheet . . . [are equal by coincidence / are necessarily equal].

are necessarily equal

3-9. Amounts on a balance sheet are generally listed with the most current items first. Correct the following list to make it accord with this practice.

Liabilities (as of December 31, 19x1):

 Bank loan payable (due next October)

 Accounts payable (due in 60 days)

 Long-term debt

Accounts payable

Bank loan payable

Long-term debt

3-10. When an entity borrows money, it may sign a written promise to repay. Such a written promise is termed a **note**. For example, if Business *A* borrows money from Business *B*, signing a note, Business *A* will record a . . . [note receivable / note payable] on its balance sheet, and Business *B* will record a . . . [note receivable / note payable].

note payable

note receivable

10-3. Both the income statement and the cash flow statement report flows during the period. The difference is that the income statement reports flows on the **accrual** basis; that is, inflows are measured as r_____s and outflows are measured as e_____s. By contrast, the cash flow statement reports inflows and outflows of c_____ .

revenues

expenses

cash

> **NOTE:** The income statement focuses on *profitability*. The statement of cash flows focuses on *liquidity*.

10-4. For example, assume that an entity sold goods for $1,000 on May 1, and the customer paid $1,000 for these goods on June 1. Its cash inflow on May 1 would be . . . [$0 / $1,000], and its revenue in May would be . . . [$0 / $1,000]. Its cash inflow on June 1 would be . . . [$0 / $1,000], and its revenue in June would be . . . [$0 / $1,000]. Its balance sheet at the end of May would include this $1,000 as an asset, called A_____ R_____ .

$0 $1,000

$1,000

$0

Accounts

Receivable

> **NOTE:** Therefore, an entity's revenues and expenses in a period do not necessarily match its cash receipts and disbursements in that period.

10-5. There are two acceptable methods of preparing the statement of cash flows. One is to summarize the debits and credits (inflows and outflows) to the Cash account directly; it is therefore called the d__ __ __ __ __ method. Most companies use the other method, which is called the ind__ __ __ __ __ method.

direct

indirect

> **NOTE:** The indirect method is more widely used because it shows the relationship between the income statement and the balance sheet and therefore aids in the analysis of these statements.

3-11. On January 3, Glendale Market borrowed $5,000 cash from a bank, giving a note therefor.

Change the following January 2 balance sheet so that it reports the financial condition on January 3. In making your changes, cross out any material to be changed and write the corrections like this:

15,000
~~10,000~~

GLENDALE MARKET
Balance Sheet as of January 2

Assets		Liabilities & Equity	
		.... $	
Cash	$10,000	Paid-in capital	$10,000
Total	$10,000	Total	$10,000

GLENDALE MARKET
Balance Sheet as of January 2

Assets		Liabilities & Equity	
Cash.... $10,000		Note payable.... $5,000	
~~Cash~~ ..... ~~$10,000~~		Paid-in capital	$10,000
Total $10,000		Total $10,000	

3-12. To record the effect of the event of January 3, _____ (how many?) change(s) in the balance sheet (not counting the new totals and the new date) were necessary. The change(s) . . . [did / did not] affect the equality that had existed between assets and liabilities + equity.

two

did not

3-13. On January 4, Glendale Market purchased inventory costing $2,000, paying cash.

Change the following January 3 balance sheet so that it reports the financial condition on January 4. Strike out any items that must be changed, and write the corrections above (or below) them.

GLENDALE MARKET
Balance Sheet as of January 3

Assets		Liabilities & Equity	
Cash	$15,000	Note payable	$ 5,000
	....	Paid-in capital	10,000
Total	$15,000	Total	$15,000

GLENDALE MARKET **4**
Balance Sheet as of January ~~3~~

Assets		Liabilities & Equity	
	13,000	Note	
Cash	~~$15,000~~	payable	$ 5,000
Inventory 2,000		Paid-in capital	10,000
Total	$15,000	Total	$15,000

Part 10

Statement of Cash Flows

Learning Objectives

In this part you will learn:

- What a statement of cash flows is.
- How it differs from an income statement.
- The meaning of the operating items.
- The content of the investing and financing sections.
- The relationship of depreciation to cash flow.
- Uses of the statement of cash flows.

10-1. A company must prepare three financial statements. We described two of them in earlier parts. The . . . [balance sheet / income statement] reports the financial status of the company as of the end of each accounting period. The . . . [balance sheet / income statement] reports financial performance during the period.

balance sheet

income statement

10-2. In this part, we describe the third required statement. It reports the **flow of cash** during the accounting period, and it is therefore called the statement of c_ _ _ _ f_ _ _ _ s.

cash flows

3-14. The event of January 4 required two changes on the balance sheet, even though . . . [only one / both] side(s) of the balance sheet was (were) affected.

only one

3-15. Each event that is recorded in the accounting records is called a **transaction**. When Glendale Market received $10,000 from John Smith and deposited it in its bank account, this qualified as a _____ under the definition given above, because it was "an event that was

__ __ __ __ __ __ __ __ in the __ __ __ __ __ __ __ __ __ __ __

__ __ __ __ __ __ __."

transaction

recorded   accounting
records

3-16. Each transaction you recorded has caused at least ——————— (how many?) change(s) on the balance sheet (not counting the changes in the totals and in the date), even when only one side of the balance sheet was affected. This is true of all transactions, and this is why accounting is called a . . . [single / double / triple]-entry system.

two

double

3-17. Earlier we described the fundamental accounting equation, assets = liabilities + equity. If we were to record only *one* aspect of a transaction, this equation . . . [would / would not] continue to describe an equality.

would not

3-18. The fundamental accounting equation, which is _____ = _____ + _____ was also referred to in Part 1 as the d__ __ __-aspect concept.

assets
liabilities   equity
dual

NOTE: When a business sells merchandise for $300 that had cost it $200, the profit of $100 represents an increase of $100 in equity. As we saw in Part 2, the Retained Earnings item is used to record changes in equity arising from the operation of the business. These facts will help you in analyzing the transactions that follow.

- The amount of capital obtained from preferred and common shareholders is the amount they paid in. The par, or stated, value of common stock is not an important number today, but it is still reported on the balance sheet.

- Cash dividends decrease the amount of equity capital. Stock dividends or stock splits do not affect the total equity.

- Retained earnings are total earnings (i.e., net income) since the entity began operations, less total dividends. (A net loss, of course, results in a decrease in retained earnings.)

- Although sometimes called "net worth," the amount of owners' equity does *not* show what the owners' interest is worth.

- In deciding on its permanent capital structure, a company attempts to strike the right balance between (1) risky but low-cost debt capital, and (2) less risky but high-cost equity capital. The balance in a given company is indicated by its debt ratio.

- Many companies have subsidiaries. The economic entity is a family consisting of the parent and the subsidiaries in which it owns more than 50% of the stock. Consolidated financial statements are prepared for such an economic entity by combining their separate financial statements and eliminating transactions among members of the family.

- The consolidated balance sheet reports all the assets owned by the consolidated entity and all the claims of parties outside the family.

- The consolidated income statement reports only revenues from sales to outside parties and expenses resulting from costs incurred with outside parties. Intrafamily revenues and expenses are eliminated.

You have completed Part 9 of this program. If you think you understand the material in this part, you should now take Post Test 9, which is in the separate booklet. If you are uncertain about your understanding, you should review Part 9.

The post test will serve both to test your comprehension and to review the highlights of Part 9. After taking the post test, you may find that you are unsure about certain points. You should review these points before continuing with Part 10.

3-19. On January 5, Glendale Market sold merchandise for $300, receiving cash. The merchandise had cost $200.

Change the following January 4 balance sheet so that it reports the financial condition on January 5. (If you cannot do this frame, skip to the next without looking at the answer to this one.)

GLENDALE MARKET
Balance Sheet as of January 4

Assets		Liabilities & Equity	
Cash	$13,000	Note payable	$ 5,000
Inventory	2,000	Paid-in capital	10,000
			....
Total	$15,000	Total	$15,000

$15,100 = $15,100

GLENDALE MARKET
Balance Sheet as of January ~~4~~ 5

Assets		Liabilities & Equity	
Cash	**13,300** $~~13,000~~	Note payable	$ 5,000
Inventory ..	**1,800** ~~2,000~~	Paid-in capital	10,000
		Retained earnings 100	
Total	$~~15,000~~ **15,100**	Total	$~~15,000~~ **15,100**

(If you answered this frame correctly, skip to Frame 3-26.)

3-20. On January 5, Glendale Market sold merchandise for $300 cash that cost $200.

To record this transaction, let's handle its individual parts separately. Change the date. Then, record only the amount of cash after the receipt of the $300. (Disregard, for the moment, any other changes, including changes in totals.)

GLENDALE MARKET
Balance Sheet as of January 4

Assets		Liabilities & Equity	
Cash	$13,000	Note payable	$ 5,000
Inventory	2,000	Paid-in capital	10,000
Total	$15,000	Total	$15,000

GLENDALE MARKET
Balance Sheet as of January ~~4~~ 5

Assets		Liabilities & Equity	
Cash	**13,300** $~~13,000~~	Note payable	$ 5,000
Inventory ..	2,000	Paid-in capital	10,000
Total	$15,000	Total	$15,000

9-85. Palm Company owns 60% of Sand Company's stock, which is a . . . [majority / minority] of the stock. Other shareholders own the other 40% of Sand Company stock; they are . . . [majority / minority] shareholders. They have an interest in the consolidated entity, and this interest is reported in the . . . [assets / liabilities and equity] side of the consolidated balance sheet. It is labeled **minority interest**.

majority

minority

liabilities and equity

9-86. The consolidated income statement reports revenues from . . . [all sales / sales to outside parties only] and expenses resulting from . . . [all costs incurred / costs incurred with outside parties]. Intrafamily revenues and expenses are e__ __ __ __ __ __ __ __ __ d.

sales to outside parties only

costs incurred with outside parties

eliminated

9-87. The consolidated financial statements report on the entity called "Palm Company and Subsidiaries." This family of corporations . . . [is / is not] an economic entity, but it . . . [is / is not] a legal entity.

is

is not

9-88. Many corporations have subsidiaries. Since the consolidated financial statements give the best information about the economic entity, many published financial statements are c__ __ __ __ __ __ __ __ __ __ d financial statements.

consolidated

NOTE: In an entity with dozens of subsidiaries, some of which have their own subsidiaries, eliminating the intrafamily transactions is a complicated task. Only the general principles have been described here.

KEY POINTS TO REMEMBER

• A company obtains its permanent capital from two sources: (1) debt (i.e., noncurrent liabilities) and (2) equity. It uses this capital to finance (1) working capital (i.e., current assets – current liabilities) and (2) noncurrent assets.

• Most debt capital is obtained by issuing bonds. Bonds obligate the company to pay interest and to repay the principal when it is due.

• Equity capital is obtained by (1) issuing shares of stock and (2) retaining earnings.

3-21. On January 5, Glendale Market sold merchandise for $300 cash that cost $200. Merchandise that had cost $200 was removed from its inventory.

Record the amount of inventory after this transaction.

GLENDALE MARKET
Balance Sheet as of January ~~4~~ 5

Assets		Liabilities & Equity	
Cash	**13,300** ~~$13,000~~	Note payable	$ 5,000
Inventory	2,000	Paid-in capital	10,000
Total	$15,000	Total	$15,000

GLENDALE MARKET
Balance Sheet as of January ~~4~~ 5

Assets		Liabilities & Equity	
Cash	**13,300** ~~$13,000~~	Note payable	$ 5,000
Inventory	**1,800** ~~2,000~~	Paid-in capital	10,000
Total	$15,000	Total	$15,000

3-22. On January 5, Glendale Market sold merchandise for $300 cash that cost $200.

Now total the assets as of the close of business on January 5, and show the new total.

GLENDALE MARKET
Balance Sheet as of January ~~4~~ 5

Assets		Liabilities & Equity	
Cash	**13,300** ~~$13,000~~	Note payable	$ 5,000
Inventory	**1,800** ~~2,000~~	Paid-in capital	10,000
Total	$15,000	Total	$15,000

GLENDALE MARKET
Balance Sheet as of January ~~4~~ 5

Assets		Liabilities & Equity	
Cash	**13,300** ~~$13,000~~	Note payable	$ 5,000
Inventory	**1,800** ~~2,000~~	Paid-in capital	10,000
Total	~~$15,000~~ **15,100**	Total	$15,000

3-23. On January 5, Glendale Market sold merchandise for $300 cash that cost $200.

GLENDALE MARKET
Balance Sheet as of January ~~4~~ 5

Assets		Liabilities & Equity	
Cash	**13,300** ~~$13,000~~	Note payable	$ 5,000
Inventory	**1,800** ~~2,000~~	Paid-in capital	10,000
Total	~~$15,000~~ **15,100**	Total	$15,000

Evidently the transaction of January 5 caused a net . . . [decrease / increase] of $_____ in the assets of Glendale Market from what they had been at the close of business on January 4.

increase

$100

9-80. In 19x1, Palm Company had sales revenue of $1,000,000, Sea Company had sales revenue of $200,000, and Sand Company had sales revenue of $400,000. Palm Company sold $30,000 of products to Sea Company. All other sales were to outside customers. On the consolidated income statement, the amount of sales reported would be $_____.

$1,570,000
(Total sales = $1,000,000 + $200,000 + $400,000 = $1,600,000. Intrafamily sales = $30,000. Consolidated sales = $1,600,000 – $30,000 = $1,570,000)

9-81. Intrafamily transactions are also eliminated from the consolidated balance sheet. For example, if Sand Company owed Palm Company $10,000, this amount would appear as Accounts . . . [Receivable / Payable] on the balance sheet of Palm Company and as Accounts . . . [Receivable / Payable] on the balance sheet of Sand Company. On the consolidated balance sheet, the Accounts Receivable and Accounts Payable would each be $10,000 . . . [more / less] than the sum of these amounts on the balance sheets of each of the family members.

Receivable

Payable

less

9-82. The balance sheet of Palm Company reports as an asset the Sand Company and Sea Company stock that it owns. This asset . . . [remains unchanged / must be eliminated] from the consolidated balance sheet. On the balance sheets of the subsidiaries, the corresponding amounts are reported as . . . [noncurrent liabilities / equity], and these amounts are also eliminated on the consolidated balance sheet.

must be eliminated

equity

9-83. Palm Company owns 40% of Gray Company stock. This asset is listed on Palm Company's balance sheet at $100,000. This asset would NOT be eliminated from the consolidated balance sheet. Why not? . . . .

Because only companies in which the parent owns more than 50% are consolidated.

9-84. Palm Company owns 60% of the stock of Sand Company. This stock was reported on the balance sheet of Palm Company as an asset, Investment in Subsidiaries, at $60,000. The equity of Sand Corporation is $100,000. On the consolidated balance sheet, the $60,000 asset would be eliminated, and because debits must equal credits, . . . [$60,000 / $100,000] of Sand Company's equity also would be eliminated.

$60,000

3-24. On January 5, Glendale Market sold merchandise for $300 that cost $200. The assets of the entity increased by $100. The increase was the result of selling merchandise at a profit. As we learned in Part 2, profitable operations result in an increase in equity, specifically in the item R_____ E_____.

Retained Earnings

3-25. On January 5, Glendale Market sold merchandise for $300 that cost $200. Add $100 of Retained Earnings and show the new total of the right-hand side.

GLENDALE MARKET
Balance Sheet as of January ~~X~~ 5

Assets		Liabilities & Equity	
Cash	*13,300* ~~$13,000~~	Note payable	$ 5,000
Inventory	*1,800* ~~2,000~~	Paid-in capital	10,000
			....
Total	~~$15,000~~ *15,100*	Total	$15,000

GLENDALE MARKET
Balance Sheet as of January ~~A~~ 5

Assets		Liabilities & Equity	
Cash	*13,300* ~~$13,000~~	Note payable	$ 5,000
Inventory	*1,800* ~~2,000~~	Paid-in capital	10,000
		Retained earnings 100	
Total	~~$15,000~~ *15,100*	Total	~~$15,000~~ *15,100*

3-26. On January 6, Glendale Market purchased merchandise for $2,000 and added it to its inventory. It agreed to pay the vendor within 30 days.

Change the following January 5 balance sheet so that it reports the financial condition on January 6. Recall that an obligation to pay a vendor is called an "Account Payable." Be sure to change the totals.

GLENDALE MARKET
Balance Sheet as of January 5

Assets		Liabilities & Equity	
Cash	$13,300		$
Inventory	1,800	Note payable	5,000
		Paid-in capital	10,000
		Retained earnings	100
Total	$15,100	Total	$15,100

GLENDALE MARKET
Balance Sheet as of January ~~5~~ 6

Assets		Liabilities & Equity	
Cash	$13,300	*Accounts Payable*	*$2,000*
Inventory	*3,800* ~~1,800~~	Note payable	5,000
		Paid-in capital	10,000
		Retained earnings	100
Total	~~$15,100~~ *17,100*	Total	~~$15,100~~ *17,100*

9-75. A corporation which controls one or more other corporations is called the **parent**, and the controlled corporations are called **subsidiaries**.

Palm Company owns 100% of the stock of Sea Company, 60% of the stock of Sand Company, and 40% of the stock of Gray Company. The **parent** company is _____ _____. The **subsidiaries** are

. . . .

. . . .

Palm Company
Sea Company and Sand Company

9-76. Since the management of the parent corporation, Palm Company, controls the activities of Sea Company and Sand Company, these three companies operate as a single entity. The e__ __ __ __ __ concept requires that a set of financial statements be prepared for this family.

entity

9-77. Each corporation is a legal entity with its own financial statements. The set of financial statements for the whole family brings together, or **consolidates**, these separate statements. The set for the whole family is therefore called a c__ __ __ __ __ __ __ __ __ __ __ d financial statement.

consolidated

9-78. For example, if Palm Company has $10,000 cash, Sea Company has $5,000 cash, and Sand Company has $4,000 cash, the whole family has $_____ cash, and this amount would be reported on the c_____ balance sheet.

$19,000
consolidated

9-79. An entity earns income by making sales to outside customers. It cannot earn income by dealing with itself. Corporations in the consolidated family may buy from and sell to one another. Transactions between members of the family . . . [do / do not] earn income for the consolidated entity. The effect of these **intrafamily transactions** therefore must be eliminated from the consolidated statements.

do not

3-27. On January 7, merchandise costing $500 was sold for $800, which was received in cash.

Change the following January 6 balance sheet so that it reports the financial condition on January 7.

GLENDALE MARKET
Balance Sheet as of January 6

Assets		Liabilities & Equity	
Cash	$13,300	Accounts payable	$ 2,000
Inventory	3,800	Note payable	5,000
		Paid-in capital	10,000
		Retained earnings	100
Total	$17,100	Total	$17,100

GLENDALE MARKET
Balance Sheet as of January ~~8~~ 7

Assets		Liabilities & Equity	
Cash	**14,100** ~~$13,300~~	Accounts payable	$ 2,000
Inventory . .	**3,300** ~~3,800~~	Note payable	5,000
		Paid-in capital	10,000
		Retained earnings . . .	**400** ~~100~~
Total	~~$17,100~~ **17,400**	Total	~~$17,100~~ **17,400**

3-28. On January 8, merchandise costing $600 was sold for $900. The customer agreed to pay $900 within 30 days. (Recall that when customers buy on credit, the entity has an asset called "Accounts Receivable.")

Change the following January 7 balance sheet so that it reports the financial condition on January 8.

GLENDALE MARKET
Balance Sheet as of January 7

Assets		Liabilities & Equity	
Cash	$14,100	Accounts payable	$ 2,000
[ ] . . . . [ ]		Note payable	5,000
Inventory	3,300	Paid-in capital	10,000
		Retained earnings	400
Total	$17,400	Total	$17,400

GLENDALE MARKET
Balance Sheet as of January ~~7~~ 8

Assets		Liabilities & Equity	
Cash	$14,100	Accounts payable	$ 2,000
Accounts Receivable 900		Note payable	5,000
Inventory . .	**2,700** ~~3,300~~	Paid-in capital	10,000
		Retained earnings . . .	**700** ~~400~~
Total	~~$17,400~~ **17,700**	Total	~~$17,400~~ **17,700**

DEBT RATIO

9-72. A common way of measuring the relative amount of debt and equity capital is the **debt ratio**, which is the ratio of debt capital to total permanent capital. Recall that **debt capital** is another name for . . . [total / current / noncurrent] liabilities. Equity capital consists of Paid-in Capital plus R_ _ _ _ _ _ _ _ E_ _ _ _ _ _ _ _ .

noncurrent

Retained Earnings

9-73. Earlier you worked with the following permanent capital structure:

LOUGEE COMPANY

Sources and Uses of Permanent Capital
As of December 31, 19x1

Uses of Capital		Sources of Capital	
Working capital	$ 6,000	Noncurrent liabilities	$ 9,000
Noncurrent assets	20,000	Equity	17,000
Total uses	$26,000	Total sources	$26,000

Calculate the debt ratio for Lougee Company.

$$\frac{\text{Debt capital (noncurrent liabilities)}}{\text{Debt capital} + \text{equity capital}} = \frac{\$ \boxed{}}{\$ \boxed{}} = \boxed{\% }*$$

$$\frac{\$\ 9,000}{\$26,000} = 35\%$$

_____
* Calculate to nearest whole percentage

9-74. Most industrial companies have a debt ratio of less than 50%. Lougee Company . . . [is / is not] in this category.

is

CONSOLIDATED FINANCIAL STATEMENTS

NOTE: If one corporation owns more than 50% of the stock in another corporation, it can control the affairs of that corporation because it can outvote all other owners. Many businesses consist of a number of corporations that are legally separate entities but, because they are controlled by one corporation, are part of a single "family."

3-29. On January 9, Glendale Market purchased a one-year insurance policy for $200, paying cash. (Recall that the right to insurance protection is an asset. For this asset, use the term "Prepaid Insurance.")

Change the following January 8 balance sheet so that it reports the financial condition on January 9.

GLENDALE MARKET
Balance Sheet as of January 8

Assets		Liabilities & Equity	
Cash	$14,100	Accounts payable	$ 2,000
Accounts receivable	900	Note payable	5,000
Inventory	2,700	Paid-in capital	10,000
		Retained earnings	700
Total	$17,700	Total	$17,700

GLENDALE MARKET
Balance Sheet as of January ~~8~~ 9

Assets		Liabilities & Equity	
Cash	**13,900** ~~$14,100~~	Accounts payable	$ 2,000
Accounts receivable	900	Note payable	5,000
Inventory	2,700	Paid-in capital	10,000
Pre-paid Insurance	**200**	Retained earnings	700
Total	$17,700	Total	$17,700

3-30. On January 10, Glendale Market purchased two lots of land of equal size for a total of $10,000. It thereby acquired an asset, Land. It paid $2,000 in cash and gave a ten-year mortgage for the balance of $8,000. (Use the term "Mortgage Payable" for the liability.)

Change the following January 9 balance sheet so that it reports the financial condition on January 10.

GLENDALE MARKET
Balance Sheet as of January 9

Assets		Liabilities & Equity	
Cash	$13,900	Accounts payable	$ 2,000
Accounts receivable	900	Note payable	5,000
Inventory	2,700		
Prepaid insurance	200	Paid-in capital	10,000
		Retained earnings	700
Total	$17,700	Total	$17,700

GLENDALE MARKET
Balance Sheet as of January ~~9~~ 10

Assets		Liabilities & Equity	
Cash	**11,900** ~~$13,900~~	Accounts payable	$ 2,000
Accounts receivable	900	Note payable	5,000
Inventory	2,700	**Mortgage Payable**	**8,000**
Prepaid insurance	200	Paid-in capital	10,000
Land	**10,000**	Retained earnings	700
Total	~~$17,700~~ **25,700**	Total	~~$17,700~~ **25,700**

9-68. In deciding on its permanent capital structure, a company must decide on the proper balance between debt capital, which has a relatively . . . [high / low] risk and a relatively . . . [high / low] cost, and equity capital, which has a relatively . . . [high / low] risk and a relatively . . . [high / low] cost.

high   low

low   high

9-69. A company runs the risk of going bankrupt if it has too high a proportion of . . . [debt / equity] capital. A company pays an unnecessarily high cost for its permanent capital if it has too high a proportion of . . . [debt / equity] capital.

debt

equity

9-70. A company that obtains a high proportion of its permanent capital from debt is said to be **highly leveraged**. If such a company does not get into financial difficulty, it will earn a high return for its equity investors, because each dollar of debt capital takes the place of a . . . [more / less] expensive dollar of equity capital.

more

9-71. However, highly leveraged companies are risky because the high proportion of debt capital and the associated requirement to pay interest . . . [increases / decreases] the chance that the company will not be able to meet its obligations.

increases

NOTE: In this introductory treatment, we focus on the basic differences between common stock and bonds. Some additional points are worth noting:

1. The interest on bonds is a tax-deductible expense to the corporation. If the annual interest expense on a 9% bond is $90,000, the corporation's taxable income is reduced by $90,000. At a tax rate of 40%, this means that the net cost to the corporation is only 60% of $90,000, or $54,000; the effective interest cost is 5.4%.

2. Preferred stock has risk and cost characteristics that are in between common stocks and bonds. However, dividends on preferred stock do not reduce a corporation's taxable income. Preferred stock is not a widely used source of capital.

3. In recent years, there has been a tremendous increase in the types of debt and equity securities. New financial instruments are structures with risk and cost characteristics designed to meet the needs of various types of investors.

3-31. On January 11, Glendale Market sold one of the two lots of land for $5,000. The buyer paid $1,000 cash and assumed $4,000 of the mortgage; that is, Glendale Market was no longer responsible for this half of the mortgage payable.

Change the following January 10 balance sheet so that it reports the financial condition on January 11.

GLENDALE MARKET
Balance Sheet as of January 10

Assets		Liabilities & Equity	
Cash	$11,900	Accounts payable	$ 2,000
Accounts receivable	900	Note payable	5,000
Inventory	2,700	Mortgage payable	8,000
Prepaid insurance	200	Paid-in capital	10,000
Land	10,000	Retained earnings	700
Total	$25,700	Total	$25,700

3-32. On January 12, Smith received an offer of $15,000 for his equity in Glendale Market. Although his equity was then only $10,700, he rejected the offer. This means that the store had already acquired goodwill with a market value of $4,300.

What changes, if any, should be made in the January 11 balance sheet so that it reports the financial condition on January 12? _____

GLENDALE MARKET
Balance Sheet as of January ~~10~~ 11

Assets		Liabilities & Equity	
Cash	**12,900** ~~$11,900~~	Accounts payable	$ 2,000
Accounts receivable	900	Note payable	5,000
Inventory	2,700	Mortgage payable	**4,000** ~~8,000~~
Prepaid insurance	200	Paid-in capital	10,000
Land	**5,000** ~~10,000~~	Retained earnings	700
Total	~~$25,700~~ **21,700**	Total	~~$25,700~~ **21,700**

The balance sheet is unchanged from that of January 11, except for the date. In accordance with the cost concept, goodwill is an asset only when it has been paid for. The balance sheet does not show the *market value* of the entity.

9-63. If the company fails to pay either the interest or the principal when due, the bondholders may force the company into bankruptcy.

Evidently bonds are a . . . [less / more] risky method of raising capital by the corporation than stock; that is, debt capital is a . . . [less / more] risky source of capital than equity capital.

more
more

9-64. Bonds are an obligation of the company that issues them, but stocks are not an obligation. Therefore, *investors* have more risk if they invest in a company's stock than if they invest in the bonds of the same company. They are not certain to get either dividends or repayment of their investment. Investors therefore expect a . . . [higher / lower] return from an investment in stock than from an investment in bonds in the same company.

higher

9-65. For example, if a company's bonds had an interest rate of 9%, investors would invest in its stock only if they expected that the return on stock would be . . . [at least 9% / considerably more than 9%]. (The expected return on stock consists of both expected dividends and an expected increase in the market value of the stock.)

considerably more than 9%

9-66. Thus, from the viewpoint of the issuing company, stock, which is . . . [debt / equity] capital, is a . . . [more / less] expensive source of capital than bonds, which are . . . [debt / equity] capital.

equity   more
debt

9-67. Circle the correct words in the following table, which shows the principal differences between debt capital and equity capital.

	Bonds (Debt)	Stock (Equity)		
Annual payments required	[Yes / No]	[Yes / No]	Yes	No
Principal payments required	[Yes / No]	[Yes / No]	Yes	No
Risk to the entity is	[High / Low]	[High / Low]	High	Low
But its cost is relatively	[High / Low]	[High / Low]	Low	High

3-33. On January 13, Smith withdrew for his personal use $200 cash from the Glendale Market bank account, and he also withdrew merchandise costing $400.

Change the following January 12 balance sheet so that it shows the financial condition on January 13.

GLENDALE MARKET
Balance Sheet as of January 12

Assets		Liabilities & Equity	
Cash	$12,900	Accounts payable	$ 2,000
Accounts receivable	900	Note payable	5,000
Inventory	2,700	Mortgage payable	4,000
Prepaid insurance	200	Paid-in capital	10,000
Land	5,000	Retained earnings	700
Total	$21,700	Total	$21,700

3-34. On January 14, Smith learned that the person who purchased the land on January 11 for $5,000, sold it for $8,000. The lot still owned by Glendale Market was identical in value with this other plot.

What changes, if any, should be made in the January 13 balance sheet so that it reports the financial condition on January 14? _____

_____

GLENDALE MARKET
Balance Sheet as of January ~~12~~ *13*

Assets		Liabilities & Equity	
	12,700		Accounts
Cash	~~$12,900~~	payable	$ 2,000
Accounts receivable ..	900	Note payable	5,000
	2,300		Mortgage
Inventory ..	~~2,700~~	payable	4,000
Prepaid insurance ...	200	Paid-in capital	10,000
			Retained *100*
Land	5,000	earnings ...	~~700~~
Total	~~$21,700~~ *21,100*	Total	~~$21,700~~ *21,100*

None. The balance sheet is identical to that of January 13, except for the date. As required by the cost concept, the land continues to be shown at its cost.

9-58. In summary, the equity section of a corporation's balance sheet has these main items:

1. Paid-in Capital from stock that has preference, called _____ stock.

    preferred

2. Paid-in Capital from common stock, which consists of (a) the . . . [par or stated value / market value] of the number of shares . . . [authorized / issued / outstanding], plus (b) the additional amount paid for the stock, called Additional P__ __ __ -in C__ __ __ __ __ __ .

    par or stated value   outstanding

    Paid-in Capital

3. Retained Earnings, which is the net difference between _____ _____ and _____ since the corporation began.

    net
    income   dividends

9-59. These items . . . [are / are not] related to the market value of the stock.

are not

BALANCE BETWEEN DEBT AND EQUITY CAPITAL

9-60. A corporation obtains some capital from retained earnings. In addition, it obtains capital from the issuance of stock, which is . . . [debt / equity] capital, and from the issuance of bonds, which is . . . [debt / equity] capital.

equity
debt

9-61. A corporation has no fixed obligations to its common shareholders; that is, the company . . . [must / need not] declare dividends each year, and . . . [must / need not] repay the amount the shareholders have invested.

need not
need not

9-62. A company has two fixed obligations to its bondholders, however:

1. . . . .

    payment of interest

2. . . . .

    repayment of principal
    (See Frame 9-12.)

3-35. On January 15, Glendale Market paid off $2,000 of its bank loan, giving cash (disregard interest).

Change the following January 14 balance sheet so that it reports the financial condition on January 15.

GLENDALE MARKET
Balance Sheet as of January 14

Assets		Liabilities & Equity	
Cash	$12,700	Accounts payable	$ 2,000
Accounts receivable	900	Note payable	5,000
Inventory	2,300	Mortgage payable	4,000
Prepaid insurance	200	Paid-in capital	10,000
Land	5,000	Retained earnings	100
Total	$21,100	Total	$21,100

3-36. On January 16, Glendale Market was changed to a corporation. John Smith received 100 shares of common stock in exchange for his $10,100 equity in the business. He immediately sold 25 of these shares for $4,000 cash.

What changes, if any, should be made in the January 15 balance sheet so that it reports the financial condition on January 16? _____

_____

NOTE: Any conceivable transaction can be recorded in terms of its effect on the balance sheet, just as you have done in this section. Although we shall describe techniques, refinements, and shortcuts in later parts, none of them changes this basic fact.

GLENDALE MARKET
Balance Sheet as of January 1̶4̶ 15

Assets		Liabilities & Equity	
Cash	10,700 $12,700	Accounts payable	$ 2,000
Accounts receivable	900	Note payable	3,000 5,000
Inventory	2,300	Mortgage payable	4,000
Prepaid insurance	200	Paid-in capital	10,000
Land	5,000	Retained earnings	100
Total	$21,100 19,100	Total	$21,100 19,100

None. There is no change, except for the date. Changing the organization to a corporation did not affect any amount on the balance sheet. (The name of the entity was changed to, say, Glendale Market Corporation, but this does not affect the numbers.) John Smith's sale of the stock did not affect the entity, Glendale Market.

9-54. Complete the following table by writing in each box the word "increases," "decreases," or "unchanged."

	Total amount of equity	Total number of shares outstanding
Cash dividend	decreases	unchanged
Stock dividend	_____	_____

unchanged   increases

STOCK SPLIT

9-55. A corporation may decide to exchange the number of shares outstanding for other shares, often two or more times the existing number. They do this in the belief that a high dollar amount is less attractive to investors. The process is called a **stock split**. In a three-for-one stock split, for example, each shareholder receives three new shares for each old share held. The total number of shares outstanding therefore . . . [increases / does not change / decreases].

increases

9-56. A stock split does not affect the total amount of equity or the percentage of stock held by each shareholder. A shareholder who owns 1% of the stock before a stock split owns _____% of it afterwards, and owns . . . [fewer / the same amount of / more] shares.

1%

more

9-57. Complete the following table by writing on each line the word "increases," "decreases," or "unchanged."

	Total amount of equity	Total number of shares outstanding
Cash dividend	decreases	unchanged
Stock dividend	unchanged	increases
Stock split	_____	_____

unchanged   increases

EQUITY AND INCOME

Please turn to Exhibit 2 in your booklet. It is a summary of the transactions for Glendale Market that you analyzed in Frames 3-3 through 3-28. We shall focus on the transactions that affected Equity.

3-37. As explained in Part 1, an entity's equity increases for either of two reasons. One is the receipt of capital from owners. On January 2, Glendale Market received $10,000 from John Smith, its owner. You recorded this as an increase in _____ and an increase in the equity item, P_____-_____ C_____.

Cash

Paid-in Capital

3-38. The other source of an increase in equity is the profitable operation of the entity. Transactions that increase profit also increase the equity item, R_____ E_____. Refer to the transactions for January 3 through 8. In the following table, show the dollar amount of the change in Retained Earnings, if any, that resulted from each transaction. If the transaction had no effect on Retained Earnings, put an X in the "No effect" column.

Retained Earnings

RETAINED EARNINGS

Date	Nature	Increased by	No effect
3	Borrowing	$	
4	Purchase		
5	Sale		
6	Purchase		
7	Sale		
8	Sale		
	Total	$	

RETAINED EARNINGS

Date	Nature	Increased by	No effect
3	Borrowing	$	X
4	Purchase		X
5	Sale	100	
6	Purchase		X
7	Sale	300	
8	Sale	300	
	Total	$ 700	

STOCK DIVIDEND

9-49. Dividends are usually paid in the form of cash. Sometimes, however, the dividend consists of shares of stock in the corporation. The latter is called a . . . [cash / stock] dividend.

stock

9-50. In a typical stock dividend, shareholders are issued additional shares of common stock amounting to 5% or 10% of the total they currently own. In a 10% stock dividend, for example, the holder of 900 shares will receive _____ additional shares of stock.

$90 (= 0.10 * 900)$

9-51. Since the number of shares received by each shareholder in a stock dividend is proportional to the number of shares that each shareholder currently owns, the percentage of the total equity owned by each stockholder . . . [increases / stays the same / decreases] as a result of a stock dividend.

stays the same

9-52. When a dividend of common stock is declared, Retained Earnings is decreased and Additional Paid-in Capital is increased by the amount of the dividend.

Write the journal entry to record a dividend of $10,000 of common stock.

Dr. _____ _____ . . . . _____

  Cr. _____ _____-____ _____ . .   _____

Retained Earnings 10,000

  Additional Paid-in Capital . . .   10,000

9-53. In a stock dividend, the Retained Earnings account decreases by an amount equal to the increase in the Additional Paid-in Capital account; therefore the total amount of equity . . . [increases / does not change / decreases].

does not change

3-39. As can be seen from the table above, three of these transactions did not affect Retained Earnings. Borrowing money . . . [does / does not] affect Retained Earnings. The purchase of merchandise . . . [does / does not] affect Retained Earnings. The sale of that merchandise, however, . . . [does / does not] affect Retained Earnings.

does not

does not

does

3-40. The amount by which equity increased as a result of operations during a period of time is called the **income** of that period. You have just calculated that the total increase during the period January 2 through 8 was $_____, so Glendale Market's i__ __ __ __ __ for that period was $_____.

$700   income

$700

3-41. The amount of income and how it was earned is usually the most important information about a business entity. An accounting report called the **income statement** explains the income of a period. Note that the income statement is for a . . . [period of time / point in time], in contrast with the other statement, the b__ __ __ __ __ __ s__ __ __ __ __, which is for a . . . [period of time / point in time].

period of time

balance sheet

point in time

3-42. The $700 increase in Retained Earnings during the period is reported on the i__ __ __ __ __ __ s__ __ __ __ __ __ __ __ __. That statement explains *why* this increase occurred.

income statement

3-43. To understand how the income statement does this, let's look at the January 5 transaction for Glendale Market. On January 5, Glendale Market sold for $300 cash some merchandise that had cost $200. This caused equity (Retained Earnings) to . . . [increase / decrease] by $_____.

increase $100

3-44. On January 5, Glendale Market sold merchandise for $300 cash that had cost $200. This transaction consists of two separate events: (1) the sale, which, taken by itself, . . . [increased / decreased] Retained Earnings by $300, and (2) the decrease in inventory, which, taken by itself, . . . [increased / decreased] Retained Earnings by $200.

increased

decreased

9-44. Retained earnings is one **source** of capital. It is reported on the . . . [left / right] side of the balance sheet. The capital is in the form of assets, and assets are reported on the . . . [left / right] side of the balance sheet.

right

left

> **NOTE:** Some people think that retained earnings are assets. Retained earnings are *not* assets.

9-45. Equity is sometimes called "net worth." This term suggests that the amount shows what the owners' claim on the assets is *worth*. Because the amounts reported on the assets side of the balance sheet . . . [do / do not] represent the real worth of these assets, this suggestion is . . . [absolutely right / dead wrong].

do not

dead wrong

9-46. The **worth** of a company's stock is what people will pay for it. This is the market price of the stock, which . . . [does / does not] appear anywhere on the balance sheet.

does not

CASH DIVIDEND

9-47. Suppose that a dividend of $5,000 is declared and paid in cash. Write the journal entry necessary to record the effect of this transaction on the Cash and Retained Earnings accounts.

Dr. _____ _____ . . . . _____

Cr. _____ . . . . _____

Retained Earnings 5,000

    Cash 5,000

9-48. In the table below, record the effects of a cash dividend on equity and on the number of shares of common stock outstanding by writing in each box the word "increases," "decreases," or "unchanged."

	Total amount of equity	Total number of shares outstanding
Cash dividend		

decreases   unchanged

3-45. Taken by itself, the increase in Retained Earnings resulting from operations is called a **revenue**. When Glendale Market sold merchandise for $300, the transaction resulted in $300 of _____ .

revenue

3-46. And taken by itself, the associated decrease in Retained Earnings is called an **expense**. When Glendale Market transferred merchandise to the customer, the transaction reduced inventory and resulted in $200 of _____ .

expense

3-47. Thus, when Glendale Market sold merchandise for $300 that cost $200, the effect of the transaction on Retained Earnings can be separated into two parts: a _____ of $_____ and an _____ of $_____ .

revenue $300
expense $200

3-48. In accounting, revenues and expenses are recorded separately. From Exhibit 2, calculate the revenues and expenses for the period January 2 through 8 by completing the following table:

Date	Revenues	Expenses		
5	$	$	$ 300	$ 200
7			800	500
8			900	600
Total	$	$	$2,000	$1,300

9-38. As you learned earlier, par value of common stock has . . . [some / practically no] significance. Because preferred stock usually does have a preferential claim on assets equal to its par value, its par value has . . . [some / practically no] significance.

practically no

some

9-39. Preferred shareholders usually have preference for a stated amount of annual dividends. Pemi Corporation has issued $100,000 of 9% preferred stock. No dividend can be paid to common shareholders until the preferred shareholders have received their full dividend of 9% of $100,000, amounting to $_____ a year.

$9,000

RETAINED EARNINGS AND DIVIDENDS

9-40. The net income of a period increases e__ __ __ __ __ . The directors may vote to distribute money to the shareholders in the form of **dividends**. Dividends decrease e__ __ __ __ __ .

equity

equity

9-41. Earnings is the same as net income. If earnings are not distributed as dividends, they are **retained** in the corporation. This amount is reported on the balance sheet as R__ __ __ __ __ __ __ E__ __ __ __ __ __ s.

Retained Earnings

9-42. The Retained Earnings account . . . [decreases / increases] by the amount of net income each period and . . . [decreases / increases] by the amount of dividends. Thus, if Retained Earnings are $100,000 at the start of a period during which a dividend of $20,000 is declared and during which net income is $30,000, Retained Earnings will be $_____ at the end of the period.

increases
decreases

$110,000
  (= $100,000 – $20,000 + $30,000)

9-43. Net income refers to the increase in equity . . . [in one year / over the life of the corporation to date], whereas **retained earnings** refers to the net increases, after deduction of dividends, . . . [in one year / over the life of the corporation to date].

in one year

over the life of the corporation to date

3-49. You can now prepare an income statement. Its heading shows the name of the accounting entity, the title of the statement, and the period covered. Complete the heading for Glendale Market's income statement for January 2–8:

GLENDALE MARKET

[   ]   Statement

    for the period   [   ]

Income

January 2–8

3-50. The income statement reports revenues and expenses for the period and the difference between them, which is income. Label the amounts in the following income statement for Glendale Market.

GLENDALE MARKET

Income Statement
for the period January 2–8

[   ] $2,000

[   ] 1,300

[   ] . . . . $ 700

Revenues

Expenses

Income

Revenues	$2,000

=

Expenses	$1,300	+	Income	$700

3-51. As the name suggests, Retained Earnings refers to the amount of income that has been r_____ in the entity. On January 13, Smith withdrew $600 of assets for his personal use. This reduced R_____ E_____ by $_____.

retained

Retained

Earnings $600

3-52. No other changes in Retained Earnings occurred. Complete the following table:

Retained Earnings, January 2	$	0	
Income	+	____	700
Withdrawal	–	____	600
Retained Earnings, January 13	$	____	100

9-32. Shareholders may sell their stock to other investors. Such sales . . . [do / do not] affect the balance sheet of the corporation. This is an example of the __ __ __ __ __ __ concept.

do not
entity

9-33. When shareholders sell their stock to other investors, the price at which the sale takes place is determined in the **marketplace**. The value at which a stock is sold in such a transaction is called the . . . [market / par / stated] value.

market

9-34. The market value of a company's stock has no necessary relation to its par value, its stated value, or the amount of paid-in capital. If the par value of a certain stock is $1, the market value . . . [will be $1 / can be any value].

can be any value

If the stated value of another stock is $10, the market value . . . [will be $10 / can be any value].

can be any value

If paid-in capital is $12 per share, the market value . . . [will be $12 / can be any value].

can be any value

9-35. The amount reported as total equity equals total assets less total liabilities. On the balance sheet, this is not likely to equal the total market value of all stock outstanding. Evidently accounting . . . [does / does not] report the market value of the shareholders' equity.

does not

PREFERRED STOCK

9-36. Some corporations issue stock that gives its owners preferential treatment over the common shareholders. As the word "preferential" suggests, such stock is called p__ __ __ __ __ __ __ ed stock.

preferred

9-37. Usually preferred shareholders have a preferential claim over the common shareholders for the par value of their stock. Thus, if the corporation were liquidated, the owner of 500 shares of $100 preferred stock would get $_____ before the common shareholders got anything.

$50,000 (= 500 ∗ $100)

The amount of Retained Earnings calculated . . . [does / does not] equal the amount shown on the balance sheet of January 13.

does

3-53. Assume that in the remainder of January Glendale Market had additional income of $800 and there were no additional withdrawals. Since Retained Earnings was $100 as of January 13, it would be $ _____ on January 31. Thus, the amount of Retained Earnings on a balance sheet is:

$900

A. the amount earned in the current period.

B. the total amount retained since the entity began operations.

B

3-54. The terms **profit**, **earnings**, and **income** all have the same meaning. They are the differences between the r__ __ __ __ __ __ __ of an accounting period and the e__ __ __ __ __ __ __ of that period.

revenues

expenses

> **NOTE:** Some people use the term **income** when they mean **revenue**; this can be confusing.

> **NOTE:** In later parts, we shall describe various revenue and expense items, such as sales revenue, interest revenue, salary expense, and rent expense. These explain in more detail the reasons for the change in Retained Earnings during a period.

3-55. Remember that the Equity section of the balance sheet reports the amount of capital that the entity has obtained from two different sources:

1. The amount paid in by the owner(s), which is called P_____-_____ C_____.

Paid-in

Capital

2. The amount of income that has been retained in the entity, which is called R_____ E_____.

Retained Earnings

9-27. If Jones's payment of $10,000 was the only equity transaction, this section of the Marple Company balance sheet would appear as follows:

Common stock . . . .$_____	$ 1,000
Additional paid-in capital . . . . _____	9,000
Total paid-in capital . . . .$_____	$10,000

9-28. Not all stocks have a par value. For these **no-par-value stocks**, the directors **state** a value. This value, called the s__ __ __ __d value, is usually set close to the amount that the corporation actually receives from the issuance of the stock. The difference between this amount and cash received is A__ __ __ __ __ __ __ __ __ __ P__ __ __-__ __ C__ __ __ __ __ __ __, just as in the case of par-value stock.

stated

Additional Paid-in
Capital

9-29. When a corporation is formed, its directors vote to **authorize** a certain number of shares of stock and to **issue** some of this authorized stock to investors. Thus, at any given time the amount of stock authorized is usually . . . [larger than / the same as / smaller than] the amount issued.

larger than

9-30. A corporation may buy back some of the stock that it had previously issued. Such stock is called **treasury stock**. The **outstanding stock** consists of the issued stock less the treasury stock.

If a company issues 100,000 shares and buys back 15,000 shares, its treasury stock is _____ shares, and its outstanding stock is _____ shares.

15,000
85,000 (= 100,000 – 15,000)

9-31. The balance sheet amount for common stock is the amount for the number of shares of stock outstanding.

Maxim Company has authorized 100,000 shares of stock. It has issued 60,000 shares, for which it received the stated value of $10 per share. As of December 31, 19x1, it has bought back 10,000 shares, paying $10 per share. These shares are its treasury stock. The balance sheet amount for common stock is $_____.

$500,000 [= (60,000 ∗ $10) – (10,000 ∗ $10)]

3-56. The two financial statements may be compared to two reports on a reservoir. One report may show how much water *flowed through* the reservoir during the period, and the other report may show how much water *was in* the reservoir as of the end of the period. Similarly, the . . . [balance sheet / income statement] reports flows during a period of time, whereas the . . . [balance sheet / income statement] reports status as of a point of time.

	income statement
	balance sheet

Thus, the income statement may be called a . . . [flow / status] report, and the balance sheet may be called a . . . [flow / status] report.

	flow
	status

3-57. Note also that withdrawals by owners (which are called dividends in a corporation) . . . [are / are not] expenses. They . . . [do / do not] appear on the income statement. They . . . [do / do not] reduce income. They . . . [do / do not] decrease retained earnings.

	are not do not
	do not
	do

3-58. If Smith sold his equity in Glendale Market on January 31, he probably would receive . . . [its equity of $100 / some other amount]. This is an illustration of the _____ concept.

	some other amount
	cost

KEY POINTS TO REMEMBER

- Every accounting transaction affects at least two items and preserves the basic equation: Assets = Liabilities + Equity. Accounting is a double-entry system.

- Some events are not transactions; they do not affect the accounting amounts. Examples in this part were: a change in the value of land, "goodwill" that was not purchased, and changing the entity from a proprietorship to a corporation.

- Other events affect assets and/or liabilities but have no effect on equity. Examples in this part were: borrowing money, purchasing inventory, purchasing insurance protection, acquiring an asset, giving a mortgage, buying land, selling land at its cost, and repaying a bank loan.

- Still other events affect equity as well as assets and/or liabilities. Revenues are increases in equity resulting from operations during a period. Expenses are decreases. Their net effect is shown in the equity item called Retained Earnings. Equity also increases when owners pay in capital, and equity decreases when owners withdraw capital, but these transactions do not affect income.

COMMON STOCK

9-25. Some stock is issued with a specific amount printed on the face of each certificate. This amount is called the **par value**. In the stock certificate shown below, for example, the par value is $_____.

$1
(See the upper right-hand corner.)

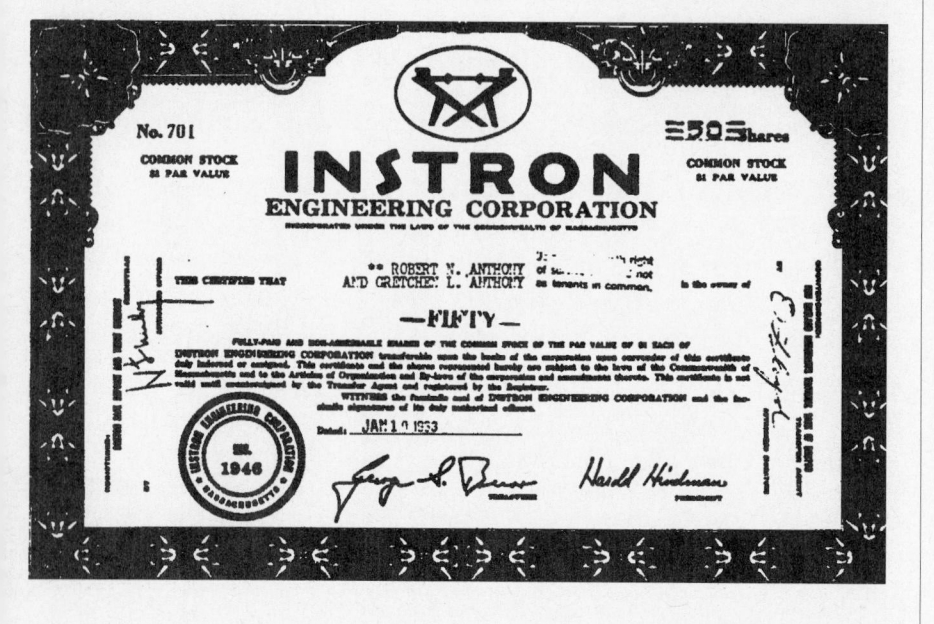

NOTE: Strangely, the par value of stock has practically no significance. It is a holdover from the days when shareholders were liable if they purchased stock for less than its par value. In order to avoid this liability, stock today is always issued for much more than its par value. Nevertheless, the par value of stock continues to be reported on the balance sheet.

9-26. The amount that the shareholders paid the corporation in exchange for their stock is **paid-in capital**. The difference between par value and the total paid-in capital is called **additional paid-in capital**.

Jones paid $10,000 cash to Marple Company and received 1,000 shares of its $1 par-value common stock. Complete the journal entry that Marple Company would make for this transaction.

Dr. Cash . . . . _____	10,000
Cr. Common stock . . . . _____	1,000 (at par value)
Cr. Additional paid-in capital . . . . _____	9,000

• A sale has two aspects: a revenue aspect and an expense aspect. Revenue results when the sale is made, whether or not cash is received at that time. The related expense is the cost of the merchandise that was sold. The income of a period is the difference between the revenues and expenses of that period.

You have completed Part 3 of this program. If you think you understand the material in this part, you should now take Post Test 3, which is in the separate booklet. If you are uncertain about your understanding, you should review Part 3.

The post test will serve both to test your comprehension and to review the highlights of Part 3. After taking the post test, you may find that you are unsure about certain points. You should review these points before continuing with Part 4.

9-21. A **partnership** is an unincorporated business owned by two or more persons jointly. If there are only a few partners, the equity of each might be shown separately.

John Black and Henry Brown are equal partners in a laundry business. On December 31, 19x1, the equity in the business totalled $100,000. The equity might be reported on that date as follows:

_____	_____ , Capital	$_____	John Black, Capital	$ 50,000

_____ _____ , Capital $_____

_____ _____ , Capital _____

Total equity $_____

John Black, Capital	$ 50,000
Henry Brown, Capital	50,000
Total equity	$100,000

9-22. Equity in a partnership consists of capital paid-in by owners, plus earnings retained in the business. Thus the item "John Black, Capital, $50,000" means (circle the correct answer):

A. John Black contributed $50,000 cash to the entity.

B. The entity owes John Black $50,000.

C. John Black's ownership interest in the assets is $50,000.

C
Not A: We don't know the amount of the original contribution.
Not B: The entity does not "owe" its owners.

9-23. Owners of a **corporation** are called **shareholders** because they hold shares of the corporation's stock. The equity section of a corporation's balance sheet is therefore labeled s__ __ __ __ __ __ __ __ __ __ e__ __ __ __ y.

shareholder

equity

9-24. There are two types of shareholders: **common shareholders** and **preferred shareholders**. The stock held by the former is called _____ stock, and that held by the latter is called _____ stock. We shall first describe accounting for common stock.

common   preferred

NOTE: Most organizations are proprietorships, partnerships, or corporations. Other forms, not described here, include limited partnerships, trusts, and S Corporations. Special rules apply to equity transactions and/or tax accounting in these organizations.

Part 4

Accounting Records and Systems

Learning Objectives

In this part you will learn:

* The nature of the **account** and how entries are made to accounts.
* The meaning of debit and credit.
* Use of the ledger and the journal.
* The closing process.
* Items reported on the income statement.
* Accounting with the computer.

THE ACCOUNT

4-1. In Part 3 you recorded the effect of each transaction by changing the appropriate items on a balance sheet. Erasing the old amounts and writing in the new amounts . . . [would / would not] be a practical method for handling the large number of transactions that occur in most entities.

would not

4-2. Instead of changing balance sheet amounts directly, in practice accountants use a device called an **account** to record each change. In its simplest form, an account looks like a large letter T, and it is therefore called a ___-account.

T

EQUITY: PAID-IN CAPITAL

9-17. Capital obtained from bonds is called . . . [debt / equity] capital. The other source of permanent capital is equity, which is called . . . [debt / equity] capital.

debt

equity

9-18. A bond is a promise to pay. Such an obligation is a liability. By contrast, equity is an ownership interest in the entity, and the entity does not promise to pay equity investors anything. Equity, therefore, . . . [is / is not] a liability.

is not

TYPES OF EQUITY CAPITAL

9-19. As noted in earlier Parts, there are two sources of equity capital:

1. Amounts paid in by equity investors, who are the entity's owners. This amount is called . . . [Paid-in Capital / Retained Earnings].

Paid-in Capital

2. Amounts generated by the profitable operation of the entity. This amount is called . . . [Paid-in Capital / Retained Earnings].

Retained Earnings

9-20. Some entities do not report these two sources separately. An unincorporated business owned by a single person is called a **proprietorship**. The equity item in a proprietorship is often reported by giving the proprietor's name, followed by the word Capital.

Mary Green is the proprietor of Green's Market. Green's Market has an equity of $10,000. Show how the owner's equity item would look by filling in the boxes.

_____ _____, _____ . . . . $_____

Mary Green, Capital $10,000

4-3. The title of the account is written on top of the T. Draw a T-account and title it "Cash."

> **NOTE:** As a matter of accounting custom, the name of an account is treated as a proper noun; that is, the first letter is capitalized.

```
                    Cash
_____|_____
                       |
                       |
                       |
                       |
```

4-4. Following is how a T-account looks at the beginning of an accounting period.

```
                    Cash
_____|_____
Beg. bal. 10,000       |
                       |
                       |
                       |
                       |
```

Evidently the amount of cash at the beginning of the accounting period was $_____.

$10,000

(Note that although the amounts are in dollars, the dollar sign is not used.)

4-5. Transactions that affect the Cash account during the accounting period can either **increase** cash or **decrease** cash. Thus, one side of the T-account is for __ __ __ __ __ __ __ __ __ s, and the other side is for __ __ __ __ __ __ __ __ s.

increases
decreases *(either order)*

4-6. Increases in cash add to the beginning balance. Because the beginning balance is recorded on the left side of the T-account, increases in cash are recorded on the . . . [left / right] side of the T-account. Decreases are recorded on the . . . [left / right] side.

left
right

9-12. When an entity issues bonds, it assumes two obligations: (1) to repay the face amount, the **principal**, on the due date; and (2) to pay **interest**, usually at semiannual intervals (i.e., twice a year). The obligation to pay the principal is usually a . . . [current / noncurrent] liability. The liability for interest that has been earned but is unpaid is a . . . [current / noncurrent] liability.

noncurrent

current

9-13. Interest on bonds is an expense and should be recognized in the accounting period to which the interest applies. Thus, if in January 19x2 an entity makes a semiannual interest payment of $3,000 to cover the last six months of 19x1, this interest expense should be recognized in 19x___. This is required by the m__ __ __ __ __ __ g concept.

19x1

matching

9-14. The $3,000 of unpaid interest that was an expense in 19x1 is recorded in 19x1 by the following entry.

Dr. I_____ E_____ 3,000

    Cr. I_____ P_____ 3,000

Interest Expense 3,000

    Interest Payable 3,000

9-15. In 19x2, when this interest was paid to the bondholders, the following entry would be made.

Dr. _____ _____ 3,000

    Cr. _____ 3,000

Interest Payable 3,000

    Cash 3,000

As the above entries indicate, the liability for the principal payment is the total face value of the bond, but the interest liability is the . . . [amount of interest expense incurred but unpaid / total amount of interest].

amount of interest expense incurred
  but unpaid

9-16. Some bonds, called **zero-coupon bonds**, do not pay interest. The buyer purchases them for less than the principal amount, and the entity promises to pay the principal amount on the due date. The buyer's return (i.e., income) is therefore the difference between the p_____ price and the p_____ amount.

purchase

principal

4-7. Here is the T-account for Cash.

Cash

(Increases)	(Decreases)
Beg. bal. 10,000	

Record in the above T-account the effect of the following transactions on Cash:

A. The entity received $300 cash from a customer.

B. The entity borrowed $5,000 from a bank.

C. The entity paid $2,000 cash to a supplier.

D. The entity sold merchandise for $800 cash.

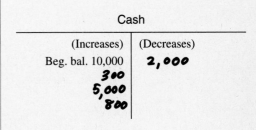

Cash

(Increases)	(Decreases)
Beg. bal. 10,000	2,000
300	
5,000	
800	

4-8. At the end of an accounting period, the increases are added to the beginning balance, and the total of the decreases is subtracted from it. The result is the **new balance**. Calculate the new balance for the Cash account shown below.

Cash

(Increases)	(Decreases)
Beg. bal. 10,000	2,000
300	
5,000	
800	
Total	Total
New balance	

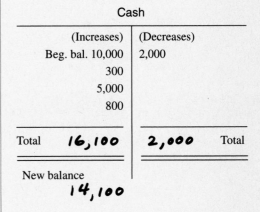

Cash

(Increases)	(Decreases)
Beg. bal. 10,000	2,000
300	
5,000	
800	
Total 16,100	2,000 Total
New balance	
14,100	

4-9. The amount of the above Cash shown on the balance sheet at the end of the accounting period would be $_____. The beginning balance of Cash in the next accounting period would be $_____.

$14,100

$14,100

9-8. A common source of debt capital is the issuance of **bonds**. A bond is a written promise to pay someone who lends money to the entity. Since a bond usually is a noncurrent liability, the payments are due . . . [within one year / sometime after one year].

sometime after one year

9-9. The total amount that must be repaid is specified on the face of a bond and is termed the **face amount**.

If Green Company issues ten-year bonds whose face amounts total $100,000, Green Company has a liability, Bonds Payable, of $_____.

$100,000

> **NOTE:** If the entity does not receive cash equal to the face amount of the bonds, there are accounting complications not discussed in this introductory program.

9-10. Suppose that Green Company receives $100,000 cash from the issuance of bonds that have a face amount of $100,000. Write the journal entry necessary to record the effect of this transaction on the Cash and Bonds Payable accounts.

Dr. _____ . . . . _____

    Cr. _____ _____ . . . . _____

Cash 100,000

  Bonds Payable   100,000

9-11. When they are issued, the bonds are . . . [current / noncurrent] liabilities. However, as time passes and the due date becomes less than one year, a bond becomes a . . . [current / noncurrent] liability. In 19x1, a bond that is due on January 1, 19x3, would be a . . . [current / noncurrent] liability. In 19x2 the same bond would be a . . . [current / noncurrent] liability.

noncurrent

current
noncurrent
current

RULES FOR INCREASES AND DECREASES

4-10. In the T-account for Cash, increases are recorded on the . . . [left / right] side. This is the rule for all asset accounts; that is, increases in _____ accounts are recorded on the _____ side.

left

asset left

4-11. Suppose Brown Company received $300 cash from Ellen Jones to settle her account receivable. In the T-account below, the increase in Brown Company's cash that results is recorded on the . . . [left / right] side. Enter the amount.

left

Cash	
(Increases)	(Decreases)
Beg. bal. 10,000	

Cash	
(Increases)	(Decreases)
Beg. bal. 10,000	
300	

4-12. Ellen Jones, a customer of Brown Company paid $300 cash to settle her account receivable. The Cash account increased by $300. Jones no longer owed $300, so the A_ _ _ _ _ _ _ _ R_ _ _ _ _ _ _ _ _ _ account decreased by $300. In the T-account below, enter the name of this second account that must be changed to complete the record of the transaction.

Accounts

Receivable

Cash					
(Increases)	(Decreases)		(Increases)	(Decreases)	
Beg. bal. 10,000			Beg. bal. 2,000		
300					

Accounts Receivable

4-13. Accounts Receivable is an asset account. The dual-aspect concept requires that if the asset account, Cash, increases by $300, the change in the other asset account, Accounts Receivable, must be a(n). . . [increase / decrease] of $300.

decrease

SOURCES OF CAPITAL

9-5. To highlight how working capital and the noncurrent assets were financed, we can rearrange the items on the balance sheet as follows:

LOUGEE COMPANY

Sources and Uses of Permanent Capital
As of December 31, 19x1

Uses of Capital		Sources of Capital	
☐	$ 6,000	Noncurrent liabilities	$ 9,000
Noncurrent assets	20,000	Equity	17,000
Total uses	$26,000	Total sources	$26,000

Fill in the box above.

9-6. The right-hand side of the balance sheet given above shows the sources of capital used to finance the working capital and the noncurrent assets. Collectively, these sources are called **permanent capital**. As the balance sheet indicates, there are two sources of permanent capital:
(1) N__ __ __ __ __ __ __ __t l__ __ __ __ __ __ __ __ __ __s, and
(2) E__ __ __ __ y. The total of these two sources is $_____,
and they are used to finance assets that also total $_____.

> **NOTE:** In this part we describe the two types of permanent capital and how they are recorded in the accounts. Although these items are called "capital," they are more accurately labelled "sources of capital."

DEBT CAPITAL

9-7. Although most liabilities are debts, the term **debt capital** refers only to noncurrent liabilities. Debt capital therefore refers to liabilities that come due . . . [within one year / sometime after one year].

Working capital

Noncurrent liabilities
Equity $26,000
$26,000

sometime after one year

4-14. Record the change in Accounts Receivable resulting from the $300 payment in the account below.

Accounts Receivable

(Increases)	(Decreases)
Beg. bal. 2,000	

Accounts Receivable

(Increases)	(Decreases)
Beg. bal. 2,000	*300*

4-15. The decrease in accounts receivable was recorded on the . . . [left / right] side of the Accounts Receivable account. This balanced the . . . [left / right] -side amount for the increase in Cash.

right

left

4-16. Another customer of Brown Company settled an $800 Account Receivable by paying $600 Cash and giving a note for $200. Record this transaction in the Brown Company's accounts, given below.

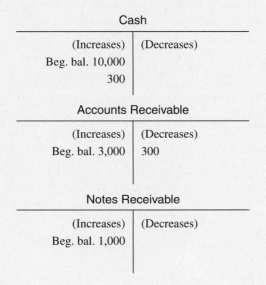

Cash

(Increases)	(Decreases)
Beg. bal. 10,000	
300	

Accounts Receivable

(Increases)	(Decreases)
Beg. bal. 3,000	300

Notes Receivable

(Increases)	(Decreases)
Beg. bal. 1,000	

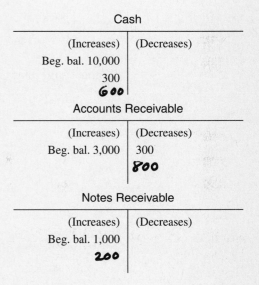

Cash

(Increases)	(Decreases)
Beg. bal. 10,000	
300	
600	

Accounts Receivable

(Increases)	(Decreases)
Beg. bal. 3,000	300
	800

Notes Receivable

(Increases)	(Decreases)
Beg. bal. 1,000	
200	

4-17. As you can see, accounting requires that each transaction give rise to . . . [equal / unequal] totals of left-side and right-side amounts. This is consistent with the fundamental equation: A__ __ __ __ __ = L__ __ __ __ __ __ __ __ __ __ + E__ __ __ __ __.

equal

Assets =

Liabilities + Equity

4-18. An **increase** in any asset account is always recorded on the left side. Therefore, since the totals of left-side and right-side amounts must equal each other, a **decrease** in any asset must always be recorded on the . . . [left / right] side.

right

LOUGEE COMPANY

Balance Sheet as of December 31, 19x1

<table>
<tr><td></td><td>[ ]</td><td></td><td>[ ] and [ ]</td><td></td><td>Assets</td><td>Liabilities and Equity</td></tr>
<tr><td>Current</td><td>[ ]</td><td>$10,000</td><td>Current [ ]</td><td>$ 4,000</td><td>Assets</td><td>Liabilities</td></tr>
<tr><td>Noncurrent</td><td>[ ]</td><td>20,000</td><td>Noncurrent [ ]</td><td>9,000</td><td>Assets</td><td>Liabilities</td></tr>
<tr><td></td><td></td><td></td><td>Paid-in capital . . . .</td><td>7,000</td><td></td><td></td></tr>
<tr><td></td><td></td><td></td><td>Retained earnings . . . .</td><td>10,000</td><td></td><td></td></tr>
<tr><td>Total</td><td>[ ]</td><td>$30,000</td><td>Total [ ]</td><td>$30,000</td><td>Assets</td><td>Liabilities and Equity</td></tr>
</table>

9-2. Current assets are assets that are expected to be turned into cash within . . . . (what period of time?). Current liabilities are obligations that come due within . . . . (what period of time?).

one year

one year

9-3. For Lougee Company, we can say that $4,000 of the $10,000 in current assets was financed by the c_ _ _ _ _ _ _ liabilities. The remaining $6,000 of current assets and the $20,000 of noncurrent assets were financed by the $9,000 of _____ _____ and the $17,000 of _____.

current

noncurrent

liabilities   equity

9-4. That part of the current assets not financed by the current liabilities is called **working capital**. Working capital is therefore the difference between c_____ a_____ and c_____ l_____. In the example given above, working capital is:

current assets   current

liabilities

$_____ – $_____ = $_____.

$10,000 – $4,000 = $6,000.

4-19. Black Company borrowed $700 from Federal Bank, signing a note.

Black Company's Cash account. . . [increased / decreased] by $700, and its Notes Payable account, which is a liability account, . . . [increased / decreased] by the same amount.

increased
increased

4-20. Black Company borrowed $700 from Federal Bank, signing a note.

The $700 increase in Black Company's cash is recorded on the . . . [left / right] side of its Cash account. In order to show equal totals of right-side and left-side amounts, the corresponding change in the Notes Payable account is recorded on the . . . [left / right] side. Record the two amounts of this transaction in the accounts below.

left

right

Cash		Notes Payable	
(Increases)	(Decreases)		

Cash	
(Increases)	(Decreases)
700	

Notes Payable	
	700

4-21. Because left-side and right-side amounts must have equal totals, and because increases in assets are always recorded on the left side, increases in liability accounts, such as Notes Payable, are always recorded on the . . . [left / right] side.

right

4-22. Similarly, because **decreases** in assets are always recorded on the *right* side, **decreases** in liabilities are always recorded on the . . . [left side / right side].

left side

Show which side of the Notes Payable account is used to record increases and which side is used to record decreases by filling in the boxes below.

Notes Payable	
	700

Notes Payable	
(Decreases)	(Increases)
	700

Part 9

Liabilities and Equity

Learning Objectives

In this part, you will learn:

- The nature of working capital.
- Types of permanent capital: debt and equity.
- How to account for debt capital.
- Accounting for equity capital in Proprietorships, Partnerships, and Corporations.
    - Paid-in capital: common and preferred stock.
    - Retained earnings and dividends.
- The debt / equity ratio.
- The nature of consolidated financial statements.

WORKING CAPITAL

9-1. In earlier parts you learned that the balance sheet has two sides with equal totals. Fill in the two missing names in the boxes in the simplified balance sheet given on the following page.

4-23. As the equation Assets = Liabilities + Equity indicates, the rules for equity accounts are the same as those for liability accounts, that is:

Equity accounts increase on the . . .[left / right] side.

right

Equity accounts decrease on the . . .[left / right] side.

left

4-24. One way to remember the above rules is to visualize the two sides of the balance sheet.

Asset accounts are on the *left* side of the balance sheet, and they increase on the . . . [left / right] side.

left

Liability and equity accounts are on the *right* side of the balance sheet, and they increase on the . . . [left / right] side.

right

4-25. The reasoning used in the preceding frames follows from the basic equation: _____ = _____ + _____ .

Assets = Liabilities + Equity

DEBIT AND CREDIT

4-26. In the language of accounting, the left side of an account is called the **debit** side, and the right side is called the **credit** side. Thus, instead of saying that increases in cash are recorded on the left side of the Cash account and decreases are recorded on the right side, accountants say that increases are recorded on the _____ side and decreases are recorded on the _____ side.

debit

credit

4-27. Debit and **Credit** are also verbs. To record an increase in cash, you _____ the Cash account. To record a decrease in cash, you _____ the Cash account. Instead of saying, "Record an amount on the left side of the Cash account," the accountant simply says, "_____ Cash."

debit

credit

Debit

- In the straight-line method, the annual depreciation expense is calculated by multiplying the asset's depreciable cost by a constant percentage. This percentage is found by dividing 1 by the number of years in the asset's estimated service life.

- Accelerated depreciation is often used for income tax purposes because it decreases the amount of taxable income in the early years. The method used is called the Modified Accelerated Cost Recovery System (MACRS).

- Taxable income may differ from pretax income reported on the income statement. If so, the reported income tax expense is calculated on the basis of accounting pretax income. The difference between this amount and the amount of tax paid is a balance sheet item, Deferred Income Taxes.

- Depletion is the process of writing off wasting assets, and amortization is the process of writing off intangible assets. The accounting for both processes is similar to depreciation, except that the credit is made directly to the asset account.

You have completed Part 8 of this program. If you think you understand the material in this part, you should now take Post Test 8 which is in the separate booklet. If you are uncertain about your understanding, you should review Part 8.

The post test will serve both to test your comprehension and to review the highlights of Part 8. After taking the post test, you may find that you are unsure about certain points. You should review these points before continuing with Part 9.

4-28. Increases in all asset accounts, such as Cash, are recorded on the . . . [debit / credit] side. To increase an asset account, you . . . [debit / credit] the account.

debit   debit

4-29. The rules we just developed in terms of "left side" and "right side" can now be stated in terms of debit and credit.

Increases in assets are . . . .[debits / credits]   debits

Decreases in assets are . . . .[debits / credits]   credits

Increases in liabilities are . . . .[debits / credits]   credits

Decreases in liabilities are . . . .[debits / credits]   debits

Increases in equity are . . . .[debits / credits]   credits

Decreases in equity are . . . .[debits / credits]   debits

4-30. In everyday language the word **credit** sometimes means "good" and **debit** sometimes means "bad." In the language of accounting, debit means only. . . [left / right], and credit means only. . . [left / right].

left   right

4-31. The word **debit** is abbreviated as "Dr.," and the word **credit** is abbreviated as "Cr." Label the two sides of the Cash account below with these abbreviations.

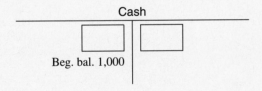

Cash
Beg. bal. 1,000

NOTE: In practice, these labels are not shown in the accounts, but we shall use them in the next frames, to help you fix them in your mind.

Cash	
(Dr.)	(Cr.)
Beg. bal. 1,000	

4-32. Exhibit 3 (in your booklet) shows the accounts for Green Company, arranged as they would appear on a balance sheet. The sum of the debit balances is $_____, and the sum of the credit balances is $_____.

$18,000 $18,000

8-86. Three terms that refer to the writing off of an asset's cost are:

    A. Depr_____tion, which refers to _____ (what type of?) assets,

           depreciation   plant

    B. Depl_____tion, which refers to _____ (what type of?) assets,

           depletion   wasting

    C. Amor_____tion, which refers to _____ (what type of?) assets.

           amortization   intangible

> **NOTE:** Although we have used the word **amortization** just for intangible assets, amortization is sometimes used as a general term for expensing the cost of all assets; that is, some people call **depreciation** and **depletion** special cases of amortization.

KEY POINTS TO REMEMBER

- When acquired, a plant asset is recorded at its cost, including installation and other costs of making the asset ready for its intended use.

- Land has an unlimited life and is rarely depreciated.

- Plant assets are depreciated over their service life. Each year, a fraction of their cost is debited to Depreciation Expense and credited to Accumulated Depreciation.

- Depreciation Expense is an estimate. We do not know how long the service life will be, nor the asset's residual value.

- The book value of a plant asset is the difference between its cost and its accumulated depreciation. When book value reaches zero or the residual value, no more depreciation expense is recorded.

- Book value does NOT report what the asset is worth.

- When an asset is sold, the difference between the sale price and book value is a gain or loss and is so reported on the income statement.

- In financial accounting, depreciation is usually calculated either by the units-of-production method or by the straight-line method.

- In the units-of-production method, the annual depreciation expense is calculated by multiplying the number of service units produced in that year by a unit cost. This unit cost is found by dividing the asset's depreciable cost by the number of service units estimated to be produced over the asset's total life.

4-33. These totals are equal in accordance with the d___ __ __-a__ __ __ __ __ concept.

dual-aspect

4-34. Record the following transactions in the accounts of Exhibit 3. Record increases in assets on the debit side and make sure that in each transaction the debit and credit amounts are equal.

  A. Inventory costing $600 was purchased for cash.

  B. Inventory costing $400 was purchased on credit.

  C. Green Company paid $300 to a creditor.

  D. Green Company received $500 in cash from a credit customer.

ACCOUNTS FOR GREEN COMPANY

Assets		Liabilities and Equity	

Cash

	(Dr.)	(Cr.)
Beg. bal.	1,000	600
	500	300

Accounts Payable

	(Dr.)	(Cr.)	
	300	2,000	Beg. bal.
		400	

Accounts Receivable

	(Dr.)	(Cr.)
Beg. bal.	3,000	500

Paid-in Capital

	(Dr.)	(Cr.)	
		7,000	Beg. bal.

Inventory

	(Dr.)	(Cr.)
Beg. bal.	4,000	
	600	
	400	

Retained Earnings

	(Dr.)	(Cr.)	
		9,000	Beg. bal.

Other Assets

	(Dr.)	(Cr.)
Beg. bal.	10,000	

4-35. Now calculate the new balances for each account and enter them in the accounts of Exhibit 3.

The new balances are:
Cash . . . . .600 Dr.
Accounts Receivable . . . . . .2,500 Dr.
Inventory . . . . .5,000 Dr.
Other Assets . . . . .10,000 Dr.
Accounts Payable . . . . .2,100 Cr.
Paid-in Capital . . . . .7,000 Cr.
Retained Earnings . . . . .9,000 Cr.

4-36. The total of the new balances of the asset accounts is $_____. The total of the new balances of the liability and equity accounts is $_____. Also, the total of the debit balances equals the total of the _____ balances.

$18,100

$18,100

credit

8-81. Depletion is usually calculated by multiplying the quantity of the resource used in a period by a unit cost. If in 19x1 Cecil Company purchased a coal mine for $3,000,000 and estimated that the mine contained 1,000,000 tons of coal, it would use a unit cost of $_____ per ton.

$3 (= $3,000,000 ÷ 1,000,000 tons)

8-82. In 19x2, Cecil Company mined 100,000 tons of coal. The cost of this coal was estimated to be $3 per ton. The depletion expense in 19x2 was $_____. How will the coal mine asset appear on the balance sheet for December 31, 19x2?

$300,000 (= $3 * 100,000)

Coal mine . . . . $

$2,700,000 (= $3,000,000 – $300,000)

INTANGIBLE ASSETS

8-83. In accordance with the cost concept, intangible items such as goodwill, trademarks, and patents are not treated as assets unless . . . [their market value can be determined / they have been acquired at a measurable cost].

they have been acquired at a measurable cost

8-84. When intangibles are recognized as assets, their cost is written off over their service life. For example, patents have a maximum life of 17 years. In no case can the life of an intangible asset exceed 40 years. The process is called **amortization**. Amortization therefore means . . . .
. . . .

writing off the cost of intangible assets.

8-85. Company A reports $1,000,000 of trademarks on its balance sheet, but Company B reports no such item. Which statement is more likely to be correct?

1. Company A has more valuable trademarks than Company B, *or*
2. Company A has purchased trademarks, but Company B has not.

2
(Refer to Frame 2-32 if you are not sure of your answer.)

NOTE: If you answered Frames 4-35 and 4-36 correctly, go to Frame 4-37. If you are not comfortable with these frames, each transaction is repeated in more detail in the following frames. These frames use the approach of first deciding on the effect of the transaction on Cash, or on an asset like Cash, and then making the second part of the entry as an offsetting Debit or Credit.

4-36a. "Inventory costing $600 was purchased for cash." There was a decrease in Cash; so there was a . . . [debit / credit] to Cash. The other entry must be a . . . [debit / credit]. It was a . . . [debit / credit] to Inventory; it was an increase in that asset.

credit

debit   debit

4-36b. "Inventory costing $400 was purchased on credit." There was an increase in Inventory, which is an asset as is Cash, so there was a . . . [debit / credit] to Inventory. The other entry must be a . . . [debit / credit]. It was a . . . [debit / credit] to Accounts Payable; it was an increase in that liability.

debit   credit

credit

4-36c. "Green Company paid $300 to a creditor." There was a decrease in Cash; so there was a . . . [debit / credit] to Cash. The other entry must be a . . . [debit / credit]. It was a . . . [debit / credit] to Accounts Payable; it was a decrease in that liability.

credit

debit   debit

4-36d. "Green Company received $500 in cash from a credit customer." There was an increase in Cash; so there was a . . . [debit / credit] to Cash. The other entry must be a . . . [debit / credit]. It was a . . . [debit / credit] to Accounts Receivable; it was a decrease in that asset.

debit

credit   credit

4-37. Because the total of the debit entries for any transaction should always equal the total of the credit entries, it is . . . [difficult / easy] to check the accuracy with which bookkeeping is done. (We owe this ingenious arrangement to Venetian merchants, who invented it more than 500 years ago.)

easy

8-77. The difference between actual income taxes paid and income tax expense is called Deferred Income Taxes. It is a liability account on the balance sheet. Refer to Exhibit 1 in your booklet. Garsden Company reported deferred income taxes as a . . . [current / noncurrent] liability of $_____. This is not to be confused with the Estimated Tax Liability, which is a . . . [current / noncurrent] liability of $_____. The latter amount is the amount it actually owed the government as of December 31, 1995, for its 1995 taxes.

noncurrent

$824,000

current $1,541,000

NOTE: Under certain circumstances, a company may have a deferred tax asset. It comes about when its taxable income is greater than its financial accounting income. For example, if a company downsizes by promising a separation bonus to employees who agree to retire early, the cost of the bonus is an expense in the year in which the decision to downsize is made, but it is not a decrease in taxable income until the year in which the bonus is paid. Accounting income will therefore be lower than taxable income in the year of the decision.

DEPLETION

8-78. Natural resources such as coal, oil, and other minerals, are called **wasting assets**. Of the following, circle those that are wasting assets.

building	natural gas	freight car
iron ore mine	cash	oil well

natural gas

iron ore mine   oil well

8-79. When the supply of oil in a well or coal in a mine is reduced, the asset is said to be **depleted**. This word, when used as the noun dep___ ___ ___ ion, is the name for the process of writing off the cost of these w___ ___ ___ ___ ___ ___ assets.

depletion

wasting

8-80. The . . . [depletion / depreciation] of a wasting asset is similar to the . . . [depletion / depreciation] of a plant asset. However, in accounting for **depletion**, the asset account is reduced directly. Therefore an accumulated depletion account . . . [is / is not] ordinarily used.

depletion

depreciation

is not

INCOME STATEMENT ACCOUNTS

4-38. The accounts in Exhibit 3 were for items that appear on the balance sheet. Accounts are also kept for items that appear on the other financial statement, the i__ __ __ __ __ statement. As we saw in Part 3, this statement reports the revenues and the expenses of an accounting period and the difference between them, which is net i__ __ __ __ __.

income

income

4-39. Revenues are. . . [increases / decreases] in equity during a period, and expenses are. . . [increases / decreases] in equity.

increases

decreases

4-40. For equity accounts, increases are recorded as . . . [debits / credits]. Because revenues are increases in equity, revenues are recorded as . . . [debits / credits].

credits

credits

4-41. Similarly, decreases in equity are recorded as . . . [debits / credits]. Because expenses are decreases in equity, expenses are recorded as. . . [debits / credits].

debits

debits

4-42. The complete set of rules for making entries to accounts is as follows:

Increases in assets are . . . .[debits / credits].	debits
Decreases in assets are . . . .[debits / credits].	credits
Increases in liabilities and equity are . . . . . .[debits / credits].	credits
Decreases in liabilities and equity are . . . . . .[debits / credits].	debits
Increases in revenues are . . . .[debits / credits].	credits
Increases in expenses are . . . .[debits / credits].	debits

> **NOTE:** It is important that you learn these rules; they govern all accounting transactions. Also, although this may seem strange, it is a fact that both increases in assets (which are good things) and increases in expenses (which are not so good) are debits. That's the way it has to be, in order to maintain the basic equation.

8-72. Taxable income and accounting income . . . [are always identical / may differ]. The tax regulations . . . [govern / do not govern] the way financial statements are prepared. Conversely, the way income is reported on a financial statement . . . [governs / does not govern] the way income is reported for tax purposes.

may differ

do not govern

does not govern

> **NOTE:** There is one important exception to the above: If LIFO is used in tax accounting, LIFO must also be used on the financial statements.

DEFERRED INCOME TAXES

8-73. If a company uses MACRS depreciation in calculating its taxable income but uses straight-line depreciation in calculating its accounting income, its taxable income in the early years will be . . . [higher / lower] than its accounting income.

lower

8-74. Manley Corporation has accounting income in 19x1 of $2,000,000 but taxable income of only $1,500,000. If the income tax rate is 40%, it will pay an income tax of $_____. If the income tax had been calculated as 40% of its accounting income, the amount of tax would be $_____.

$600,000 (= $1,500,000 * 0.40)

$800,000 (= $2,000,000 * 0.40)

8-75. Manley Corporation's actual tax payment of $600,000 is lower than the tax would be if it were calculated on its accounting income. The $600,000 does not **match** the accounting income. It is not consistent with the m_____ing concept.

matching

8-76. As required by the matching concept, the amount of income tax expense reported on the income statement is the amount of income tax calculated on the basis of accounting income, not the amount actually paid. Thus, if its accounting income was $2,000,000 and its tax rate 40 percent, Manley Corporation would report income tax expense of $_____. If it actually paid only $600,000 income tax, it would somehow have to account for the difference of $_____.

$800,000

$200,000 (= $800,000 − $600,000)

THE LEDGER AND THE JOURNAL

4-43. A group of accounts, such as those for Green Company in Exhibit 3, is called a ledger. There is no standard form, so long as there is space to record the d__ __ __ __ s and c__ __ __ __ __ s to each account. Exhibit 5 is the _____ of Glendale Market, the same company we examined in Part 3.

debits   credits
ledger

4-44. In practice, transactions are not recorded directly in the ledger. First, they are written in a record such as Exhibit 4. The title of Exhibit 4 shows that this record is called a _____ . The record made for each transaction is called a _____ entry.

journal
journal

4-45. As Exhibit 4 shows, for each journal entry, the account to be . . . [debited / credited] is listed first, and the . . . [Dr. / Cr.] amount is entered in the first of the two money columns. The account to be . . . [debited / credited] is listed below, and is indented. The . . . [Dr. / Cr.] amount is entered in the second money column.

debited   Dr.
credited
Cr.

4-46. On January 8 merchandise costing $600 was sold for $900, and the customer agreed to pay $900 within 30 days. Using the two journal entries for January 7 as a guide, record the two parts of this transaction in the journal. (If you are not sure about how to record this transaction, go to Frame 4-49.)

8	Accounts Receivable	900	
	Revenues		900
8	Expenses	600	
	Inventory		600

(If you did this correctly, jump ahead to Frame 4-49.)

4-47. On January 8 merchandise costing $600 was sold for $900, and the customer agreed to pay $900 within 30 days.

The first part of this transaction is that the business earned **revenues** of $900, and an asset, Accounts Receivable, increased by $900. Record this part of the transaction by completing the blanks below.

Dr. [   ] 900

Cr. [   ] 900

Dr. Accounts Receivable 900
Cr.   Revenues 900

8-67. In the MACRS, items of plant are assigned to one of six **recovery periods**, depending on their service lives. A schedule shows the percentage of cost that can be taken as depreciation expense in each year of a period. For example, for the seven-year recovery period, 69% of cost can be depreciated in the first half of the recovery period, and _____% in the second half. This contrasts with straight-line depreciation in which _____ % of the cost is depreciated in the first half of the asset's life and _____ % in the second half.

31%

50%

50%

8-68. Also, assets classified in a certain recovery period typically have a longer service life than the life for which that recovery period is named. For example, many machinery and equipment items are classified in the seven-year recovery period, but their actual service life is typically . . . [longer than / shorter than] seven years.

longer than

8-69. MACRS depreciation results in a . . . [higher / lower] tax depreciation expense in the early years of an asset's life and hence in . . . [higher / lower] taxable income and . . . [higher / lower] income taxes during those early years.

higher

lower

lower

8-70. In the later years of the asset's life, the MACRS system results in . . . [higher / lower] depreciation expense and . . . [higher / lower] taxable income and income taxes.

lower   higher

8-71. The higher taxable income in later years will offset the lower taxable income in earlier years. However, during the earlier years the company will have the use of the money not paid out in taxes. For this reason, most companies use _____ depreciation for calculating taxable income, rather than the slower straight-line method.

MACRS

NOTE: The government permits MACRS depreciation because it wants to encourage businesses to invest in new plant and equipment.

HINT: If in doubt as to whether a particular account is to be debited or credited, you usually can find out by referring to the other account in the entry. For example, the entry to Accounts Receivable is an increase in an asset, which is a debit, so the entry to Revenues must be a credit.

4-48. On January 8, merchandise costing $600 was sold for $900, and the customer agreed to pay $900 within 30 days.

The other part of this transaction is that the business had an **expense** of $600 because its **inventory** was decreased by $600. Record this part of the transaction by completing the blanks below.

| Dr. | [_____] | . . . . | 600 |
| Cr. | [_____] | . . . . | 600 |

| Dr. | Expenses . . . . | 600 |
| Cr. | Inventory . . . . | 600 |

4-49. Journal entries are transferred to the l_ _ _ _ _ _ (as in Exhibit 5). This process is called **posting**. The entries through January 7 have already been posted to the ledger, as indicated by the check mark opposite each one. Post the journal entries for January 8 to the proper ledger accounts in Exhibit 5, and make check marks to show that you have posted them.

ledger

Accounts Receivable	Revenues
900	300
	800
	900

Inventory	Expenses
2,000 | 200	200
2,000 | 500	500
600	*600*

4-50. To summarize, any transaction requires at least (how many?) _____ changes in the accounts. These changes are recorded first in the . . . [ledger / journal]. They are then posted to the . . . [ledger / journal].

two

journal   ledger

THE CLOSING PROCESS

4-51. The Revenues account in Exhibit 5 shows. . . [increases / decreases] in Retained Earnings during the period, and the Expenses account shows . . . [increases / decreases] in Retained Earnings. As we know, the difference between revenues and expenses is the net i_ _ _ _ _ _ of the period.

increases

decreases

income

DEPRECIATION FOR INCOME TAX PURPOSES

8-62. Corporations and individuals are subject to a tax on their income. The income tax is calculated as a percentage of taxable income. If a corporation has taxable income of $1 million, and if the income tax rate is 40%, the corporation would pay an income tax of $_____ .

$400,000 (= $1,000,000 * 0.40)

NOTE: Income tax rates are set on a sliding scale; the rates are higher for higher levels of income. In this program, we use a flat rate of 40% in order to avoid the additional arithmetic that would be necessary with the actual sliding scale.

8-63. The Internal Revenue Service publishes regulations explaining how to calculate taxable income. We refer to these regulations as **tax accounting principles**. Most tax accounting principles are consistent with financial accounting principles, but some are not. As a result, taxable income and financial accounting income . . . [may differ / are identical].

may differ

8-64. When a choice is possible, a business usually chooses the tax accounting principle that results in the . . . [higher / lower] taxable income.

lower

8-65. In its accounting income statement, a business tries to report its income as *fairly* as possible. In determining the taxes it owes, a business tries to calculate a taxable income that is as *low* as legally possible. These two objectives . . . [are / are not] the same.

are not

8-66. For income tax purposes, depreciation may be calculated according to what is called the **Modified Accelerated Cost Recovery System (MACRS)**. As the name suggests, the MACRS is a (an) . . . [straight line / accelerated] system.

accelerated

4-52. The net income for the period is an increase in the equity account, R__ __ __ __ __ __ __ E__ __ __ __ __ __ __ __. Net income is added to this account by a series of journal entries called **closing entries**.

Retained Earnings

4-53. In order to do this, we first must find the balance in the account that is to be closed. What is the balance in the Revenues account in Exhibit 5? $_____.

$2,000 (= $300 + $800 + $900)

4-54. An entry is made that reduces the balance in the account to be closed to zero and records the same amount in the Retained Earnings account. Because the Revenues account has a . . . [Dr. / Cr.] balance, the entry that reduces revenues to zero must be on the other side; that is, it must be a . . . [Dr. / Cr.].

Cr.

Dr.

4-55. In Exhibit 4, write the journal entry that closes the $2,000 balance in the Revenues account to Retained Earnings. (Date it January 8, the end of the accounting period.)

8 Revenues 2,000
      Retained Earnings   2,000

4-56. Using similar reasoning, write the journal entry that closes the $1,300 balance in the Expenses account to Retained Earnings.

8 Retained Earnings 1,300
      Expenses   1,300

4-57. Next, post these two entries to the ledger in Exhibit 5.

The accounts affected are:

Revenues	
2,000	300
	800
	900

Expenses	
200	*1,300*
500	
600	

Retained Earnings	
(Dr.)	(Cr.)
1,300	*2,000*

8-56. The difference between book value and the amount actually realized from a sale of a plant asset is called a **gain** (or **loss**) **on disposition of plant**. For example, if an asset whose book value is $10,000 is sold for $12,000, $_____ would be the . . . [gain / loss] on disposition of plant and would be so reported on the income statement.

$2,000 (= $12,000 – $10,000)   gain

8-57. When the asset is sold, its cost and its accumulated depreciation are removed from the accounts. For an asset that cost $40,000, had accumulated depreciation of $30,000, and sold for $12,000, the journal entry would be:

Cash   12,000

Accumulated Depreciation . . . .   [   ]   30,000

Plant . . . .   [   ]   40,000

Gain on disposition of plant . . . . . .   [   ]   2,000

SIGNIFICANCE OF DEPRECIATION

8-58. The purpose of depreciation is to . . . [show the decline in an asset's value / write off a fair share of the cost of the asset in each year in which it provides service].

write off a fair share of the cost of the asset in each year in which it provides service

8-59. Actually, an asset may be as valuable at the end of a year as at the beginning. Depreciation expense for a given year . . . [represents / does not represent] a decrease in the asset's real value or usefulness during the year.

does not represent

8-60. Remember that in accounting for a plant asset, original cost is . . . [known / an estimate], service life is . . . [known / an estimate], and residual value is . . . [known / an estimate].

known   an estimate
an estimate

8-61. The book value of a plant asset represents . . . [what the asset can be sold for / that portion of the cost not yet expensed]. Therefore the statement "book value reports what the asset is worth" is . . . [correct / incorrect].

that portion of the cost not yet expensed

incorrect
(This is a very common error.)

4-58. To get ready for preparing the financial statements, the balance in each asset, liability, and equity account is calculated. (Revenue and expense accounts have zero balances because of the closing process.) For the Cash account in Exhibit 5, the calculation is as follows:

Cash

(Dr.)	(Cr.)
10,000	2,000
5,000	
300	
800	
16,100	*2,000*

Balance *14,100*

NOTE: Each side is totaled. A single line is drawn above the total. A double line is drawn beneath the total. The difference between the two totals is entered beneath the double line.

Calculate the balance for each account in Exhibit 5.

(Details not shown here. The amounts can be checked against the amounts in Frame 4-60.)

4-59. Journal entries *change* the balance in the account. The *calculation* of the balance does not change the balance. Therefore the calculation of a balance. . . [does / does not] require a journal entry.

does not

4-60. The balance sheet is prepared from the balances in the asset, liability, and equity accounts. Complete the balance sheet for Glendale Market as of January 8, in Exhibit 6.

GLENDALE MARKET
Balance Sheet as of January 8

Assets		Liabilities & Equity	
Cash	$14,100	Accounts payable	$ 2,000
Accounts receivable ..	900	Note payable	5,000
Inventory ..	2,700	Paid-in capital	10,000
		Retained earnings ...	700
Total Assets	$17,700	Total Liabilities and Equity	$17,700

8-52. Refer to the following diagram:

12/31/19x1   12/31/19x2   12/31/19x3

Book value $4,000 — $3,000 — $2,000

$2,000

$3,000

etc.

Accumulated depreciation $1,000

Depreciation expense ⟶ $1,000 $1,000 $1,000

Show how the asset would be reported on the company's balance sheet at the end of 19x3.

_____ · $ [____]

Less _____ _____ · · [____]

_____ _____ · · · · · · · · · [____]

Plant $5,000

Less accumulated depreciation 3,000

Book value 2,000

8-53. After the cost of an asset has been completely written off as depreciation expense, no more depreciation is recorded, even though the asset continues to be used. In the example given above, the book value at the end of 19x5 is zero. If the asset continued to be used in 19x6, depreciation expense in 19x6 would be $_____.

0

8-54. To calculate the book value of an asset, you must subtract the _____ _____ from the original _____. Book value . . . [does / does not] report the market value of the asset.

accumulated depreciation

cost   does not

SALE OF A PLANT ASSET

8-55. The calculation of book value depends on estimates of service life and residual value. Because the actual residual value may differ from these estimates, the amount realized from the sale of a plant asset will probably be . . . [equal to / different from] its book value.

different from

4-61. The income statement is prepared from information in the Retained Earnings account. Complete the income statement in Exhibit 6.

Revenues	$2,000
Expenses	1,300
Net income	$ 700

4-62. After the closing process, the revenue and expense accounts have . . . [debit / credit / zero] balances. These accounts are therefore **temporary** accounts. They are started over at the beginning of each period. The asset accounts have . . . [debit / credit / zero] balances, and the liability and equity accounts have . . . [debit / credit / zero] balances; these balances are carried forward to the next period. Income statement accounts are . . . [temporary / permanent] accounts, and balance sheet accounts are . . . [temporary / permanent] accounts.

zero

debit

credit

temporary

permanent

4-63. Most entities report individual items of revenues and expenses (such as salary expense, maintenance expense, insurance expense) on their income statement. In order to do this, they set up an account for each item. Thus, if the income statement reported 2 revenue items and 10 expense items, there would be at least _____ (how many?) revenue and expense accounts. We shall describe these accounts in later Parts. The entries to them are made in exactly the same way as in the simple example given here.

12

4-64. Management needs more detailed information than is contained in the financial statements. For example, instead of one account, Accounts Receivable, it needs an account for each customer so that the amount owed by each customer is known. Therefore the ledger usually contains . . . [the same number of / many more] accounts than there are items on the financial statements.

many more

NOTE: Although you need to understand the bookkeeping process described in this part, you don't need to memorize the details. Our purpose is to show where the numbers in the financial statements come from. This helps you understand what the numbers mean.

8-49. The balance sheet for December 31, 19x5, would include the following items.

Plant . . . . $ [   ]

Less _____ _____ . . . . [   ]

Book value . . . . $ [   ]

Plant $10,000

Less accumulated depreciation   5,000

Book value . . . . $ 5,000

The income statement for 19x5 would include an item:

Depreciation expense . . . . $ [   ]

$1,000

8-50. Each year, the write-off of $1,000 of the cost of the asset would be recorded with the following journal entry.

Dr. _____ _____ . . . . _____

Cr. _____ _____ . _____

Depreciation expense 1,000

Accumulated depreciation . . .   1,000

8-51. The table below shows the original cost, annual depreciation expense, accumulated depreciation (at year end), and book value (at year end) for a plant asset with an original cost of $5,000, a service life of five years, and zero residual value. Complete the table.

Year	Original Cost	Depreciation Expense	Accumulated Depreciation	Book Value
19x1	$5,000	$1,000	$1,000	$4,000
19x2	5,000	1,000	2,000	3,000
19x3	5,000	1,000	3,000	2,000
19x4	5,000	1,000	4,000	1,000
19x5	5,000	[ ]	[ ]	[ ]

1,000   5,000   zero

What is the total amount charged as depreciation expense during the service life of the asset? $_____.

$5,000

A NOTE ON COMPUTERS

Most entities use a computer to do their accounting. The computer makes debit and credit entries according to exactly the same rules as those we have described. In this program, we must show the journal entries manually because what goes on inside the computer is not visible.The computer has the following advantages over the manual system we use in this program:

• The computer is much faster.

• The computer does not make copying errors. For example, when the computer writes a check, the amount of the check is always the amount credited to Cash and debited to some other account. The amounts reported on the financial statement are the same as the balances in the accounts.

• The computer assures that debit entries always equal credit entries. It will not accept an entry in which this equality does not exist.

• Once an amount has been recorded in the computer, it may be used for several purposes. For example, an entry to Accounts Receivable is used in calculating the total amount in the Accounts Receivable account, the accounts of individual customers, and the amount reported on the balance sheet.

• The computer does not make arithmetic errors.

• The computer may require that certain rules be followed. For example, the credit entry for a check is always to the Cash account.

• The computer has built-in safeguards that help detect fraudulent or erroneous entries.

However, if the initial input to the computer is made by a person, an error made by that person may not be detected. For example, if a check is supposed to be for $962 and the bookkeeper keys in $926, the computer may not detect the error. (Some input errors can be avoided by the use of automatic input devices, such as scanners that read bar codes.)

Also, despite the built-in safeguards, the computer cannot detect certain types of fraudulent entries. As examples of multimillion dollar errors reported in the

8-46. On the balance sheet, the balance in the Accumulated Depreciation account is shown as a deduction from the original cost of the asset, and the remaining amount is called **Book Value**. For example, the listing:

Plant	$10,000
Less accumulated depreciation	4,000
Book value	$ 6,000

shows that the plant originally cost $_____, that $_____ of its original cost has so far been recognized as depreciation expense, and that $_____ of book value remains to be depreciated in future years. (Part of the book value may be the estimated residual value.)

$10,000 $4,000

$6,000

8-47. If the depreciation expense on this machine was $1,000 per year, we know from the above that depreciation expense has been taken for _____ (how many?) years, and that it will be taken for _____ (how many?) more years in the future, assuming zero residual value.

four

six

8-48. Suppose that the ledger showed the following account balances on January 1, 19x5, and that annual depreciation expense was $1,000. Enter the amounts for depreciation in 19x5.

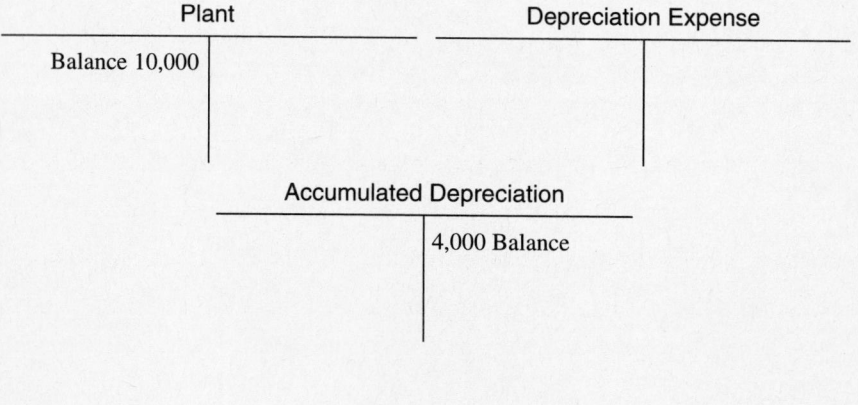

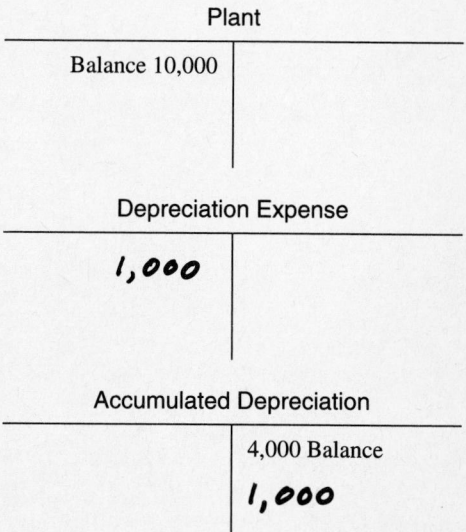

press demonstrate, there is no guarantee that errors do not exist. Therefore, there must be an audit function to check the possibility of fraud or error.

Although the computer may perform most of the bookkeeping functions, it cannot replace the accountant. The accountant specifies the rules to be followed in routine transactions, but, as we shall see, some transactions require judgment as to the accounts affected and the amounts; the accountant must tell the computer how to make these entries. If the accountant makes an incorrect decision, the accounts will be incorrect.

KEY POINTS TO REMEMBER

- **Debit** refers to the left side of an account and **credit** to the right side.

- Increases in asset and expense accounts are debits.

- Increases in liability, equity, and revenue accounts are credits.

- Decreases are the opposite.

- For any transaction, debits must equal credits. For the whole set of accounts, debit balances must equal credit balances.

- Transactions are first recorded in a journal. Amounts are then posted to the accounts in a ledger.

- Revenue and expense accounts are temporary accounts. At the end of each accounting period, they are closed to Retained Earnings. The difference between the revenues of a period and the expenses of the period is the net income of the period. These revenues and expenses are reported on the income statement.

- Net income is the increase in retained earnings from operating performance during the period.

- Asset, liability, and equity accounts are permanent accounts. Their balances are carried forward to the next accounting period.

You have completed Part 4 of this program. If you think you understand the material in this part, you should now take Post Test 4, which is in the separate booklet. If you are uncertain about your understanding, you should review Part 4.

The post test will serve both to test your comprehension and to review the highlights of Part 4. After taking the post test, you may find that you are unsure about certain points. You should review these points before continuing with Part 5.

8-41. Similarly, if a company purchased a three-year insurance policy in advance for $9,000 on December 31, 19x1, the following journal entry would be made to record Insurance Expense in 19x2.

Dr. _____ _____ . . . . _____

    Cr. _____ _____ . . . . _____

Insurance expense 3,000	
Prepaid expense	3,000
(*or* Prepaid insurance)	

8-42. In accounting for depreciation, the procedure is similar. First, we recognize the appropriate amount of expense for the period. In this case the title of the expense account is D_____ Expense.

Depreciation

8-43. Next, we must recognize an equal . . . [decrease / increase] in the amount of the asset. However, accountants prefer to show the original cost of plant assets on the balance sheet at all times. Therefore, decreases in the amount of a plant asset . . . [are / are not] shown as a direct reduction in the asset amount.

decrease

are not

8-44. Instead, decreases in the asset amount of a plant asset because of depreciation expense are accumulated in a separate account called **Accumulated Depreciation**.

A decrease in an asset is always a . . . [debit / credit]. Accumulated Depreciation is a decrease in an asset, and therefore has a . . . [Dr. / Cr.] balance. (Accumulated Depreciation is a contra-asset account.)

credit
Cr.

8-45. Suppose $1,000 of depreciation expense is recognized for a given year. What would be the appropriate journal entry?

Dr. D_____ e_____ . . . . _____

    Cr. A_____ d_____ .   _____

Depreciation expense 1,000	
Accumulated depreciation . . .	1,000

Part 5

Revenues and Monetary Assets

Learning Objectives

In this part you will learn:

- The accounting period.
- What accrual accounting is.
- Three more of the nine basic accounting concepts:
  - Conservatism concept.
  - Materiality concept.
  - Realization concept.
- How revenue items are measured.
- How monetary assets are measured.
- The days' sales uncollected ratio.

5-1. In Part 4 we introduced the idea of income, which is the difference between r__ __ __ __ __ __ __ and e__ __ __ __ __ __ __ .

revenues   expenses

5-2. Income increases Retained Earnings. Retained Earnings is an item of . . . [liabilities / equity] on the balance sheet. Any increase in Retained Earnings is also an increase in . . . [liabilities / equity].

equity
equity

> **NOTE:** Net income results from the profitable operation of an entity. The amount of net income is one of the most important items of information that accounting reports. In this part we describe how the revenue portion of net income is measured.

8-38. There are many ways of calculating accelerated depreciation amounts. The following table shows one of them. The asset has a depreciable cost of $15,000 and a service life of five years. Enter the amounts for straight-line depreciation and show whether accelerated depreciation is larger or smaller in each of the five years.

Year	Accelerated Depreciation	Straight-line Depreciation	Accelerated is		
1	$ 5,000	$_____	larger/smaller	$3,000	larger
2	4,000	_____	larger/smaller	3,000	larger
3	3,000	3,000	same	3,000	same
4	2,000	_____	larger/smaller	3,000	smaller
5	1,000	_____	larger/smaller	3,000	smaller
Total	$15,000	$ 15,000			

Accelerated depreciation is used principally in calculating taxable income, as we shall see in a later section.

ACCOUNTING FOR DEPRECIATION

8-39. In Part 6 we described how certain types of assets were converted into expenses with the passage of time. When this occurs, there is a . . . [Dr. / Cr.] entry to the asset account, which shows the . . . [decrease / increase] in the amount of the asset, and there is an equal . . . [Dr. / Cr.] to the expense account.

Cr.   decrease

Dr.

8-40. For example, if an entity had a fuel oil asset of $2,000 at the beginning of March and used $500 of fuel oil during March, the entity will recognize $_____ of fuel oil expense for March, and it will also recognize an equal decrease of $_____ in the fuel oil asset. On the balance sheet of March 31, the fuel oil asset will be reported at $_____.

$500

$500

$1,500 (= $2,000 – $500)

ACCOUNTING PERIOD

5-3. An income statement reports the amount of net income . . . [at a moment in time / over a period of time]. The period of time covered by one income statement is called the **accounting period**.

over a period of time

5-4. For most entities, the official accounting period is one year. However, financial statements, called **interim statements**, usually are prepared for shorter periods. In Part 4 you prepared an income statement for Glendale Market for the period January 2 through January 8. This was an . . . [annual / interim] statement, and the accounting period was one . . . [week / month / year.]

interim   week

5-5. For most entities, the accounting period is the **calendar year**, that is, the year that ends on the last day of the calendar, which is _____ (what date?).

December 31

5-6. Some entities end their year when activities are at a relatively low level. For example, a school might end its year on June 30, when students have left for the summer. The accounting period for these entities is the . . . [calendar year / natural business year.] The period selected is called the **fiscal year**.

natural business year

5-7. Entities don't fire their employees and cease operations at the end of an accounting period. They continue from one accounting period to the next. The fact that accounting divides the stream of events into a__ __ __ __ __ __ __ __ __ __ periods makes the problem of measuring revenues and expenses in a single accounting period . . . [an easy / the most difficult] problem in accounting.

accounting
the most difficult

ACCRUAL ACCOUNTING

5-8. On January 3, Glendale Market borrowed $5,000 from a bank. Its cash therefore . . . [increased / decreased / did not change]. A liability . . . [increased / decreased / did not change].

increased

increased

8-34. Complete the following table.

If the estimated life of an asset is:	The straight-line depreciation rate is:	
2 years	☐ %	50%
3 years	☐ %	33-1/3%
4 years	☐ %	25%
5 years	20%	

8-35. In the straight-line method, the amount of **depreciation expense** for a given year is found by multiplying the depreciable cost by the depreciation rate. Thus, if the depreciable cost is $9,000 and the depreciation rate is 20%, the amount of depreciation expense each year will be $_____ .

$1,800 (= $9,000 * 0.20)

ACCELERATED DEPRECIATION

8-36. If you want an automobile to go faster, you press down on the accelerator. **Accelerated Depreciation** writes off the cost of an asset . . . [faster / slower] than straight-line depreciation.

faster

8-37. In accelerated depreciation, more depreciation expense is reported in the early years of the asset's service life and therefore . . . [more / less] in the later years. The total amount of depreciation expense is the same as in the straight-line method.

less

5-9. Revenues are increases in equity. The receipt of $5,000 cash from the bank on January 3 . . . [increased / decreased / did not change] revenues and therefore . . . [increased / decreased / did not change] equity.

did not change

did not change

5-10. On January 4, Glendale Market purchased $2,000 of inventory, paying cash. This was an increase in one asset and a decrease in another asset. Since equity was unchanged, the payment of cash on January 4 . . . [was / was not] associated with an expense.

was not

5-11. On January 8, Glendale Market sold merchandise for $900, and the customer agreed to pay $900 within 30 days. This transaction resulted in . . . [an increase / a decrease / no change] in cash. Revenue was $_____ . This revenue . . . [was / was not] associated with a change in cash on January 8.

no change $900

was not

5-12. Evidently revenues and expenses . . . [are / are not] necessarily accompanied, at the same time, by changes in cash. Moreover, changes in cash . . . [are / are not] necessarily coupled with corresponding changes in revenues or expenses.

are not

are not

5-13. Increases or decreases in cash are changes in an . . . [equity / asset] account. Revenues or expenses are changes in an . . . [equity / asset] account.

asset

equity

5-14. Income is measured as the difference between . . . [cash increases and cash decreases / revenues and expenses].

revenues and expenses

5-15. Income measures the increase in e__ __ __ __ __ during an accounting period that was associated with the entity's operations.

equity

STRAIGHT-LINE DEPRECIATION

8-31. The depreciation of a plant asset with a cost of $10,000, no residual value, and a five-year life, may be graphed as follows:

Amount not yet depreciated   Annual depreciation

$10,000

8,000

6,000

4,000

2,000 $2,000

0

End of year   During year

The line showing depreciation expense as a function of time is . . . [straight / vertical].

straight

8-32. Because of this, charging off an equal fraction of the asset cost each year is called the s__ __ __ __ __ __ __-line method of depreciation. Most companies use this method.

straight

8-33. The percentage of cost charged off each year is called the depreciation rate. In the straight-line method, we obtain the rate by finding:

$$\frac{1}{\text{number of years of service life}}$$

For example, if an asset is to be depreciated over five years, the d_____ r_____ is _____%.

depreciation rate   20% (1/5)

5-16. Many individuals and some small businesses keep track only of cash receipts and cash payments. This type of accounting is called c_ _ _ _ accounting. If you keep a record of your bank deposits, the checks you write, and the balance in your bank account, you are doing _ _ _ _ _ accounting. Cash accounting . . . [does / does not] measure changes in equity.

cash

cash   does not

5-17. Most entities, however, account for revenues and expenses, as well as for cash receipts and cash payments. This type of accounting is called **accrual accounting**. Evidently, accrual accounting is . . . [simpler / more complicated] than cash accounting, but accrual accounting . . . [does / does not] measure changes in equity. The most difficult problems in accounting are problems of . . . [cash / accrual] accounting.

more complicated

does

accrual

5-18. Because net income is the change in equity and measures the entity's financial performance, accrual accounting provides . . . [more / less] information than cash accounting.

more

5-19. In order to measure the income of a period, we must measure r_ _ _ _ _ _ _ s and e_ _ _ _ _ _ _ s of that period, and this requires the use of _ _ _ _ _ _ _ accounting.

revenues   expenses

accrual

> **NOTE:** In this part, we describe the measurement of revenues. The measurement of expenses is described in later parts. First, we shall introduce three more accounting concepts: conservatism, materiality, and realization.

CONSERVATISM CONCEPT

5-20. Suppose that in January Lynn Jones agreed to buy an automobile from Ace Auto Company; the automobile is to be delivered to Jones in March. Because Ace Auto Company is in the business of selling automobiles, it . . . [would / would not] be happy that Jones has agreed to buy one.

would

8-28. The difference between the cost of a plant asset and its residual value is called the **depreciable cost**. Thus, if an automobile purchased for $10,000 is expected to have a six-year life, and to have a residual value of $1,000 at the end of that life, $10,000 is the _____ and $9,000 is the _____ _____.

cost (*or* gross cost)

depreciable cost

8-29. Here is a list of factors that are relevant to the depreciation of an asset:

1. original cost
2. residual value
3. service life

Which factors are used in arriving at the depreciable cost? ....

1 and 2

The amount of depreciation expense in a given year? ....

1, 2, and 3

Which factors are estimates? ....

2 and 3

> **NOTE:** There are many methods of calculating the cost that is to be recorded as depreciation expense in each year of the estimated service life. In the following sections we describe three of them:
>
> 1. Units-of-production depreciation;
> 2. Straight-line depreciation;
> 3. Accelerated depreciation.

UNITS-OF-PRODUCTION DEPRECIATION

8-30. In the units-of-production method, a cost per unit of production is calculated, and depreciation expense for a year is found by multiplying this unit cost by the number of units that the asset produced in that year.

Grady Company purchased a truck in 19x1 for $44,000. It estimated that the truck would provide services for 100,000 miles and would have a residual value of $4,000.

Its depreciable cost was $_____.

$40,000 (= $44,000 − $4,000)

Its estimated cost per mile was $_____.

$0.40 (= $40,000 ÷ 100,000)

In 19x2, the truck was driven 15,000 miles. Its depreciation expense in 19x2 was $_____.

$6,000 (= $0.40 ∗ $15,000)

5-21. Jones agreed in January to buy an automobile for delivery in March. Although Jones is . . . [likely / unlikely] to take delivery in March, it is possible that she will change her mind. The sale of this automobile therefore is . . . [absolutely certain / uncertain].

likely

uncertain

5-22. Jones agreed in January to buy an automobile for delivery in March.

Because in January the sale of this automobile is uncertain, accounting . . . [does / does not] recognize the revenue in January. If Jones does accept delivery in March, accounting recognizes r__ __ __ __ __ __ in March. This is a . . . [conservative / liberal] way to account for the transaction.

does not
revenue
conservative

5-23. Increases in equity are recognized only when they are **reasonably certain**. To be conservative, decreases in equity should be recognized as soon as they probably occurred. Suppose an automobile was stolen from Ace Auto Company in January, and the company waits until March to decide that the automobile is gone for good. Conservatism requires that the decrease in equity be recognized when it is **reasonably possible**; that is, in . . . [January / March].

January

5-24. The conservatism concept therefore has two parts:

1. Recognize **increases** in equity only when they are reasonably . . . [certain / possible].

certain

2. Recognize **decreases** in equity as soon as they are reasonably . . . [certain / possible].

possible

> **NOTE:** These are general ideas only. Specifics will be given in later Parts of this program.

8-23. To summarize:

1. Depreciation is the process of converting the cost of an asset into expense over its service life.
2. This process recognizes that an asset gradually loses its usefulness.
3. An asset can lose its usefulness for either of two reasons:

   a. ....   it wears out

   b. ....   it becomes obsolete
4. The asset's service life is the . . . [longer / shorter] of these two   shorter

   causes.

8-24. In the summary above, no mention was made of market value.
Depreciation . . . [is / is not] related to changes in the market value of an   is not
asset. This is consistent with the _____ concept.   cost

8-25. In some cases, an entity expects to be able to sell the plant asset at
the end of its service life. The amount that it expects to sell it for is
called its **residual value**. If an entity buys a truck for $20,000 and expects to sell it for $4,000 five years later, the estimated residual value is
$_____. $4,000

8-26. In most cases, an entity expects that a plant asset will be worthless
at the end of its service life. If so, its residual value is _____   zero
(how much?).

> **NOTE:** Residual value, as such, does not appear in the accounts. It is merely
> a number used to calculate depreciation.

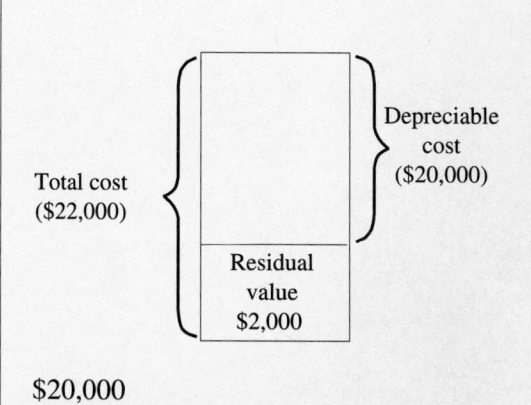

8-27. Suppose a restaurant oven that cost $22,000 is expected to have a
residual value of $2,000 at the end of its 10-year life. In this case, the
total amount of depreciation that should be recorded during the service
life of the asset is only $_____. The depreciation expense for $20,000
each of the ten years would be $_____. $2,000 (= 1/10 * $20,000)

MATERIALITY CONCEPT

5-25. A brand new pencil is a(n) . . . [asset / liability / equity] of the entity that owns it.

asset

5-26. Every time an employee writes with a pencil, part of the asset's value . . . [increases / decreases], and the entity's equity also . . . [increases / decreases].

decreases   decreases

5-27. Would it be possible, theoretically, to find out each day the number of partly used pencils and to make a journal entry showing the amount of pencils that were used up and the corresponding "pencil expense" of that day? . . . [Yes / No] Would it be practical? . . . [Yes / No]

Yes   No

5-28. The accountant considers that the asset value of pencils was entirely used up at the time they were purchased or issued to the user. To do otherwise would be a waste of time. This solution is simple and . . . [impractical / practical], but . . . [more / less] exact than the theoretically correct treatment.

practical

less

5-29. The treatment of pencils is an example of the **materiality** concept. The materiality concept states that the accountant may disregard im__ __ __ __ __ __ __ __ transactions. When accountants consider the asset value of pencils to be entirely used up at the time of purchase, they are applying the __ __ __ __ __ __ __ __ __ __ __ concept.

immaterial

materiality

NOTE: Material transactions are those that make a difference in understanding an entity's financial affairs. Deciding which transactions are material is a matter of judgment. There are no mechanical rules.

8-17. When a machine or other item of plant is acquired, we . . . [know / do not know] how long it actually will be of service. Therefore, we . . . [can know with certainty / must estimate] its service life.

do not know

must estimate

8-18. Since some portion of a plant asset is used up during each year of its service life, a portion of the cost of the asset is treated as a(n) . . . [revenue / expense] in each year. For example, suppose a computer is purchased at a cost of $50,000. It has an estimated service life of five years and will be worthless then. It would be reasonable to charge _____ (what fraction?) or $_____ as expense in each of the five years.

expense

1/5
$10,000 (= 1/5 * $50,000)

8-19. The process of recognizing a portion of the cost of a plant asset as an expense during each year of its estimated service life is called **depreciation**. The $10,000 recorded as an expense during each one of the five years of service life of the computer that cost $50,000 is called the _____ expense for that year.

depreciation

8-20. A plant asset can become useless for either of two reasons: (1) it may wear out physically; or (2) it may become obsolete (i.e., no longer useful). The latter reason is called **obsolescence**. Loss of usefulness because of the development of improved equipment, changes in style, or other causes not related to the physical condition of the asset are examples of _____.

obsolescence

8-21. The **service life** of an asset considers both physical wear and obsolescence. The service life is the shorter of the two periods. Thus an asset with an estimated physical life of ten years that is estimated to become obsolete in five years has an estimated service life of . . . [five / ten] years.

five

8-22. Since depreciation considers obsolescence, it is . . . [correct / not correct] to regard depreciation and obsolescence as two different things.

not correct

5-30. The other side of the coin is that the financial statements must disclose all material facts. For example, if a large fraction of a company's inventory is found to be worthless, the m_____ concept requires that this fact be disclosed.

materiality

5-31. The materiality concept therefore has two parts: (1) . . . [disregard / disclose] trivial (i.e., unimportant) matters, and (2) . . . [disregard / disclose] all important matters.

disregard

disclose

5-32. To review, the conservatism concept is: recognize increases in equity only when they are r__ __ __ __ __ __ __ __ __ c__ __ __ __ __ __ , but recognize decreases as soon as they are r__ __ __ __ __ __ __ __ __ p__ __ __ __ __ __ __ . The materiality concept is: . . . [disregard / disclose] trivial matters, but . . . [disregard / disclose] all important matters.

reasonably certain

reasonably

possible   disregard

disclose

REALIZATION CONCEPT

5-33. Consider an entity that manufactures goods and then sells them. In accounting, the revenue from these goods is recognized at the time they are delivered to the customer, *not* at the time they are manufactured.

Suppose that in 19x2 an entity delivers to a customer an item that it manufactured in 19x1. The revenue is recognized in . . . [19x1 / 19x2].

19x2

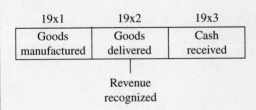

5-34. If a company sells services rather than goods, revenue is recognized at the time the services are . . . [contracted for / delivered].

delivered

5-35. Goods (such as shoes) are *tangible* products. Services (such as repairing TV sets) are *intangible* products. Both goods and services are products. Thus, the general rule is that revenue from a product is recognized when the product is . . . [manufactured / contracted for / delivered].

delivered

8-12. Even though the entity does not own the item, a capital lease is treated like other plant assets. A capital lease is an exception to the general rule that assets are property or property rights that are _ _ _ _ _ by the entity.

owned

> **NOTE:** Special rules apply to accounting for capital leases. They are beyond the scope of this introductory treatment.

DEPRECIATION

8-13. Except in rare cases, land retains its usefulness indefinitely. Land therefore continues to be reported on the balance sheet at its acquisition cost, in accordance with the _____ concept.

cost

If Hanover Hospital purchased a plot of land in 1970 at a cost of $100,000, it would have been reported at $_____ on the December 31, 1970 balance sheet. If Hanover Hospital still owned the land in 1996, and its market value then was $300,000, it would be reported on the December 31, 1996, balance sheet at . . . [$100,000 / $300,000].

$100,000

$100,000

8-14. Unlike land, plant assets eventually become useless. They have a(n) . . . [limited / unlimited] life.

limited

8-15. Plant assets will become completely useless at some future time. At that time, the item is no longer an asset. Usually this process occurs gradually; that is, a portion of the asset is used up in each year of its life, until finally it is scrapped or sold and therefore is no longer _ _ _ ful to the entity. At that time, it . . . [is / is not] an asset.

useful

is not

8-16. The period of time over which a plant asset is estimated to be of **service** to the company is called its s_ _ _ _ _ _ life.

service

5-36. At the time of delivery, revenue is said to be realized. The realization concept is that revenue is recognized and recorded in the period in which it is r__ __ __ __ __ ed.

realized

5-37. In January, Smith Company contracts to paint Herbert's house. The house is painted in February, and Herbert pays Smith Company in March. Smith Company should recognize revenue in _____ (what month?).

February

January	February	March
Services ordered	Services delivered	Cash received

Revenue recognized

5-38. Gordon Company manufactures some imitation carrots in May. In June it receives an order from Peter Rabbit, Esq., for one carrot. Gordon Company delivers the carrot in July. Peter Rabbit pays the bill in August and eats the carrot in September. Gordon Company would recognize revenue in _____, which is . . . [before / after] the order was received and . . . [before / after] the cash was received.

July   after

before

5-39. Revenue is realized when a *sale* is completed by the delivery of a product. Because of this, the word "sales" is often used along with revenue, as in the phrase "s_____ r_____."

sales revenue

5-40. A salesperson may say that he or she has "made a sale" when the order was written, even though the product is to be delivered at some future time. In accounting, writing a sales order . . . [is / is not] a sale because the revenue has not yet been __ __ __ __ __ __ ed.

is not

realized

NOTE: Revenue may be recognized (1) before, (2) during, or (3) after the period in which the cash from the sale is received. First, let's consider a case in which revenue is recognized in the same period as when the cash is received.

8-8. If an entity constructs a machine or a building with its own personnel, all costs incurred in construction are included in the asset amount.

Thayer Company built a new building for its own use. It spent $200,000 in materials, $900,000 in salaries to workers directly engaged in the building's construction, and $200,000 in overhead costs related to the building. This building should be recorded in the accounts at its cost, $_____.

$1,300,000 (= $200,000 + $900,000 + $200,000)

CAPITAL LEASES

8-9. Most assets are *owned* by the entity. When an entity leases (i.e., rents) a building, a machine, or other tangible item, the item is owned by someone else (the **lessor**); the entity . . . [does / does not] own it. In other words, most leased items . . . [are / are not] assets of the entity that leases them (the **lessee**).

does not
are not

8-10. However, if an entity leases an item for a long period of time, it has as much control over the use of that item as if it owned it. A lease for a long time—almost the whole life of the asset—is called a **capital lease**. Because the entity controls the item for almost its whole life, a c__ __ __ __ __ __ l__ __ __ __ is recorded as an asset.

capital lease

8-11. The amount recorded for a capital lease is the amount the entity would have paid if it had purchased the item rather than leased it. If an entity leased a machine for 10 years, agreeing to pay $10,000 per year, and if the purchase price of this machine was $70,000, this c__ __ __ __ __ __ l__ __ __ __ would be recorded as an asset at an amount of . . . [70,000 / 100,000], as in this entry:

capital lease
$70,000

Capital lease . . . . _____

70,000

Lease obligation . . . . _____

70,000

5-41. In January, Loren Company sold and delivered a motorcycle to Jerry Paynter, who paid $1,800 cash.

In this example, revenue is recognized in the . . . [month before / same month as / month after] the related cash receipt.

same month as

5-42. In January, Loren Company sold a motorcycle for $3,800 and de-livered it to Jean Matthews. Matthews agreed to pay for the motorcycle in 30 days.

In this case revenue is recognized in the . . . [month before / same month as / month after] the related cash receipt.

month before

5-43. When revenue is recognized before the related cash receipt, as in the preceding transaction, the revenue is accompanied by the right to col-lect the cash, which is an Account Receivable. Thus, the entry for the sale of the motorcycle on credit was:

Dr. _____ _____ 3,800

    Cr. _____ _____ 3,800

Dr. Accounts Receivable 3,800

    Cr. Sales Revenue 3,800

5-44. When a customer pays an entity for a credit purchase, the entity records an increase in Cash and a corresponding decrease in Accounts Receivable. Thus, when Loren Company receives a check for $3,800 from Matthews in February, Loren Company makes the following entry:

Dr. _____ 3,800

    Cr. _____ _____ . . . 3,800

Dr. Cash 3,800

    Cr. Accounts Receivable 3,800

Revenue . . . [was / was not] recognized in February.

was not

8-3. On the balance sheet, tangible noncurrent assets are often labeled **fixed assets**, or **property, plant, and equipment**. Equipment is a . . . [current / noncurrent] and . . . [tangible / intangible] asset.

noncurrent   tangible

8-4. For brevity, we shall use the word **plant** for all tangible noncurrent assets except land. Thus, buildings, equipment, and furniture are items of _____. These assets are expected to be useful for longer than _____ _____.

plant
one year

ACCOUNTING FOR ACQUISITIONS

8-5. When an item of plant is acquired, it is recorded in the accounts at its _____ (what value?) in accordance with the fundamental accounting concept known as the _____ concept.

cost
cost

8-6. The cost of an asset includes all costs incurred to make the asset ready for its intended use.

Bird Corporation paid $50,000 for a plot of land. It also paid $1,500 as a brokers' fee, $600 for legal fees, and $5,000 to tear down the existing structures in order to make the land ready for a new building. The land should be recorded in the accounts at an amount of $_____.

$57,100 (= $50,000 + $1,500 + $600 + $5,000)
(Note: Some accountants charge the $5,000 as a cost of the new building.)

8-7. Transportation and installation costs are usually included as part of equipment cost.

Plymouth Bank purchased a computer for $40,000. The bank also paid $200 in freight charges and $1,000 in installation charges. This equipment should be recorded in the accounts at its cost, $_____.

$41,200 (= $40,000 + $200 + $1,000)

5-45. So far we have treated the cases in which

1. revenue is recognized *in the same period* as the associated cash receipt; and

2. revenue is recognized *before* the associated receipt of cash.

There remains the case in which

3. revenue is recognized _____ the associated receipt of cash.

after

5-46. When a customer pays an entity in advance of delivery of the product, the entity has an obligation to deliver the product. This obligation is a(n) . . . [asset / liability / equity]. It is listed on the . . . [left / right] side of the balance sheet with the title **Advances from Customers**.

liability   right

5-47. Thus, when an entity receives cash in advance of delivery, it records a debit to Cash and a corresponding credit to the liability, Advances from Customers.

In March, Maypo Company received $3,000 cash in advance from a firm to prepare an advertising brochure. Write the entry that Maypo Company should make in March to record this transaction.

Dr. _____ 3,000

Cr. _____ _____ _____ 3,000

Dr. Cash 3,000

Cr. Advances from Customers   3,000

5-48. In March, Maypo Company received $3,000 in advance from a firm to prepare an advertising brochure. It delivered the brochure in June. It therefore no longer had the liability, Advances from Customers. Write the entry that should be made in June.

Dr. _____ _____ _____ 3,000

Cr. S_____ R_____ 3,000

Dr. Advances from Customers .. 3,000

Cr. Sales Revenue 3,000

March	April	May	June
Cash received	Product made		Product delivered

Revenue recognized

Part 8

Noncurrent Assets and Depreciation

Learning Objectives

In this part you will learn:

- How plant assets are recorded in the accounts.
- The meaning and significance of depreciation.
- Straight-line, accelerated, and units of production methods of depreciation.
- How depreciation is recorded.
- Differences between income-tax principles and accounting principles.
- The meaning of depletion and how it is recorded.
- How intangible assets are recorded.

NONCURRENT ASSETS

8-1. Earlier, you learned that current assets are cash or items likely to be converted to cash within one _____ (what time period?). Evidently, **noncurrent assets** are expected to be of use to the entity for longer than _____ _____.

year

one year

8-2. Tangible assets are assets than can be touched. Intangible assets are assets that have no physical substance (other than pieces of paper) but give the entity valuable rights. Which of the following are tangible assets?

Current Assets	Noncurrent Assets
1. Account receivable	5. Land
2. Notes receivable	6. Goodwill
3. Inventory	7. Buildings
4. Prepaid rent	8. Investment in another entity

(3), (5), and (7)
(Note: Although a note receivable is evidenced by a paper that can be touched, the asset is the sum of money that is promised. This is an intangible asset.)

5-49. A magazine publisher received a check for $50 in 19x1 for a magazine subscription. The magazines will be delivered in 19x2. Write the entry that the publisher should make in 19x1.

Dr. _____ 50

    Cr. _____ _____ _____ 50

Dr. Cash 50

    Cr. Advances from Customers 50

> **NOTE:** The terms "Deferred Revenue," "Precollected Revenue," and "Unearned Revenue" are sometimes used instead of "Advances from Customers."

5-50. A publisher received $50 for a magazine subscription in 19x1. In 19x2, when the magazines are delivered, the publisher recognizes the $50 revenue and records a corresponding decrease in the liability, Advances from Customers.

Write the names of the accounts and the amounts for the entry that should be made in 19x2.

Dr. _____ _____ _____ ☐

    Cr. _____ _____ ...... ☐

Dr. Advances from Customers .. 50

    Cr. Sales Revenue 50

5-51. The customer's advance may provide for revenue that will be earned over several future accounting periods. Suppose in 19x1 a publisher received $80 for a magazine subscription, with the magazines to be delivered in 19x2 and 19x3. The entry for 19x1 should be:

Dr. _____ .... ☐

    Cr. _____ _____ _____ ☐

Dr. Cash 80

    Cr. Advances from Customers 80

The amount of the liability at the end of 19x1 would be . . . [$80 / $40 / $20 / $0].

$80

KEY POINTS TO REMEMBER

- If an entity has no record of the cost of the specific items that were sold during a period, it deduces Cost of Sales by (1) adding purchases to the beginning inventory, which gives the goods available for sale, and (2) subtracting the cost of the ending Inventory.

- In doing this, it must make an assumption as to which items were sold.

- The First-In First-Out (FIFO) method assumes that the oldest items are the first to be sold.

- The Last-In First-Out (LIFO) method assumes that the most recently purchased items are the first to be sold. In periods of rising prices, it results in a higher Cost of Sales and hence a lower taxable income than the FIFO method.

- The average-cost method charges both Cost of Sales and the ending Inventory at the average cost of the goods available for sale.

- The inventory method that a company selects does not necessarily reflect the physical flow of its goods.

- If the market value of items in inventory decreases below their cost, the inventory is written down to market.

- The cost of goods produced in a manufacturing company is the sum of their direct materials cost, direct labor cost, and production overhead cost.

- Period costs are those that are charged as expenses in the period in which the costs were incurred. Product costs become Cost of Sales in the period in which the products are sold, which may be later than the period in which the products were manufactured.

- Overhead is charged to products by means of an overhead rate, such as a rate per direct labor hour.

- The inventory turnover ratio shows how many times the inventory turned over during a year.

You have now completed Part 7 of this program. If you think you have understood the material in this part, you should now take Post Test 7 which is in the separate booklet. If you are uncertain about your understanding, you should review Part 7.

The post test will serve both to test your comprehension and to review the highlights of Part 7. After taking the post test, you may find that you are unsure about certain points. You should review these points before continuing with Part 8.

5-52. In 19x1 a publisher received $80 for a magazine subscription, with the magazines to be delivered in 19x2 and 19x3. The entry for 19x2 would be:

Dr. _____ _____ _____ ☐

Cr. _____ _____ . . . . . . ☐

Dr. Advances from Customers . .   40

    Cr. Sales Revenue   40

At the end of 19x2 . . . [$80 / $40 / $20 / $0] would be reported as a liability on the balance sheet.

$40

5-53. In 19x1 a publisher received $80 for a magazine subscription, with the magazines to be delivered in 19x2 and 19x3. The entry for 19x3 would be:

Dr. _____ _____ _____   40

Cr. _____ _____   40

Dr. Advances from Customers . .   40

    Cr. Sales Revenue   40

At the end of 19x3, . . . [$80 / $40 / $20 / $0] would be reported as a liability on the balance sheet.

$0

> **NOTE:** The effect of recording these transactions is to assign the total subscription of $80 to the years in which the magazine will be delivered—$40 to each year.

SERVICE REVENUE

5-54. Revenue is recognized in the period in which services are delivered. If a landlord receives cash from a tenant in January and in return permits the tenant to use an apartment in February, March, and April, the landlord recognizes revenue in . . . [January / February / March / April].

February, March, April

INVENTORY TURNOVER

7-67. In earlier parts we described ratios and percentages that are useful in analyzing financial statements. Find the gross margin percentage from the following facts:

$$\frac{\boxed{}\quad \$\ 600{,}000}{\boxed{}\quad \$1{,}500{,}000} = \underline{\hspace{1cm}} \%\ \text{Gross Margin}$$

$$\frac{\text{Gross Margin}}{\text{Sales (or Sales Revenue)}} = 40\% \text{ Gross Margin}$$

7-68. A useful ratio for analyzing inventory is the **inventory turnover ratio**. This ratio shows how many *times* the inventory turned over during a year. It is found by dividing Cost of Sales for a period by I__ __ __ __ __ __ __ __ at the end of the period (or by the average inventory during the period).

Inventory

7-69. Cost of Sales for 19x1 was $1,000,000. Inventory on December 31, 19x1, was $200,000. Calculate the inventory turnover ratio to determine how many times the inventory turned over in 19x1.

$$\frac{\boxed{}}{\boxed{}} = \frac{\$\ \boxed{}}{\$\ \boxed{}} = \boxed{}\ \text{times}$$

$$\frac{\text{Cost of Sales}}{\text{Inventory}} = \frac{\$1{,}000{,}000}{\$200{,}000} = 5 \text{ times}$$

7-70. Slow-moving inventory ties up capital and increases the risk that the goods will become obsolete. Thus, an inventory turnover of 5 times is generally . . . [better / worse] than an inventory turnover of 4 times. However, if inventory is too small, orders from customers may not be filled promptly, which can result in lost sales revenue. This would reduce . . . [cash receipts / income / both cash and income].

better

both cash and income

7-71. Look back at the calculation of the inventory turnover ratio. The turnover ratio can be increased either by selling . . . [more / less] goods with the same level of inventory or by having . . . [more / less] inventory for the same amount of sales volume.

more

less

5-55. In January, a tenant paid the landlord $2,400 cash covering rent for February, March, and April. This type of revenue is called **rental revenue**. How much revenue would the landlord recognize each month, and how much liability would be reported at the end of each month?

	Rental Revenue for the month	Liability at the end of month
January	$	$
February	$	$
March	$	$
April	$	$

	Rental Revenue for the month	Liability at the end of month
January	$ 0	$2,400
February	$800	$1,600
March	$800	$ 800
April	$800	$ 0

5-56. When a bank lends money, it delivers a service; that is, the bank provides the borrower with the use of the money for a specified period of time. The bank earns revenue for the service it delivers during this period. This type of revenue is called **interest revenue**. In accordance with the realization concept, interest revenue is recognized in the period(s) . . . [in which the interest is received / in which the borrower has the use of the money].

in which the borrower has the use of the money

> **NOTE:** The term "interest income" is sometimes used, but the amount actually is revenue, not income. Income is always a *difference* between revenue and expense.

5-57. Interest revenue is similar to rental revenue. Banks deliver a service when they "rent" money; landlords deliver a service when they rent apartments. In both cases, revenue is realized in the period(s) in which the service is d _ _ _ _ _ _ _ _ _ _ .

delivered

5-58. To summarize, accountants recognize revenue before the related cash receipt by crediting Revenues and debiting a(n) . . . [asset / liability / equity] account entitled A_ _ _ _ _ _ _ _ R_ _ _ _ _ _ _ _ _ _ _ .

asset

Accounts Receivable

7-63. . . . [Period / Product] costs reduce income in the period in which the costs are incurred . . . [Period / Product] costs reduce income in the period in which the products are sold, which is often a later period.

Period

Product

OVERHEAD RATES

> **NOTE:** One overhead problem is how to divide the total product overhead cost among the various products produced. For example, how much of the cost of heating a shoe factory should be charged to each pair of shoes made in the factory? Any of several methods may be used to charge overhead costs to various products. Usually these methods make use of an overhead rate.

7-64. Lee Shoe Company incurred $40,000 of production overhead costs during January. If 5,000 hours of direct labor were used during January, then $_____ of overhead cost might be charged for each hour of direct labor. This amount per hour is the o__ __ __ __ __ __ __ __ r__ __ __ .

$8 (= $40,000 ÷ 5,000)

overhead

rate

7-65. If a certain pair of shoes requires 1/2 hour of direct labor, and if the overhead rate is $8 per direct labor hour, the amount of overhead cost charged to those shoes would be $_____ .

$4 (= 0.5 * $8)

7-66. Suppose the direct materials used in a certain pair of shoes cost $10. One-half hour of direct labor at $12 per hour was also used. The overhead rate is $8 per direct labor hour. The cost of the shoes is recorded at $_____ .

$20 [= $10 + (0.5 * $12) + (0.5 * $8)]

> **NOTE:** There are many other types of overhead rates: a rate per machine hour, a rate per labor dollar, or a rate per material dollar. Whatever the rate, its purpose is to assign a fair share of overhead cost to each product.

5-59. Accountants recognize revenue *after* the related cash receipt by debiting Cash and crediting a(n) . . . [asset / liability / equity] account when the cash is received. Revenue is recognized when the product is d_ _ _ _ _ _ _ _ _ in accordance with the r_ _ _ _ _ _ _ _ _ _ _ concept.

liability

delivered

realization

> **NOTE:** There are exceptions to the principle that revenue is recognized when a product is delivered. They involve certain types of installment sales, certain long-term contracts, and a few other special situations. They are outside the scope of this introductory treatment.

AMOUNT OF REVENUE

> **NOTE:** The realization concept describes *when* revenue is recognized. The conservatism concept governs both *when* and *how much* revenue is recognized.

5-60. Loren Company sold a motorcycle to James Austin for $3,000 on credit, but Austin never paid the $3,000. Since Loren Company's assets decreased by one motorcycle but there was no actual increase in another asset, Loren Company's equity actually . . . [increased / stayed the same / decreased] as a result of this transaction. Loren Company . . . [did / did not] realize revenue from this transaction.

decreased

did not

5-61. Obviously, if Loren Company knew in advance that Austin would not pay for the motorcycle, Loren would not have delivered it. Although Loren . . . [would / would not] knowingly sell a motorcycle to someone who is not going to pay, experience indicates that some customers do not pay; in this case there is a **bad debt**. Loren . . . [must / need not] take this possibility into account in measuring its income. It does this by estimating the amount of revenue that it is **reasonably certain** to receive from all its sales during the accounting period.

would not

must

7-58. Product costs do not affect income until the product is sold. At that time, product costs become Cost of Sales. Thus, if $10,000 of overhead is counted as a product cost in 19x1, and if the goods with which these product costs were associated are sold in 19x2, the $10,000 of overhead costs will appear as a part of Cost of Sales in . . . [19x1 / 19x2].

19x2

7-59. By contrast, costs that are classified as **period** costs are treated as part of the operating expenses of the period in which they are incurred. For example, if 19x1 period costs in Jones Manufacturing Company were $50,000, and if the products produced in 19x1 were not sold until 19x2, the $50,000 of period costs would be an expense in . . . [19x1 / 19x2].

19x1

7-60. Suppose that in January the total overhead costs in Lee Shoe Company were $100,000, and that 40% of this overhead was associated with the production activities of the business and 60% with the sales and general activities.

$40,000 (= 0.4 ∗ $100,000)

In this example, the amount of overhead that is a product cost is $_____, and the amount that is a period cost is $_____.

$60,000 (= 0.6 ∗ $100,000)

7-61. Since Lee Shoe Company recognized $60,000 as a period cost for January, this $60,000 will be charged (i.e., debited) as an expense . . . [in January / whenever the products manufactured in January are sold]. (The word "charged" means "debited.")

in January

7-62. Suppose the shoes manufactured in January are sold in February. The $40,000 of product overhead costs will be included in _____ (what account?) at the end of January and will be part of Cost of Sales in _____ (what month?).

Inventory
February

		January	February
Product cost		Inventory cost $40,000	Expense $40,000
January overhead $100,000			
Period cost		Expense $60,000	

5-62. Recognizing only the amount of revenue that is reasonably certain to be received is required by the . . . [conservatism / materiality / realization] concept.

conservatism

5-63. In 19x1 Loren Company sold $500,000 of motorcycles to customers, all on credit. It estimated that 2% of these credit sales would never be collected; that is, they would become **bad debts**. Its estimate of bad debts for 19x1 was $_____, and its increase in equity in 19x1 was therefore only $_____.

$10,000 (= .02 ∗ $500,000)
$490,000 (= $500,000 − $10,000)

5-64. Loren Company recorded each sale as revenue at the time the motorcycles were delivered. In order to measure its increase in equity properly, it must . . . [increase / decrease] the total amount of the increase in equity by $_____.

decrease
$10,000

5-65. After this decrease, the amount recognized as revenue is $_____. This is the amount that is . . . [possible / reasonably certain] to be realized. This is in accordance with the . . . [conservatism / materiality] concept.

$490,000   reasonably certain
conservatism

5-66. Since the Accounts Receivable account includes amounts from customers who probably will never pay their bills, it overstates the real asset value. Thus, if the Loren Company decreases its equity by $10,000, it must also . . . [increase / decrease] its Accounts Receivable account by $10,000. Otherwise, the equality of Assets = Liabilities + Equity will not be maintained.

decrease

5-67. However, accountants usually can't decrease the Accounts Receivable account directly because they don't know *which* customers will not pay their bills. Therefore, accountants usually set up a separate account, called **Allowance for Doubtful Accounts**. They record the estimated amount of bad debts as an increase in this account. Accounts Receivable, like all asset accounts, has a . . . [debit / credit] balance. Allowance for Doubtful Accounts, which is subtracted from Accounts Receivable, therefore must have the opposite balance; that is, a . . . [debit / credit] balance.

debit

credit

7-54. The process of assigning production costs to products is called **cost accounting**. The assignment of costs to various services in banks, schools, hotels, and all types of service organizations also involves c__ __ __ a__ __ __ __ __ __ __ __ __ __ . We shall describe some of its major aspects.

cost

accounting

PRODUCT COSTS AND PERIOD COSTS

7-55. Costs are divided into two categories, which are treated differently for purposes of accounting:

1. **product costs**—those that are associated with the production of products, and
2. **period costs**—those that are associated with the sales and general activities of the accounting period.

For example, the cost of heating the offices of the sales department would be considered a . . . [product / period] cost. The cost of heating the production plant itself would be a . . . [product / period] cost.

period

product

7-56. It is relatively easy to keep track of the first two elements of the product cost mentioned earlier: the _____ _____ and the _____ _____. The measurement of overhead costs is more difficult.

direct labor

direct materials
(either order)

19x1				19x2
Materials	$ 20,000			
Labor	100,000		Cost of sales	
Overhead	10,000		$130,000	
Total	$130,000			

7-57. Overhead costs that are classified as product costs are added to direct labor costs and direct material costs in order to find the amount at which the products are costed in the Inventory account. If, during 19x1, Jones Manufacturing Company spent $10,000 on production overhead, $100,000 on direct labor and $20,000 on direct materials, and if no products were sold, its Inventory item on the balance sheet will . . . [decrease / increase] by $_____. If these products (and no others) were sold in 19x2, Cost of Sales in 19x2 would be $_____.

	19x1	19x2
Inventory, Dec. 31	$130,000	$ 0
Cost of Sales	0	130,000

increase

$130,000 (= $10,000 + $100,000 + $20,000)

$130,000

> **NOTE:** The Allowance for Doubtful Accounts is called a **contra-asset** account. It is subtracted from the asset, Accounts Receivable. Because asset accounts have a debit balance, a contra-asset account has a credit balance.

5-68. Although this decrease in equity theoretically resulted from the overstatement of revenue, accountants record it as an account called **Bad Debt Expense**. The amount recorded as Bad Debt Expense would be $_____. An increase in expense has the same effect on equity as a(n) . . . [decrease / increase] in revenue.

$10,000

decrease

5-69. The entry to record Loren Company's estimate that Bad Debt Expense should be increased by $10,000 and an Allowance for Doubtful Accounts of $10,000 should be established is:

Dr. _____ _____ _____ 10,000

    Cr. _____ _____

        _____ _____ 10,000

Dr. Bad Debt Expense 10,000

    Cr. Allowance for

        Doubtful Accounts 10,000

5-70. On December 31, 19x1, Loren Company had $125,000 of Accounts Receivable before subtracting the Allowance for Doubtful Accounts. Fill in the amounts that would be reported on Loren Company's December 31, 19x1, balance sheet.

Accounts receivable, gross	$
Less Allowance for doubtful accounts . . . . −	
Accounts receivable, net	$

$125,000

10,000
_____

$115,000

5-71. Sometime in 19x2, Loren Company decides it is never going to collect the $3,000 owed by Austin. It therefore *writes off* the bad debt. It does this by decreasing Accounts Receivable and also decreasing Allowance for Doubtful Accounts. Write the entry for this transaction.

Dr. _____ _____

    _____ _____ 3,000

    Cr. _____ _____ 3,000

Dr. Allowance for

    Doubtful Accounts 3,000

    Cr. Accounts Receivable 3,000

7-50. In a **manufacturing** company, the cost of a finished product consists of three elements:

1. cost of materials used directly in that product;
2. cost of labor used directly on that product;
3. a fair share of overhead, or general, costs associated with the production process.

materials

labor

overhead

Circle one word in each of 1, 2, and 3 above that best summarizes the whole phrase.

7-51. Some materials, such as oil for lubricating machinery, are not used directly on a product. The materials that are used *directly* in the product are called d__ __ __ __ __ materials. Similarly, the labor used directly to make the product is called _____ labor.

direct

direct

7-52. Production overhead consists of all other production costs; that is, costs that are not d_____ m_____ or d_____ l_____.

direct materials   direct

labor

NOTE: In some manufacturing companies, computers and automated machine tools replace workers, so direct labor cost is relatively small. These companies combine labor costs and production overhead costs into a single item called **Other Production Costs**.

7-53. The three elements of production cost—**direct labor**, **direct materials**, and **overhead**—are added together to determine the total cost of the finished product. Until the product is sold, this amount is held in inventory. When the product is sold, this amount becomes Cost of Sales. Thus, if a product requires $5 of direct labor, $7 of direct materials, and $3 of overhead, the product will be costed at $_____ as long as it is in the Inventory account. When it is sold, C__ __ __ of S__ __ __ __ __ will be $_____.

$15 (= $5 + $7 + $3)

Cost of

Sales $15

5-72. Loren Company's equity in 19x1 was reduced by the estimated bad debts on sales made in 19x1, but its equity in 19x2 . . . [was / was not] affected by this write-off of a bad debt.

was not
(Since equity was decreased in 19x1, it should not be decreased again for the same motorcycle.)

5-73. The write-off . . . [increased / decreased / had no effect on] the "Accounts Receivable, Net" item on the balance sheet. As shown by the above entry, the Gross Accounts Receivable was reduced by $3,000 and the Allowance for Doubtful Accounts was also reduced by $3,000.

had no effect on

MONETARY ASSETS

5-74. Monetary assets are cash and promises by an outside party to pay the entity a specified amount of money. Which of the following assets are monetary assets?

A. Inventory

D. Buildings

B. Accounts receivable

E. Equipment

B, C, and F

C. Notes receivable

F. Bonds owned by the entity

5-75. As with accounts receivable, other monetary assets are usually reported on the balance sheet at the amounts that are r __ __ __ __ __ __ __ __ __ __ c __ __ __ __ __ __ __ to be received. By contrast, nonmonetary assets, such as buildings and equipment, are reported at their c __ __ __ .

reasonably

certain

cost

DAYS' SALES UNCOLLECTED

5-76. In Part 2 we described the current ratio, which is:

$$\frac{\text{current a} \_\_ \_\_ \_\_ \_\_ \text{ s}}{\text{current l} \_\_ \_\_ \_\_ \_\_ \_\_ \_\_ \_\_ \_\_ \text{ s}}$$

$$\frac{\text{current assets}}{\text{current liabilities}}$$

7-45. In "writing down" inventory, the Inventory account is . . . [debited / credited], and Cost of Sales is . . . [debited / credited].

credited
debited

7-46. If inventory is written down by $20, what would the appropriate journal entry be?

Dr. _____ ____ _____   20

   Cr. _____   20

Cost of Sales   20

   Inventory   20

INVENTORY IN A MANUFACTURING COMPANY

7-47. Retail stores, wholesalers, and distributors are . . . [merchandising / manufacturing] companies. A company that makes shoes is a . . . [merchandising / manufacturing] company.

merchandising
manufacturing

7-48. A company that sells finished goods that it purchased from other companies is a . . . [merchandising / manufacturing] company. A company that converts raw materials into finished goods and then sells these goods is a . . . [merchandising / manufacturing] company.

merchandising

manufacturing

7-49. A merchandising company buys its goods in salable form and receives an invoice showing the cost for each item. The costs on these invoices are the amounts used to record the additions to inventory. A manufacturing company adds value to the raw material it buys; it must include these **conversion costs** in its inventory and in its cost of sales.

Measuring inventory and cost of sales is more complicated in a . . . [merchandising / manufacturing] company.

manufacturing

5-77. Another useful ratio is Days' Sales Uncollected. This is the number of days of sales that are in Accounts Receivable at the end of the accounting period. Sales per day are total credit sales for the year divided by 365. The formula is:

$$\text{Days' Sales Uncollected} = \frac{\boxed{A} \quad \boxed{R}}{\text{Credit sales} \div 365}$$

$$\frac{\text{Accounts Receivable}}{\text{Credit sales} \div 365}$$

5-78. Calculate the Days' Sales Uncollected ratio for Worley Company from the following data:

Accounts Receivable, December 31, 19x1 . . . .$50,000

Credit sales for the year 19x1 . . . .$365,000

$$\text{Days' Sales Uncollected} = \frac{\boxed{\$ \qquad}}{\boxed{\$ \qquad} \div 365} = \boxed{\qquad} \text{ days}$$

$$\frac{\$50,000}{\$365,000 \div 365} = 50 \text{ days}$$

5-79. The Days' Sales Uncollected ratio indicates whether customers are paying their bills when they are due. If Worley Company expects customers to pay within 30 days from the date of the sale, the ratio of 50 days indicates that customers . . . [are / are not] paying on time.

are not

> **NOTE:** This is only a rough indication; it assumes that sales are made evenly throughout the year, which is not the case with seasonal sales.

KEY POINTS TO REMEMBER

- The official accounting period is one year, but financial statements can be prepared for shorter periods. They are called interim statements.

- Accrual accounting measures revenues and expenses during an accounting period and the difference between them, which is net income. Accrual accounting is more complicated, but more useful, than accounting only for cash receipts and cash payments.

7-40. In calculating income taxes, cost of sales is one of the items subtracted from revenue in order to find taxable income.

Assume the revenue of Lewis Fuel Company was $1,000. Disregarding other expenses, if cost of sales was $470, taxable income would be $_____. If cost of sales was $400, taxable income would be $_____.

$530
$600

7-41. As can be seen from the above, the higher the cost of sales, the . . . [lower / higher] the taxable income. The lower the taxable income, the . . . [lower / higher] the income tax based on that income will be.

lower
lower

7-42. Companies usually prefer to pay as low an income tax as they legally can. Therefore, they prefer the method that results in the . . . [lower / higher] cost of sales. If prices are rising, this is usually the . . . [FIFO / LIFO] method.

higher
LIFO

> **NOTE:** Any of the methods described above is permitted in calculating taxable income in the United States. However, a company cannot switch back and forth between methods from one year to the next. In many countries, the LIFO method is not permitted.

INVENTORY VALUATION: ADJUSTMENT TO MARKET

7-43. We have assumed so far that inventory is recorded at its cost. Suppose, however, that the market value of the inventory falls below its original cost. The conservatism concept requires that we reduce the inventory to the . . . [higher / lower] amount.

lower

7-44. For this reason, if the market value of an item of inventory at the end of an accounting period is lower than its original cost, the item is "written down" to its m_____ v_____. For example, an item whose original cost was $100 and whose current market value is $80 should be written down by $_____. (This is an exception to the general rule that nonmonetary assets are reported at cost.)

market value

$20 (= $100 – $80)

- The conservatism concept: Recognize increases in equity only when they are reasonably certain; recognize decreases as soon as they are reasonably possible.

- The materiality concept: Disregard trivial matters, but disclose all important matters.

- The realization concept: Revenue is usually recognized when goods and services are delivered.

- If revenue is recognized before the cash receipt, an asset, Accounts Receivable, is debited (increased). If cash is received before revenue is recognized, a liability, Advances from Customers, is credited (increased). The liability is debited (decreased) in the period(s) in which revenue is recognized.

- The equity and accounts receivable balances in a period are reduced by estimated bad debt losses. A Bad Debt Expense account is used to record the decrease in equity. When specific bad debts are later discovered, Accounts Receivable is reduced, but revenue is unaffected.

- Monetary assets are reported at the amounts reasonably certain to be realized, but nonmonetary assets are reported at cost.

- The days' sales uncollected ratio is

$$\frac{\text{Accounts Receivable}}{\text{Credit sales} \div 365}$$

It indicates whether customers are paying their bills on time.

You have completed Part 5 of this program. If you think you understand the material in this part, you should now take Post Test 5, which is in the separate booklet. If you are uncertain about your understanding, you should review Part 5.

The post test will serve both to test your comprehension and to review the highlights of Part 5. After taking the post test, you may find that you are unsure about certain points. You should review these points before continuing with Part 6.

7-35. In the LIFO section in Exhibit 9, enter the amount available for sale, $1,090, calculate the ending inventory, and subtract to find the cost of sales.

Goods available	$1,090

Ending inventory:

400 units @ $1.00 = $400	
300 units @ $1.10 = 220	
Total 600 units	620
Cost of sales	$ 470

LIFO Method

Goods available $1,090	Purchase April 20 $360	Cost of sales $470
	Purchase April 10 $330	
	Inventory April 1 $400	Ending inventory $620 400 @ $1.00 = 400 200 @ $1.10 = 220

AVERAGE COST METHOD

7-36. The third method is the **average-cost** method. It calculates the cost of both the ending inventory and the cost of sales at the average cost per unit of the goods available. In Exhibit 9, the number of units available in April was _____, and the total cost of these goods was $_____, so the average cost per unit was $_____.

1,000

$1,090 $1.09 (= $1,090 ÷ 1,000)

7-37. Using the average cost of $1.09 per unit, complete the average cost section of Exhibit 9.

$$\frac{\$1,090}{1,000} = \$1.09 \text{ cost per unit}$$

Ending inventory: 600 units @ $1.09 = $654
Cost of sales: 400 units @ $1.09 = $436

COMPARISON OF INVENTORY METHODS

7-38. Most businesses try to sell their oldest goods first, so the goods that were first out are likely to be the goods . . . [first in / last in]. The . . . [FIFO / LIFO] method reflects this practice.

first in

FIFO

7-39. From Exhibit 9, we see that cost of sales under FIFO was $_____ and under LIFO it was $_____. Cost of sales was . . . [lower / higher] under LIFO. In most companies, during periods of rising prices (i.e., inflation) this same relationship holds.

$400 $470
higher

Part 6

Expense Measurement; The Income Statement

Learning Objectives

In this part you will learn:

- The difference between "expense" and "expenditure."
- How the expenses of a period are measured.
- The last of the nine basic accounting concepts:
    - The matching concept.
- The meaning of items reported on an income statement.
- Methods of analyzing an income statement.

6-1. In Part 5 you learned that the revenues recognized in an accounting period were not necessarily associated with the cash receipts in that period. If $1,000 of goods were delivered to a customer in August, and the customer paid cash for these goods in September, revenue would be recognized in . . . [August / September].

August

6-2. Revenues are . . . [increases / decreases] in equity during an accounting period. Expenses are . . . [increases / decreases] in equity during an accounting period. Just as revenues in a period are not necessarily the same as cash receipts in that period, the expenses of a period . . . [are / are not] necessarily the same as the cash payments in that period.

increases
decreases

are not

7-32. Earlier, you found the amount of goods available for sale to be $1,090. Enter this amount in your calculation, and subtract the ending inventory of $690 from it. The difference is the FIFO c_____ of s_____, which is $_____.

cost of
sales $400

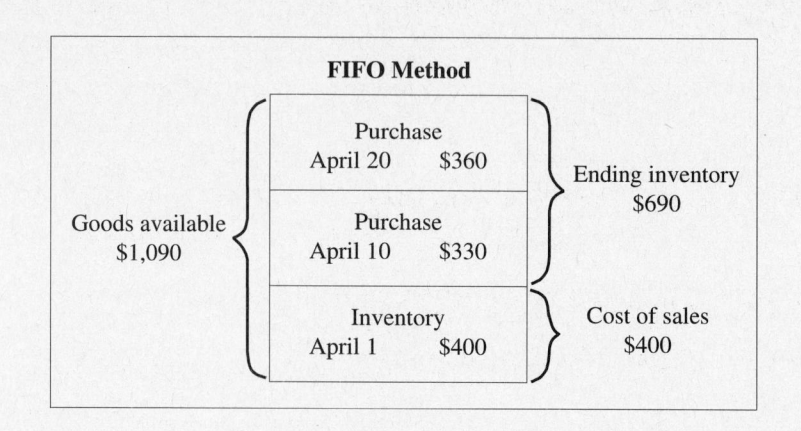

FIFO Method

Goods available $1,090	Purchase April 20 $360	Ending inventory $690
	Purchase April 10 $330	
	Inventory April 1 $400	Cost of sales $400

LAST-IN, FIRST-OUT (LIFO) METHOD

7-33. The FIFO method assumes that the oldest units—that is, those F_____ I_____—were the first to be sold; that is, that they were the F_____ O_____. The **LIFO** method assumes the opposite, namely, that the . . . [oldest / newest] units, which were the Last In, were the first to be sold; that is, that they were . . . [Last Out / First Out], hence the name **L**ast-**I**n **F**irst-**O**ut.

First In
First Out
newest
First Out

7-34. Because the LIFO method assumes that the last units purchased were the first ones to be sold, the ending inventory is assumed to consist of any remaining units in beginning inventory, plus the earliest units purchased. In Exhibit 9, the ending inventory was 600 units, and in the LIFO method these 600 units are assumed to be the _____ (how many?) units in beginning inventory plus _____ (how many?) of the 300 units purchased on April _____.

400
200
April 10

EXPENSE AND EXPENDITURE

6-3. When an entity acquires goods or services, it makes an **expenditure**. In August, Mogul Shop purchased goods for its inventory at a cost of $1,000, paying cash; it had an e_ _ _ _ _ _ _ _ _ _ _ _ of $1,000 in August. It would record this transaction with the following journal entry:

expenditure

    Dr. I_____ 1,000

        Cr. C_____ 1,000

Inventory 1,000	
Cash	1,000

6-4. If in August Mogul Shop purchased $2,000 of goods for inventory, agreeing to pay in 30 days, it had an e_ _ _ _ _ _ _ _ _ _ _ of $2,000 in August. Accounts Payable, which is a liability account, increased. Mogul would record this transaction with the following journal entry:

expenditure

    Dr. I_____ 2,000

        Cr. A_____ P_____ ... 2,000

Inventory 2,000	
Accounts Payable	2,000

6-5. Thus, an expenditure results either in a decrease in the asset C_____ or an increase in a l_____, such as Accounts Payable.

Cash   liability

> **NOTE:** Occasionally an expenditure results in a decrease in an asset other than cash. For example, when an old automobile is traded in for a new automobile, part of the expenditure is the decrease in the asset, Automobiles.

6-6. Mogul Shop had e_ _ _ _ _ _ _ _ _ _ _ _ s of $3,000 in August for the purchase of goods for inventory. If $500 of these goods were sold in August, there was an **expense** in August of $500. The remaining $2,500 of goods are still in inventory at the end of August; they therefore are an **asset**. Thus, the expenditures of a period are either _____ of the period or _____ s at the end of the period.

expenditures

expenses   assets

7-27. The problem now is: What unit cost should we assign to the ending inventory? There are three choices: (1) we could assume that the older fuel oil was sold, leaving the . . . [older / newer] fuel oil in inventory; (2) we could assume that the newer fuel oil was sold, leaving the . . . [older / newer] fuel in inventory; or (3) we could assume that a mixture of old and new oil was sold. Because the fuel oil has been mixed together in the storage tank, we . . . [have / do not have] a record of the cost of the specific quantities of fuel oil actually sold during the month. Therefore the solution . . . [is / is not] clearcut.

newer

older

do not have

is not

FIRST-IN, FIRST-OUT (FIFO) METHOD

7-28. In this situation, many companies make the **First-In First-Out** (**FIFO**) assumption. They assume that the goods that came into the inventory . . . [first / last] are the . . . [first / last] to move out.

first   first

7-29. If you applied the FIFO method to the data of Exhibit 9, you would assume that the . . . [newer / older] fuel oil was sold during the month and that the . . . [newer / older] fuel oil remains in the ending inventory.

older

newer

7-30. The FIFO method assumes that the older units were sold during the period; therefore, the ending inventory of 600 units of fuel oil is assumed to be the most recently purchased fuel oil; namely, the 300 units purchased on April _____ at $_____ per unit, and the 300 units purchased on April _____ at $_____ per unit.

20    $1.20

10    $1.10

7-31. In the "FIFO Method" section of Exhibit 9, enter these amounts and calculate the ending inventory.

Ending inventory

	300 units @ $1.20 =	$360
	300 units @ $1.10 =	330
Total	600 units	$690

6-7. Mogul Shop sold the remaining $2,500 of goods in September. In September it had an . . . [expenditure / expense] of $2,500, but it did not have any . . . [expenditure / expense] for these goods in September.

expense

expenditure

6-8. In August, Mogul Shop paid an employee $2,000 cash for services rendered in August. It had both an _____ and an _____ of $2,000 for labor services in August.

expense

expenditure
(either order)

6-9. When an asset is used up or consumed in the operations of the business, an expense is incurred. Thus, an asset gives rise to an . . . [expenditure / expense] when it is acquired, and to an . . . [expenditure / expense] when it is consumed.

expenditure

expense

6-10. Suppose that Irwin Company purchased a supply of fuel oil in 19x1, paying $10,000 cash. No fuel oil was consumed in 19x1. In 19x2, $8,000 of fuel oil was consumed, and in 19x3, $2,000 was consumed. There was an expenditure in _____ (when?), and there were expenses in _____ (when?).

19x1

19x2 and 19x3

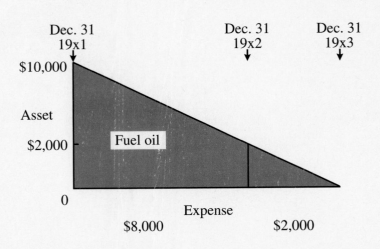

6-11. Between the time of their purchase and the time of their consumption, the resources of a business are assets. Thus, when fuel oil is purchased, there is an expenditure. The fuel oil is an _____ until consumed. When consumed, it becomes an _____.

asset

expense

INVENTORY VALUATION: ASSUMPTIONS

> **NOTE:** In the preceding frames, we assumed that all units of a given item, such as all Refrigerators #602, were purchased at the same time. Actually, the cost of goods purchased at different times may differ. For example, because inflation leads to increases in cost, the cost of goods purchased recently may be higher than the cost of the same goods purchased some time ago. In the following frames, we describe the three principal methods of finding cost of sales and ending inventory in such a situation.

7-23. Complete the following table, filling in all empty boxes.

	Quantity	Unit Cost	Total Cost
Beginning inventory, April 1	400	$1.00	$
Purchases, April 6	300	1.00	
Purchases, April 20	300	1.00	
Total goods available		1.00	
Ending inventory, April 30	600	1.00	
Cost of sales, April			

Quantity	Unit Cost	Total Cost
400	$1.00	$ 400
300	1.00	300
300	1.00	300
1,000	1.00	1,000
600	1.00	600
400	1.00	400

7-24. Lewis Fuel Company deals in fuel oil. Its inventory and purchases during April are shown in the top section of Exhibit 9 in the separate booklet. Fill in the two empty boxes in the column titled "Units."

Total goods available   1,000
Cost of sales, April   400

7-25. The "Unit Cost" column of Exhibit 9 shows that fuel oil entered the inventory at . . . [identical / different] unit costs during April.

different

7-26. In Exhibit 9 fill in the first four boxes in the column headed "Total Cost."

Units	Unit Cost	Total Cost
400	$1.00	$ 400
300	1.10	330
300	1.20	360
1,000		1,090

6-12. Irwin Company purchased a two-year supply of fuel oil in 19x1, paying $10,000. None of it was consumed in 19x1, $8,000 was consumed during 19x2, and $2,000 in 19x3. The balance sheet item for the asset Fuel Oil Inventory will show the following amounts:

As of December 31, 19x1 .... $ [   ] $10,000

As of December 31, 19x2 .... $ [   ] $ 2,000

As of December 31, 19x3 .... $ [   ] $ 0

6-13. Irwin Company purchased a two-year supply of fuel oil in 19x1, paying $10,000. None was consumed in 19x1, $8,000 was consumed in 19x2, and $2,000 in 19x3. The item Fuel Oil Expense on the income statements will be as follows:

For the year 19x1 .... $ [   ] $ 0

For the year 19x2 .... $ [   ] $8,000

For the year 19x3 .... $ [   ] $2,000

6-14. Over the life of a business, most expenditures . . . [will / will not] become expenses, but in a single accounting period, expenses . . . [are / are not] necessarily the same as expenditures.

will

are not

UNEXPIRED AND EXPIRED COSTS

6-15. Expenditures result in costs. When inventory or other assets are acquired, they are recorded at their acquisition c_ _ _ . Expenses are the c_ _ _ of the resources used up in an accounting period.

cost

cost

6-16. Costs that are used up or consumed in a period are e_ _ _ _ _ _ s. Costs that are represented by resources on hand at the end of the period are a_ _ _ _ s.

expenses

assets

7-20. To summarize, many entities . . . [do / do not] keep track of individual items in inventory. They find their cost of sales by the process of **deduction**. This requires a . . . [perpetual / physical] inventory. An automobile dealership finds its cost of sales directly from its . . . [perpetual / physical] inventory records.

do not

physical
perpetual

7-21. These entities find cost of sales by subtracting the ending inventory from the total goods available, as in the following table:

	Cost (000 omitted)
Beginning inventory	$ 200
Purchases	600
Total goods available	[ ]
Ending inventory	300
Cost of sales	[ ]

	Cost (000 omitted)
Beginning inventory	$ 200
Purchases	600
Total goods available	800
Ending inventory	300
Cost of sales	500

7-22. The same situation is shown in the following diagram. Fill in the boxes.

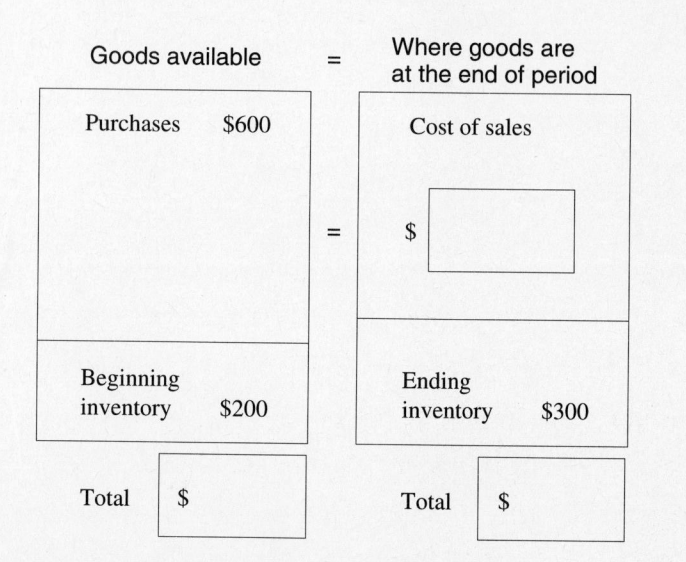

$500

$800 $800

NOTE: Entities that use the perpetual inventory method count physical inventory at least annually. This inventory may reveal that the actual ending inventory is lower than is indicated in the perpetual inventory records, because of theft, errors in record keeping, or items that have been discarded. If so, the ending inventory is reduced by a credit entry. The offsetting debit entry is to an expense account, Loss on Inventory.

6-17. Costs that have been consumed are gone; they have **expired**. Costs of resources still on hand are **unexpired**. You will find it useful to think of expenses as . . . [expired / unexpired] costs and assets as . . . [expired / unexpired] costs.

expired   unexpired

6-18. Irwin Company purchased $10,000 of fuel oil in 19x1, consumed $8,000 of it in 19x2, and consumed $2,000 in 19x3. At the end of 19x1, the total expenditure of $10,000 was an . . . [asset / expense] because none of the cost had expired. In 19x2, $8,000 of the cost expired, and $8,000 was therefore an . . . [asset / expense] in 19x2. At the end of 19x2, $2,000 was an unexpired cost and therefore an . . . [asset / expense]. The remaining $2,000 expired in 19x3, so it was an . . . [asset / expense] in 19x3.

asset

expense
asset
expense

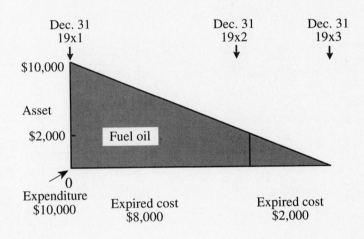

MATCHING CONCEPT

6-19. An important task of the accountant is to measure the income of an accounting period. Income is the difference between r__ __ __ __ __ __ __ s and e__ __ __ __ __ __ __ s of the period. Expenses are . . . [expired / cash] costs.

revenues
expenses   expired

6-20. As you learned in Part 5, the concept governing the recognition of revenues of a period is the r__ __ __ __ __ __ __ __ __ __ __ __ concept; **revenue** is recognized in the period in which goods or services are d__ __ __ __ __ __ __ ed.

realization

delivered

7-13. Therefore, the **goods available for sale** in a period are the sum of the b_____ inventory plus the p_____ during the period.

beginning   purchases

7-14. On January 1, 19x1, Cantal Hardware had an inventory that cost $200,000. During 19x1 it purchased $600,000 of additional merchandise. The cost of goods **available for sale** in 19x1 was $_____.

$800,000 (= $200,000 + $600,000)

7-15. Accountants assume that goods available for sale during a period either are in inventory at the end of the period or they were sold. Thus, if goods costing $800,000 were available for sale during 19x1 and goods costing $300,000 were in inventory on December 31, 19x1, cost of sales in 19x1 is assumed to be $_____.

$500,000 (= $800,000 – $300,000)

7-16. At the end of each accounting period, all goods currently on hand are counted. This process is called **taking a physical inventory**. Since its purpose is to find the cost of the goods that were sold, each item is reported at its . . . [cost / selling price].

cost

7-17. In order to determine the ending inventory of one period and the beginning inventory of the next period, how many physical inventories must be taken? _____

One (Because the ending inventory on
December 31, 19x1 is also the begin-
ning inventory on January 1, 19x2.)

7-18. "Cost of sales" means the same as "Cost of goods sold." We use the shorter term, **cost of sales**. In the deduction method for determining cost of sales, the rationale is as follows: Goods are assumed to have been sold if they . . . [are / are not] in inventory at the . . . [beginning / end] of the period.

are not   end

7-19. Sometimes goods in inventory are stolen, damaged, or spoiled. Therefore, the assumption that goods not in the closing inventory have been sold . . . [is / is not] necessarily valid. However, steps are taken to discover and record this **shrinkage**.

is not

6-21. The concept governing the recognition of expenses of a period is the **matching** concept. It is that **costs associated with the revenues of a period are** . . . [cash payments / expenses] **of that period**.

expenses

6-22. To illustrate, consider an automobile that Bryan Company, an automobile dealer, purchased for $15,000 in March and sold (i.e., delivered) for $18,000 in May. At the end of March, the automobile was in the Bryan Company inventory, so its cost was . . . [expired / unexpired]. At the end of April, its cost was . . . [expired / unexpired].

unexpired
unexpired

6-23. Bryan Company purchased an automobile for $15,000 in March and sold it for $18,000 in May.

In May, Bryan Company recognizes $18,000 of _____ from the sale of this automobile. It must m__ __ __ __ the $15,000 of cost with the revenue from the sale of the same automobile. Thus, its expense in May is $15,000. The $18,000 of revenue and the $15,000 of expense relate to the same automobile. The expense **matches** the revenue.

revenue
match

OTHER ASSETS THAT WILL BECOME EXPENSES

6-24. When products are delivered, their costs are matched with revenues in the period in which the sale takes place. These costs become expenses of that period. This is one application of the m__ __ __ __ __ __ __ concept. Other costs associated with activities of the current period are also expenses, even though they are not directly related to the products delivered in the period.

matching

6-25. If expenditures were made in an earlier period, the unexpired costs are a__ __ __ __ s until the period in which the expense is recognized. We shall consider several examples. The first is an intangible asset.

assets

7-8. Refrigerators that cost $1,800 were sold in May for $2,500. Complete the following partial income statement, assuming these were the only items sold.

Income Statement
May

Sales Revenue	$
Cost of sales	
G_____ m_____	$

Income Statement
May

Sales revenue	$2,500
Cost of sales	1,800
Gross margin	$ 700

FINDING COST OF SALES BY DEDUCTION

7-9. If an entity has a p_____ inventory, as illustrated above, finding cost of sales in a month is easy. We shall next show how to deduce cost of sales in a business that does not have this record. This method is the process of **deduction**.

perpetual

7-10. Many stores, such as hardware stores, carry so many relatively low-value items that keeping a perpetual inventory record for each separate item is not practical. When the salesperson rings up a sale on the cash register, a record is made of the . . . [cost of sales / sales revenue] but not the . . . [cost of sales / sales revenue].

sales revenue

cost of sales

NOTE: With computers, many more companies use the perpetual inventory method. The cash register (point-of-sale terminal) then records both sales revenue and the cost of sales.

7-11. If a hardware store does not keep a record of the cost of each item in inventory, it . . . [can arrive at cost of sales directly / must deduce cost of sales by an indirect method].

must deduce cost of sales by an indirect method

7-12. Items in a hardware store's **beginning inventory** on January 1, 19x1 . . . [are / are not] available for sale during 19x1. Additional items **purchased** and placed on the shelves during 19x1 . . . [are / are not] available for sale during 19x1.

are

are

6-26. A **tangible asset** has physical substance; an **intangible asset** does not have physical substance. Buildings, equipment, and inventories of goods are . . . [tangible / intangible] assets. The protection provided by an insurance policy is a(n) . . . [tangible / intangible] asset.

tangible

intangible

6-27. The general name for intangible assets that will become expenses in a future period is **prepaid expenses**. The asset account may identify the particular type of prepaid expense. Thus, the name of the asset account that shows the cost incurred for insurance protection in future periods is P_____ Insurance.

Prepaid

6-28. Bryan Company purchased a two-year insurance policy on December 31, 19x1, for $2,000.

The effect of this expenditure is a decrease in Cash and an increase in the asset Prepaid Insurance. Record the journal entry for this transaction.

Dr. _____ _____ 2,000

  Cr. _____ 2,000

Prepaid Insurance 2,000

  Cash   2,000

6-29. Bryan Company purchased a two-year insurance policy on December 31, 19x1, for $2,000.

During 19x2 Bryan Company used up half of this insurance protection, thereby incurring $1,000 of insurance expense. The effect on the accounts in 19x2 is a decrease in the asset Prepaid Insurance and an increase in Insurance Expense. Record the journal entry for 19x2.

Dr. _____ _____ . . . . . . _____

  Cr. _____ _____ . . . . . .   _____

Insurance Expense 1,000

  Prepaid Insurance   1,000

On December 31, 19x2, the balance in the asset account, Prepaid Insurance, was $_____.

$1,000

This is called a **perpetual inventory** record. "Receipts" are . . . [increases / decreases] in inventory, and "Shipments to Customers" are . . . [increases / decreases] in inventory.

increases

decreases

7-6. Information in the perpetual inventory records corresponds to that in the Inventory account. From the previous frame, we see that the beginning balance for refrigerator #602 in the Inventory account on May 1 was $_____. There were receipts during May of $_____, which added to Inventory; these were . . . [Dr. / Cr.] to the Inventory account. Shipments during May decreased inventory by $_____ which were . . . [Dr. / Cr.] to the inventory account. This decrease in inventory was Cost of Sales in May, which was $_____.

$800 $2,000
Dr.
$1,800
Cr.
$1,800

7-7. Using the *totals* in the perpetual inventory record, enter the inventory transactions for May in the T-accounts given below. (The inventory purchases were on credit.)

Inventory
Beg. bal. 800

Accounts Payable

Cost of Sales

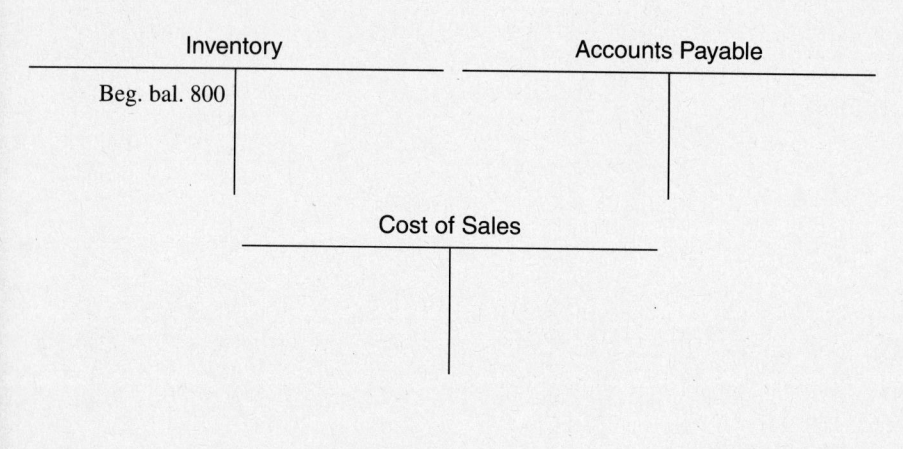

Inventory
Beg. bal. 800
2,000 | 1,800

Accounts Payable
| 2,000

Cost of Sales
1,800 |

> *Refer back to Frame 7-6 if you are uncertain. Remember that debits must equal credits.*

6-30. Bryan Company purchased a two-year insurance policy on December 31, 19x1, for $2,000.

During 19x3 Bryan Company received the remaining $1,000 of insurance protection. Make the journal entry for 19x3.

Dr. _____   _____ . . . . _____

Cr. _____   _____ . . . . . . _____

Insurance Expense 1,000	
Prepaid Insurance	1,000

On December 31, 19x3, the amount of insurance protection has completely expired. The balance in the Prepaid Insurance account on that date therefore was $_____.

zero

> **NOTE:** If you were uncertain about the responses to these frames, refer back to Frames 6-10 through 6-13.

6-31. Similarly, if Carter Company made an advance payment of $1,800 to its landlord on January 31 for two months' rent, its asset account P__ __ __ __ __ __ Rent would have a balance of $_____ on January 31, a balance of $_____ on February 28, and a balance of $_____ on March 31. Its rent expense would be $_____ in February and $_____ in March.

Prepaid $1,800
$900
$0 $900
$900

6-32. Buildings and equipment also benefit future periods. They are assets like Prepaid Insurance and Prepaid Rent, except that they usually have a longer life and therefore benefit . . . [more / fewer] future periods. The amount reported as an asset on the balance sheet is the . . . [expired / unexpired] cost as of the balance sheet date.

more
unexpired

6-33. Also, as with insurance and rent, the amount of building and equipment cost that is reported as an expense in each period is the amount of . . . [expired / unexpired] cost in that period.

expired

7-2. In some entities, matching cost of sales and sales revenue is easy. For example, an automobile dealer keeps a record of the cost of each automobile in its inventory. If the dealer sold two automobiles during a given month, one for $18,000 that had cost $16,000, and the other for $10,000 that had cost $7,500, sales revenue for the period would be recorded as $_____ and cost of sales as $_____. This is the **specific identification** method.

$28,000 (= $18,000 + $10,000)

$23,500 (= $16,000 + $7,500)

7-3. A dealer sold an automobile costing $16,000 for $18,000 cash. Write the journal entry that records the effect of this transaction solely on the Sales Revenue and Cash accounts:

Dr. _____ .... _____

    Cr. _____ _____ ... _____

Cash 18,000

   Sales Revenue   18,000

7-4. A dealer sold an automobile costing $16,000 for $18,000 cash. Write the journal entry that records the effect of this transaction solely on the Inventory and Cost of Sales accounts:

Dr. _____ _____ _____ .... _____

    Cr. _____ .... _____

Cost of Sales 16,000

   Inventory   16,000

7-5. A dealer that sells refrigerators might keep a record of its inventory of each type of refrigerator, something like the following:

Item: Refrigerator #602, Cost $200 each

Date	Receipts		Shipments to Customers		On Hand	
	Quantity	Cost	Quantity	Cost	Quantity	Cost
May 1					4	800
6			1	200	3	600
10	10	2,000			13	2,600
13			6	1,200	7	1,400
31			2	400	5	1,000
Totals	10	2,000	9	1,800	5	1,000

6-34. The expired cost for buildings and equipment is called **Depreciation Expense**. If Bryan Company bought a machine for $5,000 and expected it to provide service for five years, the amount of expired cost in each year would be 1/5 of $5,000. In each of the five years D__ __ __ __ __ __ __ __ __ __ __ __ E__ __ __ __ __ __ __ would be reported as $_____. Accounting for depreciation is discussed in more detail in Part 8.

Depreciation Expense

$1,000

EXPENSES THAT CREATE LIABILITIES

> **NOTE:** We have described expenditures that first were assets and then became expenses as the costs expired. We now describe expenses for which the related expenditures are liabilities.

6-35. Amounts earned by the employees of Eastman Company for services performed in 19x1 are e__ __ __ __ __ __ __ s of 19x1. If Eastman paid its employees one week after the week they worked, the amounts earned in the last week of 19x1 would be a cash disbursement in 19x__ (what year?).

expenses

19x2

6-36. Employees of Eastman Company earned $10,000 in the last week of 19x1, for which they were paid in 19x2. The $10,000 was . . . [an expense / an expenditure / both an expense and an expenditure] in 19x1.

both an expense and expenditure

On December 31, 19x1, Eastman Company owed its employees $10,000. It would report a l__ __ __ __ __ __ __ __ y of $10,000 on its December 31, 19x1, balance sheet.

liability

	Dec. 31	
	19x1	19x2
	Employees earn $10,000	Employees paid $10,000
Expenditure	Yes	No
Expense	Yes	No
Cash paid	No	Yes

Liability
$10,000

Part 7

Inventories and Cost of Sales

Learning Objectives

In this part you will learn:

- How the cost of sales is calculated.
- Methods of arriving at inventory amounts.
- When inventory amounts on the balance sheet are reduced.
- How inventory is measured in a manufacturing company.
- The distinction between product costs and period costs.
- How overhead rates are calculated.

FINDING COST OF SALES

7-1. In the income statement in Part 6, the first item subtracted from sales revenue was called **Cost of sales**. It is the cost of the same products whose revenues are included in the sales amount. This is an example of the m____ ____ ____ ____ ____ ____ ____ concept. (Some businesses call this item **Cost of goods sold**.) In most businesses the cost of sales is the . . . [smallest / largest] item of expense, amounting to as much as 85% of sales revenues in a profitable supermarket, and 60–70% in a profitable manufacturing company.

matching

largest

6-37. Liabilities for expenses incurred but not yet paid for are called **accrued liabilities**. Account titles may describe the nature of the liability, in this case A__ __ __ __ __ __ Salaries.

Accrued

6-38. In the last week of 19x1, Eastman Company had a salary expense of $10,000, which was not paid to its employees. Write the journal entry for this transaction.

Dr. _____ _____ . . . . _____

Cr. _____ _____ . . .   _____

Salary Expense 10,000

    Accrued Salaries   10,000

> **NOTE:** Employees are not paid the total amount that they earn. Part of their salary is withheld by the employer, who pays it to the federal government for income taxes. Amounts are also deducted for social security taxes and for other reasons. We shall disregard these complications and assume that total earnings are paid in cash to the employees.

6-39. In January 19x2, Eastman Company employees were paid the $10,000 owed them for work done in 19x1. This payment decreases the liability Accrued Salaries. The journal entry for this transaction is:

Dr. _____ _____ . . . . _____

Cr. _____ . . . .   _____

Accrued Salaries 10,000

    Cash   10,000

FRINGE BENEFITS

6-40. Many companies agree to pay employees a pension when they retire. Employees earn the right to their pension benefits when they work. Therefore, if an employee earns a $2,000 pension benefit in 19x1 because he or she worked in 19x1, the $2,000 is an expense in . . . [19x1 / when he or she retires]. It is a liability in . . . [19x1 / when he or she retires]. The liability is called **Accrued Pensions**.

19x1

19x1

• Percentages are calculated for various income statement items, especially gross margin and net income, taking sales revenue as 100 percent.

You have completed Part 6 of this program. If you think you understand the material in this part, you should now take Post Test 6, which is in the separate booklet. If you are uncertain about your understanding, you should review Part 6.

The post test will serve both to test your comprehension and to review the highlights of Part 6. After taking the post test, you may find that you are unsure about certain points. You should review these points before continuing with Part 7.

6-41. Joan Eaton earned a pension benefit of $2,000 in 19x1. The journal entry for this transaction is:

Dr. Pension Expense   2,000

Cr. _____ _____   2,000   Accrued Pensions

6-42. Joan Eaton retired in 19x7. She was paid a pension of $6,000 in 19x8. The journal entry for the 19x8 payment is:

Dr. _____ _____   6,000   Accrued Pensions

Cr. Cash   6,000

> **NOTE:** Many companies transfer amounts earned for pensions to an insurance company or bank, which makes the actual payments. The effect on the company's financial position is nevertheless the same as that illustrated in the above journal entries.

6-43. Many companies agree to pay for health care or other benefits to retired employees. These fringe benefits are called **Other Post Employment Benefits**, abbreviated to the initials __ __ __ __ .   OPEB

6-44. OPEB are accounted for in the same way as pensions; that is, the expense is incurred . . . [in the years in which the employee earns the right to them / when the benefits are paid]. The liability is incurred . . . [in the years in which the employee earns the right to them / when the benefits are paid]. When the benefit is paid, there . . . [is / is not] an expense.

in the years in which the employee earns the right to them

in the years in which the employee earns the right to them

is not

RENT EXPENSE

6-45. Eastman Company will pay its December rent of $5,000 in January. In December 19x1, it records the Rent Expense of December and the related liability, Accrued Rent, by the following journal entry:

Dr. _____ _____ . . . . _____   Dr. Rent Expense 5,000

Cr. _____ _____ . . . . . . _____   Cr. Accrued Rent   5,000

6-95. Conservatism concept: Revenues are recognized when they are reasonably c＿ ＿ ＿ ＿ ＿ ＿ ＿ . Expenses are recognized when they are reasonably p＿ ＿ ＿ ＿ ＿ ＿ ＿ .

certain

possible
(See Frames 5-20 to 5-24.)

6-96. Materiality concept: Disregard . . . . matters. Disclose . . . . matters.

insignificant

all important
(See Frames 5-25 to 5-32.)

6-97. Realization concept: Revenues are recognized when goods or services are ＿＿＿＿＿＿＿＿＿＿ .

delivered
(See Frames 5-33 to 5-53.)

6-98. The **mat**＿ ＿ ＿ ＿ ＿ **concept** states that the expenses of a period are costs associated with the revenues or activities of the period.

matching
(See Frames 6-19 to 6-39.)

KEY POINTS TO REMEMBER

- Expenditures are made when goods or services are acquired. If these goods or services are used up during the current period, they are expenses of the period. If not used up, they are assets at the end of that period. These assets will become expenses in future periods as they are used up.

- Some expenditures result in liabilities that will be paid in future periods. An example is accrued salaries.

- Expenses are expired costs. Assets are unexpired costs.

- Matching concept: Costs associated with the revenues or activities of a period are expenses of the period.

- Expenses of a period are (1) cost of the products (i.e., goods and services) that were delivered to customers during the period; (2) other expenditures that benefit operations of the period; and (3) losses, that is, decreases in assets from fire, theft, and other unusual reasons, and increases in liabilities from unusual events, such as lawsuits.

- The income statement summarizes revenues and expenses of the period. Its "bottom line," or net income, shows the increase in equity resulting from activities during the period.

- Dividends are a distribution of earnings to shareholders. Dividends are *not* expenses.

- Retained Earnings at the beginning of the period + Net Income – Dividends = Retained Earnings at the end of the period.

6-46. In January 19x2, Eastman Company paid $5,000 to its landlord for the December 19x1 rent. The journal entry in January is:

Dr. _____ _____ . . . . _____

    Cr. _____ . . . . _____

Accrued Rent 5,000

    Cash 5,000

6-47. Earlier we saw that if rent is paid *prior to* the period in which the expense was incurred, the amount is first debited to Prepaid Rent, which is a(n) . . . [asset / liability] account. As the previous frame indicates, if rent is paid *after* the period in which the expense was incurred, the entry is made to Accrued Rent, which is a(n) . . . [asset / liability] account.

asset

liability

6-48. Prepaid expenses are turned into expenses by a debit to the . . . [asset / expense] account and a credit to the . . . [asset / expense] account. Accrued Liabilities are discharged by a debit to . . . [Cash / Accrued Liabilities] and a credit to . . . [Cash / Accrued Liabilities].

expense   asset
Accrued Liabilities
Cash

6-49. Of course, many items of expense are paid for in cash during the accounting period. Salaries of $90,000 earned in 19x1 and paid in cash in 19x1 is recorded in the following entry.

Dr. _____ _____ . . . . _____

    Cr. _____ . . . . _____

Dr. Salary Expense 90,000

    Cr. Cash 90,000

LOSSES

6-50. Assets provide benefits to future periods. Suppose Bryan Company owned an uninsured machine that was destroyed by fire in 19x1. The machine . . . [will / will not] benefit future periods. The asset amount carried for the machine therefore expired in 19x1, and this amount is recorded as an . . . [expense / expenditure] in 19x1.

will not

expense

> **NOTE:** The net income of many American manufacturing corporations is roughly 5% to 10% of sales revenue, but there is a wide variation from company to company.

REVIEW OF BASIC CONCEPTS

> The nine basic concepts described in this program are listed in the following frames, together with some guides that will refresh your memory as to their meaning. Complete the meaning of each concept. (These concepts are not stated as such in accounting literature, but most accountants would agree that they are the basic underpinnings of accounting.)

6-90. Dual-aspect concept: _____ = _____ +

_____

Assets = Liabilities + Equity
(See Frames 1-20 to 1-39.)

6-91. Money-measurement concept: Accounting reports only facts that can be expressed . . . .

in monetary amounts
(Note: If you have the general idea, fine. Your words need not be exactly like those given here.)
(See Frames 1-40 to 1-49.)

6-92. Entity concept: Accounts are kept for an _____ as distinguished from the p__ __ __ __ __ __ associated with that entity.

entity

persons
(See Frames 1-50 to 1-56.)

6-93. The accounting concept that assumes that an entity will continue to operate indefinitely and that it is not about to be sold is the **g__ __ __ __ - c__ __ __ __ __ __ concept**.

going-

concern
(See Frames 2-1 to 2-5.)

6-94. Cost concept: Accounting focuses on the c_____ of non-monetary assets, rather than on their . . . .

cost

market value
(See Frames 2-6 to 2-20.)

6-51. Thus, even though an asset does not provide benefits during a period, it is an expense of that period if its cost has expired for any reason. Such expenses are called **losses**. A loss is recorded as an expense . . . [in the period in which the loss occurs / over the periods that the asset was supposed to benefit].

in the period in which the loss occurs

6-52. A loss is recorded as an expense if it is **reasonably possible** that the loss occurred, even though it is not certain. Thus, if a customer sues Bryan Company in 19x1, and if it seems reasonably possible that Bryan Company will lose the law suit, the estimated loss is recorded as an expense . . . [in 19x1 / when the law suit is settled]. This is in accordance with the concept that requires expenses to be recognized when they are reasonably possible, which is the c_ _ _ _ _ _ _ _ _ _ _ m concept.

in 19x1

conservatism

SUMMARY OF MATCHING CONCEPT

6-53. Three types of costs are expenses of the current period. First, there are the costs of the goods and services that are **delivered** in the current period and whose r_ _ _ _ _ _ _ are recognized in that period.

revenues

NOTE: The period in which revenues are recognized is determined first, according to the principles described in Part 5. Then the associated costs are matched with those revenues. Costs are matched against revenues, not vice versa.

6-54. Second, there are costs that are **associated with activities of the period**. The expenditures for these costs were made either in the current period or in an earlier period. If made in an earlier period, these amounts are a_____ on the balance sheet as of the beginning of the current period.

assets

6-86. Remember that dividends are . . . [an expense / a distribution of earnings to owners]. Dividends are *not*. . . . [an expense / a distribution of earnings to owners].

a distribution of earnings to owners

an expense

NOTE: The "package" of required financial reports also includes a Statement of Cash Flows. This statement is described in part 10.

INCOME STATEMENT PERCENTAGES

6-87. In an analysis of a business's performance, **percentages** of certain income statement items are usually calculated. The base (i.e., 100 percent) is **Sales revenue**. One percentage is the **gross margin percentage**; it is found by dividing g_ _ _ _ m_ _ _ _ _ by s_ _ _ _ r_ _ _ _ _ _ _.

gross margin
sales revenue

6-88. Calculate the gross margin percentage for Garsden Company in 19x2.

Gross margin $ _____

_____ = _____ = [ ] %*

Sales revenue $ _____

*Show the nearest percent.

$\dfrac{\$23,251}{\$75,478} = 31\%$

6-89. An even more important percentage is the **net income percentage**. Calculate it for Garsden Company.

Net income $ _____

_____ = _____ = [ ] %*

Sales revenue $ _____

*Show the nearest percent.

$\dfrac{\$6,122}{\$75,478} = 8\%$

Part 6 Expense Measurement; The Income Statement **111**

6-55. Third, there are **losses** that are recognized in the current period. These may recognize a reasonably possible decrease in a(n) . . . [asset / liability] because of fire, theft, or other reasons. Or, they may recognize a reasonably possible increase in a(n) . . . [asset / liability] arising from events occurring in the period, such as a law suit.

asset

liability

6-56. The cash payments associated with any of these expenses may have been made in a prior period, or in the current period, or they may be made in a future period, when the . . . [assets / liabilities] are paid.

liabilities

6-57. The balance sheet at the beginning of a period reports assets obtained as a result of e_ _ _ _ _ _ _ _ _ _ s made in earlier periods. Part of these assets will expire and therefore are e_ _ _ _ _ _ s of the current period. The remainder will be carried forward to future periods and will be reported as a_ _ _ _ _ on the balance sheet at the end of the current period.

expenditures

expenses

assets

NOTE: The next set of frames is an extended example of the use of the matching and realization concepts. If you now are comfortable with these concepts, skip to Frame 6-67. If you want additional practice, proceed with Frame 6-58.

AN EXAMPLE OF MATCHING

NOTE: Homes, Inc., is a company that buys and sells houses. Exhibit 7 in your booklet describes some of its transactions during May, June, and July. These events relate to the sale of two houses, House *A* and House *B*.

We will measure the income for Homes, Inc., for the month of June.

6-58. Delivery of the deed to a house is delivery of the ownership of the house. Exhibit 7 states that for House A this happened in _____ (what month?); therefore, revenue from the sale of House A is recognized in _____ (what month?).

June

June

A PACKAGE OF ACCOUNTING REPORTS

6-79. An income statement is a summary of certain changes in
R_____ E_____ that have taken place during
an A_____ P_____.

Retained Earnings

Accounting Period

6-80. Also, a(n) _____ _____ (what account-
ing report?) reports certain changes in Retained Earnings that have taken
place between two _____ _____ (what accounting
reports?).

income statement

balance sheets

6-81. Thus, a useful accounting "report package" consists of a(n)
_____ _____ *at the beginning of* the accounting
period, a(n) _____ _____ *for* the period, and
a(n) _____ _____ *at the end of* the period.

balance sheet

income statement

balance sheet

6-82. Exhibit 8 shows a financial report package consisting of an income
statement and two balance sheets. Exhibit 8 shows that Retained
Earnings on December 31, 19x1, was $_____.

$13,640,000

6-83. During 19x2 profitable operations resulted in net income of
$_____, which increased Retained Earnings by this amount.
(Net income is the **bottom line** on the income statement.)

$6,122,000

6-84. Retained Earnings decreased by $4,390,000, representing a dis-
tribution to the shareholders in the form of _____.

dividends

6-85. As a result, the total Retained Earnings on December 31, 19x2,
was $_____.

$15,372,000 (= $13,640,000 +
$6,122,000 – $4,390,000)

6-59. The amount of revenue for House A is measured by two transactions. List these below and find the revenue for House A.

Date	Transaction*	Amount
May 2	_____ _____	$
June 5	_____	
	Revenue from House A	$

*Write a brief description of the transaction.

Date	Transaction	Amount
May 2	Down payment	$ 16,000
June 5	Payment	144,000
	Revenue from House A	$160,000

6-60. Now consider the costs that are associated with the total revenue from the sale of House A, $160,000, in June. One of these costs was the cost of House A, which was $_____.

$140,000

6-61. Two of the cash payments related specifically to the sale of House A. What were these cash decreases?

Date	Transaction	Amount
May ____	_____	$
July ____	_____	
	Total	$

Date	Transaction	Amount
May 15	Commission	$ 800
July 2	Commission	7,200
	Total	$8,000

6-62. The **matching** concept requires that the costs associated with the revenues of a period be recognized as expenses of that period. Therefore, the two commissions associated with House A, totaling $_____, should be recognized as expenses in _____ (what month?), even though they were not paid in that month.

$8,000

June

6-63. In accordance with the realization concept, the $24,000 down payment received on House B in June . . . [was / was not] revenue in June. It will be revenue in _____ (what month?). Because Homes, Inc., has an obligation to deliver the house, the $24,000 is a(n) . . .[asset / liability] on the balance sheet at the end of June.

was not

July

liability

6-72. Exhibit 8 shows that _____ _____ are subtracted from Gross margin, giving the item _____ _____ _____ .

operating expenses
Income
before taxes

6-73. In accordance with the m__ __ __ __ __ __ __ concept, these expenses include costs related to the c__ __ __ __ __ __ period, and costs that do not benefit f__ __ __ __ __ periods (i.e., losses).

matching
current
future

6-74. The next item on Exhibit 8, _____ _____ _____ _____ , is shown separately because it is an especially important expense.

Provision for
income taxes

6-75. The final item (the bottom line) on an income statement is called _____ _____ (or **net loss**, if expenses were larger than revenues).

Net income

6-76. To arrive at net income, **dividends** . . . [are / are not] subtracted from revenues. Dividends . . . [are / are not] an expense. Dividends are a distribution of earnings to shareholders.

are not
are not

6-77. Revenues are defined as . . . [increases / decreases] in the _____ _____ item on the balance sheet. Expenses are . . . [increases / decreases] in that item. Net income is the difference between _____ and _____ .

increases
retained earnings
decreases
revenues   expenses

6-78. Because income is always supposed to be the *difference* between sales revenue and expenses, a term such as "sales income" . . . [is / is not] a misleading term. However, it is sometimes used.

is

6-64. The matching concept says that general costs of operations during any period are expenses of that period. Thus the $4,000 general costs of operations in June are expenses in _____ (what month?).

June

6-65. Refer to Frames 6-59 through 6-64 and complete the income statement for Homes, Inc., for the month of June, applying the realization concept and the matching concept.

HOMES, INC.

Income Statement for June

Sales Revenue	$ _____	$160,000 (= $16,000 + $144,000)
Expenses:		
Cost of House	$ _____	$140,000
Commission Expense	_____	8,000 (= $800 + $7,200)
General Expense	_____	4,000
Total Expense	_____	152,000
Net Income	$ _____	$8,000

INCOME STATEMENT, JUNE

6-66. According to Exhibit 7, cash transactions in June were:

June	Event	Cash Increases	Cash Decreases
2	Down payment on House B	$ 24,000	
5	Final payment on House A	144,000	
30	Commission on House B		$1,200
	General expenses for June		4,000

Revenue

May payment—A	$ 16,000
June payment—A	144,000
Total Revenue	160,000

Expenses

Cost of house	140,000
May Commission—A	800
June Commission—A	7,200
June Expenses	4,000
Total expenses	152,000
Net Income	$ 8,000

In June, Cash increased by a net amount of $_____. This increase . . . [was approximately the same as / had no relation to] the $8,000 net income for June.

$162,800 (= $168,000 – 5,200)

has no relation to

THE INCOME STATEMENT

6-67. The equity section of a balance sheet shows the two sources of equity capital: (1) the capital supplied by equity investors (i.e., proprietors, partners, shareholders), which is called Paid-in C__ __ __ __ __ __ ; and (2) that portion of the earnings resulting from profitable operations that have been retained in the entity, which is called R__ __ __ __ __ __ __ __ E__ __ __ __ __ __ __ __ .

Capital

Retained
Earnings

6-68. The amount added to Retained Earnings as a result of profitable operations during a period is the **income** of the period. An i__ __ __ __ __ __ statement explains how this income was earned.

income

> **NOTE:** The income statement is also called a Profit and Loss, or Earnings, statement.

6-69. There is no standard format for an income statement. The lower portion of Exhibit 8 shows one common format. The first item on this income statement is _____ _____, which is the amount of products (i.e., goods and services) _____ during the period.

Sales Revenue
delivered to customers, or sold

6-70. The item on the second line is labeled _____ _____ _____. It reports the cost of the goods or services whose revenue is reported on the first line. This is an example of the _____ concept.

cost of
sales
matching

6-71. The difference between sales and cost of sales is called _____ _____ in Exhibit 8. Write an equation, using the terms **cost of sales**, **sales revenue**, and **gross margin**.

Gross
margin

_____ = _____ − _____

gross margin = sales revenue − cost of sales

Exhibits

EXHIBIT 1

GARSDEN COMPANY

**Balance Sheet
as of December 31, 1995
(000 omitted)**

ASSETS		LIABILITIES AND EQUITY	
CURRENT ASSETS		**CURRENT LIABILITIES**	
Cash	$ 1,449	Accounts payable	$5,602
Marketable securities	246	Bank loan payable	1,000
Accounts receivable, net	9,944	Accrued liabilities	876
Inventories	10,623	Estimated tax liability	1,541
Prepaid expenses	389	Current portion of long-term debt	500
Total current assets	22,651	Total current liabilities	9,519
NONCURRENT ASSETS		**NONCURRENT LIABILITIES**	
Property, plant, equipment at cost	$26,946	Long-term debt, less current portion	2,000
Accumulated depreciation	−13,534	Deferred income taxes	824
Property, plant, equipment, net	13,412		
Investments	1,110	Total liabilities	12,343
Patents and trademarks	403		
Goodwill	663	**EQUITY**	
		Common stock	1,000
		Additional paid-in capital	11,256
		Total paid-in capital	12,256
		Retained earnings	13,640
		Total equity	25,896
TOTAL ASSETS	$38,239	TOTAL LIABILITIES AND EQUITY	$38,239

EXHIBIT 2

GLENDALE MARKET

	Assets		Liabilities and Equity	
January 2. Glendale market received $10,000 from John Smith and banked the money.	Cash	$ 10,000	Paid-in capital	$ 10,000
		$ 10,000		$ 10,000
January 3. Glendale Market borrowed $5,000 from a bank, giving a note therefor.	Cash	$ 15,000	Note payable .... Paid-in capital	$ 5,000 10,000
		$ 15,000		$ 15,000
January 4. Glendale Market purchased inventory costing $2,000, paying cash for it.	Cash .... Inventory	$ 13,000 2,000	Note payable .... Paid-in capital	$ 5,000 10,000
		$ 15,000		$ 15,000
January 5. Glendale Market sold merchandise for $300 cash that cost $200.	Cash .... Inventory	$ 13,300 1,800	Note payable .... Paid-in capital .... Retained earnings	$ 5,000 10,000 100
		$ 15,100		$ 15,100
January 6. Glendale Market purchased and received merchandise for $2,000, agreeing to pay within 30 days.	Cash .... Inventory	$ 13,300 3,800	Accounts payable.............. Note payable .... Paid-in capital .... Retained earnings	$ 2,000 5,000 10,000 100
		$ 17,100		$ 17,100
January 7. Merchandise costing $500 was sold for $800, which was received in cash.	Cash .... Inventory	$ 14,100 3,300	Accounts payable.............. Note payable .... Paid-in capital .... Retained earnings	$ 2,000 5,000 10,000 400
		$ 17,400		$ 17,400
January 8. Merchandise costing $600 was sold for $900, the customer agreeing to pay $900 within 30 days.	Cash .... Accounts receivable.......... Inventory	$ 14,100 900 2,700	Accounts payable.............. Note payable .... Paid-in capital .... Retained earnings	$ 2,000 5,000 10,000 700
		$ 17,700		$ 17,700

EXHIBIT 3

ACCOUNTS FOR GREEN COMPANY

ASSETS	LIABILITIES AND EQUITY

Cash

(Dr.)	(Cr.)
Beg. bal. 1,000	

Accounts Receivable

(Dr.)	(Cr.)
Beg. bal. 3,000	

Inventory

(Dr.)	(Cr.)
Beg. bal. 4,000	

Other Assets

(Dr.)	(Cr.)
Beg. bal. 10,000	

Accounts Payable

(Dr.)	(Cr.)
	2,000 Beg. bal.

Paid-in Capital

(Dr.)	(Cr.)
	7,000 Beg. bal.

Retained Earnings

(Dr.)	(Cr.)
	9,000 Beg. bal.

EXHIBIT 4

JOURNAL

19x1		Accounts		Dr.	Cr.
Jan.	2	Cash	√	10,000	
		Paid-in Capital	√		10,000
	3	Cash	√	5,000	
		Notes Payable	√		5,000
	4	Inventory	√	2,000	
		Cash	√		2,000
	5	Cash	√	300	
		Revenues	√		300
	5	Expenses	√	200	
		Inventory	√		200
	6	Inventory	√	2,000	
		Account Payable	√		2,000
	7	Cash	√	800	
		Revenues	√		800
	7	Expenses	√	500	
		Inventory	√		500

EXHIBIT 4 (continued)

JOURNAL

19		Transactions		Dr.	Cr.
Jan.					

EXHIBIT 5

GLENDALE MARKET LEDGER

Cash			Accounts Payable		Revenues	
10,000	2,000			2,000		300
5,000						800
300						
800						

Accounts Receivable			Note Payable		Expenses	
				5,000	200	
					500	

Inventory			Paid-in Capital		Retained Earnings	
2,000	200			10,000		
2,000	500					

EXHIBIT 6 FINANCIAL STATEMENTS

GLENDALE MARKET

Balance Sheet as of January 8

Assets		Liabilities and Equity	
Cash	$14,100	Accounts payable	$
Accounts receivable		Note payable	
Inventory		Paid-in capital	
		Retained earnings	
Total Assets	$	Total Liabilities and Equity	$

Income Statement
for the period January 2–8

Revenues	$
Expenses	
Net Income	$

EXHIBIT 7

TRANSACTIONS OF HOMES, INC.

Date	Event	Effects on Cash
May 2	Able agrees to buy House *A* from Homes, Inc., and makes a $16,000 down payment.	increase $16,000
May 15	Homes, Inc., pays $800 commission to the salesperson who sold House *A* (5% of cash received).	decrease $800
May	Homes, Inc., general expenses for May were $4,400 (assume for simplicity these were paid in cash in May).	decrease $4,400
June 2	Baker agrees to buy House *B*, and makes a $24,000 down payment.	increase $24,000
June 5	Able completes the purchase of House *A*, paying $144,000 cash. Homes, Inc., delivers the deed to Able thereby delivering ownership of the house. (House *A* cost Homes, Inc., $140,000.)	increase $144,000
June 30	Homes, Inc., pays $1,200 commission to the salesperson who sold House *B*.	decrease $1,200
June	Homes, Inc., general expenses for June were $4,000.	decrease $4,000
July 2	Homes, Inc., pays $7,200 additional commission to the salesperson who sold House *A*.	decrease $7,200
July 3	Baker completes the purchase of House *B*, paying $216,000 cash. Homes, Inc., delivers the deed to Baker, thereby delivering ownership of the house. (House *B* costs Homes, Inc., $200,000.)	increase $216,000
July 30	Homes Inc., pays $10,800 commission to the salesperson who sold House *B*.	decrease $10,800
July	Homes Inc., general expenses for July were $4,800.	decrease $4,800

EXHIBIT 8

A "PACKAGE" OF ACCOUNTING REPORTS
(000 omitted)

GARSDEN COMPANY

Condensed Balance Sheet
As of December 31, 19x1

Assets

Current assets	$22,651
Buildings and equipment	13,412
Other assets	2,176
Total Assets	$38,239

Liabilities and Equity

Liabilities	$12,343
Equity:	
Paid-in capital	12,256
Retained earnings	13,640
Total Liabilities and Equity	$38,239

Condensed Balance Sheet
As of December 31, 19x2

Assets

Current assets	$24,062
Buildings and equipment	14,981
Other assets	3,207
Total Assets	$42,250

Liabilities and Equity

Liabilities	$14,622
Equity:	
Paid-in capital	12,256
Retained earnings	15,372
Total Liabilities and Equity	$42,250

Income Statement
For the Year 19x2

Sales revenue	$75,478
Less cost of sales	52,227
Gross margin	23,251
Less operating expenses	10,785
Income before taxes	12,466
Provision for income taxes	6,344
Net income	$6,122

Statement of Retained Earnings

Retained earnings, 12/31/x1	$13,640
Add Net income, 19x2	6,122
	19,762
Less Dividends	4,390
Retained earnings, 12/31/x2	$15,372

EXHIBIT 9

Lewis Fuel Company

	Units	Unit Cost	Total Cost
Beginning inventory, April 1	400	1.00	
Purchase, April 10	300	1.10	
Purchase, April 20	300	1.20	
Total goods available			
Ending inventory, April 30	600		
Cost of sales, April			

FIFO Method

Goods available .... $_____

Ending inventory:

_____ units @ $_____   = $_____

_____ units @ $_____   =   _____

Total 600 units ....   _____

    Cost of sales   _____

LIFO Method

Goods available .... $_____

Ending inventory:

_____ units @ $_____   = $_____

_____ units @ $_____   =   _____

Total 600 units ....   _____

    Cost of sales   _____

Average-Cost Method

Average cost of $_____

                       _____   = _____ cost per unit

                       _____

Goods available $1,090

    Ending inventory 600 units @ $ _____ = _____

    Cost of sales   400 units @ $ _____ = _____

EXHIBIT 10

ARLEN COMPANY
Balance Sheets
(000 Omitted)

Assets

	As of December 31			
	19x2		19x1	
Current assets				
Cash		$ 20		$ 7
Accounts receivable		40		42
Inventory		60		56
Prepaid expenses		20		20
Total current assets		140		125
Noncurrent assets				
Land		$ 30		$ 30
Plant, at cost	$120		$108	
Less accumulated depreciation	70	50	64	44
Goodwill and patents		10		10
Total Assets		230		209

Liabilities and Equity

Current liabilities				
Accounts payable		$ 30		$ 33
Accrued wages		10		6
Income taxes payable		20		20
Total current liabilities		60		59
Noncurrent liabilities				
Mortgage bonds payable		40		34
Total liabilities		100		93
Shareholder equity				
Paid-in capital (4,800 shares outstanding)		$ 60		$ 60
Retained earnings		70		56
Total shareholder equity		130		116
Total Liabilities and Equity		230		209

Income Statement, 19x2
(000 Omitted)

		Percentage
Sales revenue	$300	100.0
Less cost of sales	− 180	60.0
Gross margin	120	40.0
Less depreciation expense	− 6	2.0
other expenses	− 72	24.0
Earnings before interest and taxes	42	14.0
Interest expense	− 5	1.7
Earnings before income taxes	37	12.3
Provision for income taxes	− 13	4.3
Net income	24	8.0
Less dividends	− 10	
Addition to equity	14	

EXHIBIT 11

ARLEN COMPANY
Statement of Cash Flows, 19x2

Cash Flow from Operating Activities

Net income		$ 24
Decrease in accounts receivable	$	
Increase in inventory	(. . . . .)	
Decrease in accounts payable	(. . . . .)	
Increase in accrued wages	. . . . .	
Change in working capital	(. . . . .)	
Depreciation expense	. . . . .	
Total adjustments to net income		. . . . .
Total cash flow from operations		. . . . .

Cash Flow from Investing Activities:

Purchase of Plant and Property		(. . . . .)

Cash Flow from Financing Activities:

Issuance of long-term debt	. . . . .	
Dividends paid	(. . . . .)	(. . . . .)
Net increase in cash and cash equivalents		$. . . . .

Note: Parentheses indicate decreases in cash.

EXHIBIT 12

Independent Auditors' Report

Garsden Company,
its directors and shareholders:

We have audited the balance sheets of Garsden Company as of December 31, 1995 and 1994 and the related income statements and statements of cash flows for each of the three years in the period ended December 31, 1995. These financial statements are the responsibility of the company's management. Our responsibility is to express an opinion on these financial statements based on our audits.

We conducted our audits in accordance with generally accepted auditing standards. These standards require that we plan and perform the audit to obtain reasonable assurance about whether the financial statements are free of material misstatements. An audit includes examining, on a test basis, evidence supporting the amounts and disclosures in the financial statements. An audit also includes assessing the accounting principles used and significant estimates made by management, as well as evaluating the overall financial statement presentation. We believe that our audits provide a reasonable basis for our opinion.

In our opinion, such financial statements present fairly, in all material respects, the financial position of Garsden Company at December 31, 1995 and 1994 and the results of its operations and its cash flows for each of the three years in the period ended December 31, 1995, in conformity with generally accepted accounting principles.

Deane and Burnham

Boston, Massachusetts
February 21, 1996

EXHIBIT 13

ARLEN COMPANY
Factors Affecting Return on Equity

PROFITABILITY

Gross margin
120 ÷ 300 = 40%

Cost of sales
180

+

Other expenses
96

=

Sales revenue
300

–

Expenses
276

=

Net income
24

Profit margin
24 ÷ 300 =
8.0%

=

Return on
equity
(ROE)
18.5%

CAPITAL UTILIZATION

Days'
sales uncollected
40
———
300 ÷ 365
= 49 days

Inventory
turnover
180 ÷ 60
= 3 times

Current ratio
140 ÷ 60 = 2.3

Quick ratio
80 ÷ 60 = 1.3

Current Assets

Cash	20
Accts. receivable	40
Inventory	60
Prepaid expense	20
Total	140

–

Current
liabilities
60

=

Noncurrent
assets
90

+

Working
capital
80

=

Permanent
capital
170

–

Debt
capital
40

=

Equity
capital
130

Debt ratio
40 ÷ 170 =
24%

÷

EXHIBIT 14

SOME COMMON RATIOS

Overall Performance	Numerator	Denominator
1. Return on equity (ROE)		
2. Earnings per share		
3. Price-earnings ratio		
4. Return on permanent capital		
Profitability		
5. Gross margin %		
6. Profit margin %		
7. EBIT margin %		
Capital utilization		
8. Days' sales uncollected		
9. Inventory turnover		
10. Current ratio		
11. Quick ratio		
12. Debt ratio		
13. Capital turnover		

Post Tests

POST TEST 1

1. Give the accounting name for the following terms:

   (a) Things of value owned

       by an entity   _____ .

   (b) Money   _____ .

   (c) Claims of creditors   _____ .

   (d) Claims of investors   _____ .

2. List the two types of sources of funds; list first the type having the stronger claim on an entity's assets:

   Stronger claim   _____

   Lesser claim   _____

3. A balance sheet reports the status of an entity . . . [at a point in time / over a period of time].

4. Give the fundamental accounting equation:

_____ =_____ +_____

5. The above equation is consistent with what concept? ....

6. Why are amounts in accounting stated in monetary terms? ....

7. A balance sheet does not report all the facts about a business. What concept limits the amount or type of information that can be reported? ....

8. Brown Company has $10,000 cash. Fred Foy, its sole owner, withdraws $100 for his own use. Fred Foy is . . . [better off / worse off / no better or worse off] than he was before. Brown Company now has . . . [the same amount of / less] cash. The fact that this event affects Fred Foy differently than it affects Brown Company is an illustration of the _____ concept.

9. The entity concept states that ....

10. On December 31, 19x1, Lewis Corporation has $12,000 in cash on hand and in the bank. It owns other things of value that total $25,000. Its only debt is a bank loan of $10,000. Prepare a balance sheet for Lewis Corporation as of December 31, 19x1, using the form below:

_____

_____		_____	
_____	$ _____	_____	$ _____
_____	_____	_____	_____
Total $ _____		Total $ _____	

Answers for Post Test 1 are on page 31.

1. What is the going-concern concept? ....
....
....
....

2. What is the cost concept? ....
....
....
....

3. Two reasons why nonfinancial assets are usually reported at their cost, rather than at their current market value:

    (a) ....
....

    (b) ....
....

4. An item can be reported as an asset only if it passes three of the following tests. Circle "yes" for these and "no" for the others.

    (a) Item is valuable.   yes   no

    (b) Item is located in a building owned by the entity.   yes   no

    (c) Item is used by the entity.   yes   no

    (d) The entity has ordered the item. yes   no

    (e) Item was acquired at a measurable cost.   yes   no

    (f) Item is owned or controlled by the entity.   yes   no

5. "Goodwill" refers to what things? ....
....
....
....
....

6. An asset is classified as "current" if it is cash or is expected to be converted into cash in the near future, usually within .... [what time period?].

7. Marketable securities are ... [current / non-current] assets. Investments are. . . [current / non-current] assets.

8. Give an example of inventory ....
....
....
....

9. Give an example of a prepaid expense ....
....
....
....
....

10. Give an example of property and plant ....
....
....
....
....

11. On December 31, 19x1, Ace Company owed Chemical Bank $10,000, of which $5,000 is due July 1, 19x2, and $5,000 is due July 1, 19x3. How should this liability be reported?

(a) $10,000 as a current liability

(b) $5,000 as a current liability and $5,000 as a noncurrent liability

(c) $10,000 as a noncurrent liability

12. Parker Company operates a furniture store. On December 31, 19x1, it had 30 desks that it was holding for sale. These would be reported as _____. The desk that is used by the president of Parker Company would be reported as _____.

13. Indicate whether the following statements about the balance sheet of a corporation are true or false.

(a) Assets list all the valuable things owned by the entity .... T   F

(b) The amount reported for the paid-in-capital item is approximately the market value of the stock ..... T   F

(c) The amount reported for total equity is approximately the market value of the corporation's stock .... T   F

(d) Total equity (also called "net worth") shows approximately what the entity is worth .... T   F

(e) Retained earnings is the amount of cash retained in the entity ...... T   F

(f) Land is reported at approximately what it is worth .... T   F

14. Give the numerator and the denominator of the current ratio:

Numerator _____
Denominator

Answers for Post Test 2 are on pages 31–32.

POST TEST 3

1. On January 2, John Brown started the Brown Company. In January, Brown Company did the following things.

(a) It received $5,000 cash from John Brown as its capital.

(b) It borrowed $10,000 from a bank, giving a note therefor.

(c) It purchased $4,000 of inventory for cash.

(d) It sold $2,000 of its inventory for $6,000 to a customer, who paid $3,500 cash and agreed to pay $2,500 within 30 days.

(e) It purchased an auto for $7,000. It paid $2,000 down and gave a note to the automobile dealer for the remaining $5,000.

(f) Brown withdrew $1,000 cash for his personal use.

(g) Brown was offered $10,000 for his equity in the business, but he refused the offer.

Prepare a balance sheet for Brown Company as of the close of business January 31, and prepare an income statement for January.

2. Brown Company's income was $4,000, but its Retained Earnings was only $3,000. Explain the difference.

3. John Brown claims that the inventory as of January 31 is worth $6,000, as shown by the fact that inventory costing $2,000 was actually sold for $6,000. Would you change the balance sheet? _____ Why or why not? ....
....
....
....
....
....
....

Answers for Post Test 3 are on page 32.

POST TEST 4

1. The following transactions occurred in Kay Company in March. Prepare journal entries for each of them in the journal given on the next page:

March 5: Purchased $6,000 of inventory, paying cash.

March 10: Made a $15,000 sale to a customer who paid $6,000 cash and agreed to pay the other $9,000 in 30 days. The merchandise sold had cost $8,000.

2. Post these entries to the ledger accounts on the next page.

3. Prepare closing entries for March in the journal and post these entries.

4. Prepare a balance sheet as of March 31 and an income statement for March.

5. Complete the following table by placing an X in the proper column.

	Debits	Credits
Increases in asset accounts are	_____	_____
Decreases in asset accounts are	_____	_____
Increases in liability accounts are	_____	_____
Decreases in liability accounts are	_____	_____
Increases in equity accounts are	_____	_____
Decreases in equity accounts are	_____	_____
Increases in revenue accounts are	_____	_____
Increases in expense accounts are	_____	_____

6. A critic said that the company had $25,000 cash at the beginning of March and $25,000 at the end of March, and since its cash balance was unchanged, it couldn't be said to have any income in March. Explain why this criticism is incorrect.

19x1	Account	Dr.	Cr.

Cash	Accounts Payable	Revenues
Bal. 25,000	16,000 Bal.	

Accounts Receivable	Paid-in Capital	Expenses
Bal. 11,000	60,000 Bal.	

Inventory	Retained Earnings	Property and Plant
Bal. 40,000	30,000 Bal.	Bal. 30,000

Answers for Post Test 4 are on page 33.

1. What are the two parts to the conservatism concept?

(a) ....

....

(b) ....

....

2. What are the two parts to the materiality concept?

(a) ....

....

(b) ....

....

3. What is the length of the usual accounting period? .... Financial statements prepared for shorter periods are called _____ statements.

4. Cash accounting reports only items that increase or decrease cash. Accrual accounting reports items that change .... (what balance sheet category?), even though these changes may not affect cash.

5. Increases in equity associated with the entity's operations during a period are _____; decreases are _____. The difference between them is labeled _____.

6. The realization concept states that revenues are recognized when goods or services are _____.

7. Hartwell Company manufactures a table in August and places it in its retail store in September. Ralph Smith, a customer, agrees to buy the table in October, it is delivered to him in November, and he pays the bill in December. In what month is the revenue recognized? ....

8. The receipt of cash is a debit to Cash. What is the offsetting credit for the following types of sales transaction?

		Account credited
(a)	Cash received prior to delivery	_____
(b)	Cash received in same period as delivery	_____
(c)	Cash received after the period of delivery	_____

9. Similarly, revenue is a credit entry. What is the offsetting debit when revenue is recognized in each of these periods?

		Account debited
(a)	Revenue recognized prior to receipt of cash	_____
(b)	Revenue recognized in same period as receipt of cash	_____
(c)	Revenue recognized in period following receipt of cash	_____

10. In February, Hartwell Company agrees to sell a table to a customer for $600, and the customer makes a deposit of $100 at that time. The cost of the table is $400. The table is delivered to the customer in March, and the customer pays the remaining $500 in April. Using the journal on the next page, give the entries (if any) that would be made in February, March, and April for both the revenue and expense aspects of this transaction. Be sure to label each entry with the proper month.

Month	Account	Dr.	Cr.

11. At the end of 19x1, Maypo Company had accounts receivable of $200,000, and it estimated that $2,000 of this amount was a bad debt. Its revenue in 19x1, with no allowance for the bad debts, was $600,000.

(a) What account should be debited for the $2,000 bad debt?......................................
....

(b) What account should be credited? ....
....

(c) What amount would be reported as *net* accounts receivable on the balance sheet?

_____

(d) What amount would be reported as revenue on the 19x1 income statement?

_____

12. In 19x2, the $2,000 of bad debt was written off.

(a) What account should be debited for this write off? ....

(b) What account should be credited?..............
....

_____

Answers for Post Test 5 are on page 34.

1. An expenditure occurs in the period in which goods or services are . . . [acquired / consumed]. An expense occurs in the period in which goods or services are . . . [acquired / consumed].

2. For each of the following events, state the month in which the expenditure and the expense should be recorded.

	Month of Expenditure	Expense
(a) Inventory is ordered in February, received in March, paid for in April, delivered to a customer in May; customer pays in June.	_____	_____
(b) Wages are earned in February and paid to employees in March.	_____	_____
(c) Fuel oil was received in February, paid for in March, and consumed in April.	_____	_____
(d) Rent was paid in February for the use of the premises in March.	_____	_____

3. A certain asset was acquired in May. There was therefore an _____ in May. At the end of May, the item was either on hand, or it was not. If it was on hand, it was an _____; if not on hand, it was an _____ in May.

4. Productive assets are . . . [expired / unexpired] costs. Expenses are . . . [expired / unexpired] costs.

5. State the matching concept: ....
....
....
....

6. The three categories of expenses of a period are:

(a) ....
....
....

(b) ....
....
....

(c) ....

7. If Brown Company pays rent prior to the period that the rent covers, the amount is initially reported as a credit to cash and a debit to _____ Rent, which is a(n) . . . [asset / liability] account. If Brown Company pays rent after the period covered, the amount is initially recorded as a debit to Rent Expense and a credit to _____ Rent, which is a(n) . . . [asset / liability] account.

8. A brand new machine owned by Fay Company was destroyed by fire in 19x1. It was uninsured. It had been purchased for $10,000 with the expectation that it would be useful for five years. The expense (i.e., loss) recorded in 19x1 should be . . . [$2,000 / $10,000].

9. What is gross margin? ....
....

10. Give the numerator and the denominator of the gross margin percentage:

Numerator
_____
Denominator

11. The term *net income* means ....

....

....

12. Dividends are not an expense. They are ....

....

13. Give an equation that uses the terms (a) net income, (b) dividends, (c) retained earnings at the beginning of the period, and (d) retained earnings at the end of the period.

_____

_____

Answers for Post Test 6 are on pages 34–35.

POST TEST 7

1. A dealer sells a television set for $800 cash. It had cost $600. Write journal entries for the *four* accounts affected by this transaction.

Dr. _____ _____

   Cr. _____ _____

Dr. _____ _____

   Cr. _____ _____

2. What is meant by the perpetual inventory method? ....

....

....

....

....

3. Write an equation that shows how the cost of sales is determined by deduction ....

....

....

....

4. In the equation above, how were the following amounts found?

   (a) Ending inventory ....

      ....

   (b) Beginning inventory ....

      ....

5. From the information given below, calculate cost of sales for July and inventory at the end of July by the (a) FIFO, (b) LIFO, and (c) average cost methods.

	Quantity of Units	Unit Cost	Total Cost
Inventory, July 1	400	$1.00	
Purchase, July 15	200	1.20	
Total goods available			
Inventory, July 31	300		

Method Used	Cost of Sales	Inventory July 31
(a) FIFO	$	$
(b) LIFO		
(c) Average Cost		

6. In periods of inflation, many companies use the LIFO method in calculating their taxable income. Why? ....

....

....

....

7. A company discovers that the market value of its inventory is $1,000 lower than its cost. What journal entry should it make?

Dr. _____ _____

  Cr. _____ _____

8. In a manufacturing business, what three elements enter into the cost of a manufactured item?

....

9. In what period do period costs become an expense? ....

....

....

10. In what period do product costs become an expense? ....

....

....

11. A given finished item requires $50 of direct materials and 5 hours of direct labor at $8 per hour. The overhead rate is $4 per direct labor hour. At what amount would the finished item be shown in inventory? $_____ .

12. An inventory turnover of 5 is generally . . . [better / worse] than an inventory turnover of 4. Why? ....

....

....

....

Answers for Post Test 7 are on page 35.

POST TEST 8

1. The amount at which a new plant asset is recorded in the accounts includes its purchase price plus what other elements of cost? ....

....

....

....

....

....

2. A plant asset is acquired in 19x1. It is expected to be worn out at the end of 10 years and to become obsolete in five years. What is its service life? _____ years

3. Land is ordinarily not depreciated. Why not?

....

....

4. A plant asset is acquired in 19x1 at a cost of $20,000. Its estimated service life is 10 years, and its estimated residual value is $2,000.

(a) The estimated depreciable cost of the asset is $_____.

(b) If the straight-line depreciation method is used, the depreciation rate for this asset is _____.

(c) What amount will be recorded as depreciation expense in each year of the asset's life? $_____.

(d) What account will be debited and what account will be credited to record this depreciation expense?

Dr ....

   Cr ....

(e) After five years have elapsed, how would this asset be reported on the balance sheet?

    (1)* .... $ _____
    (2)* .... _____
    (3)* .... _____

_____
*Fill in the name below.

(1) ....
(2) ....
(3) ....

5. A machine is purchased on January 1, 19x1, for $20,000, and it has an expected life of five years and no estimated residual value.

(a) If the machine is still in use six years later, what amount of depreciation expense will be reported for the sixth year? ....

(b) What amount, if any, will be reported on the balance sheet at the end of the sixth year?

Answer: (1) It will not be reported.

or

(2) It will be reported as follows:

_____ .... $ _____
_____ .... _____
_____ .... _____

6. A machine is purchased on January 1, 19x1, for $50,000. It has an expected service life of 10 years and no residual value. Eleven years later it is sold for $3,000 cash.

(a) There will be a . . . [loss / gain] of $_____ .

(b) What account will be debited and what account credited to record this amount?

Dr. ....

   Cr. ....

7. Give an example of each of the following types of assets, and give the name of the process used in writing off the cost of the second and third type.

Asset type	Example	Write-off process
Plant asset	_____	Depreciation
Wasting asset	_____	_____
Intangible asset	_____	_____

8. Conoil Company purchased a producing oil property for $10,000,000 on January 1, 19x1. It estimated that the property contained one million barrels of oil and that the property had a service life of 20 years. In 19x1, 40,000 barrels of oil were recovered from the property. What amount should be charged as an expense in 19x1? $ _____ .

9. Wasting assets and intangible assets are reported on the balance sheet in a different way than building, equipment, and similar plant assets. What is this difference? ....
....
....
....

10. In calculating its taxable income, a company tries to report its income as _____ as it can. In calculating its financial accounting income, a company tries to report its income as _____ as it can.

11. As compared with straight-line depreciation, accelerated depreciation writes off . . . [more / the same / less] depreciation in the early years of an asset's life and . . . [more / the same / less] in the later years. Over the whole life of the asset, accelerated depreciation writes off . . . [more / the same / less] total cost as straight-line depreciation.

12. Why do companies usually use accelerated depreciation in tax accounting? ....
....
....
....

13. Assume an income tax rate of 40%. If a company calculated its financial accounting income (before income taxes) in 19x1 as $6 million and its taxable income as $4 million, what amount would it report as income tax expense on its 19x1 income statement? $_____.

14. Fill in the missing name on the following table.

Income tax expense	$100,000
Income tax paid	− 60,000
....	$ 40,000

The $40,000 would be reported on the balance sheet as a(n) . . . [asset / liability].

Answers for Post Test 8 are on page 36.

POST TEST 9

1. The term *working capital* means ....
....
....
....

2. The two principal sources of a company's permanent capital are: ....
.... and
....

3. Bonds obligate the company to ....
.... and also
....
Bonds are . . . [never / sometimes / always] current liabilities.

4. The two principal sources of equity capital are
....
and ....

5. A corporation issues 1,000 shares of $1 par value common stock in exchange for $10,000 cash. Complete the journal entry for this transaction.

Dr. ____Cash____   10,000

  Cr._____   _____

    _____   _____

6. The equity section of a balance sheet is as follows:

Common stock (1,000 shares, no par value) $10,000

Other paid-in capital 20,000

Retained earnings 40,000

      Total equity... $70,000

Circle the correct answer to the following:

  (a) The stated value per share is: $10, $30, $70, can't tell.

  (b) The company received from its shareholders: $10,000, $30,000, $70,000, can't tell.

  (c) The shareholders' equity is worth: $10,000, $30,000, $70,000, can't tell.

  (d) The company has cash of at least: $20,000, $40,000, $70,000, can't tell.

  (e) The company's income to date has totaled: $40,000, at least $40,000, can't tell.

  (f) If the company is liquidated, the shareholders will receive at least: $10,000, $30,000, $70,000, can't tell.

7. The dollar amount reported for common stock on the balance sheet is the amount for the number of shares . . . [authorized / issued]. This amount is called the amount _____ .

8. Kay Company had 200,000 shares of stock authorized. It issued 150,000 shares. It later bought back 10,000 shares. The 10,000 shares are called _____ stock. The total shareholder equity on the balance sheet would be the amount for _____ shares.

9. Preferred shareholders usually have preference as to _____ and also as to

....

....

10. A cash dividend . . . [increases / decreases / does not change] shareholder equity. A stock dividend . . . [increases / decreases / does not change] shareholder equity. A stock dividend . . . [increases / decreases / does not change] the number of shares of stock outstanding.

11. Circle the correct words in the following table, which shows the principal differences between debt capital and equity capital.

	Bonds (Debt)	Stock (Equity)
Annual payments are required.	[Yes / No]	[Yes / No]
Principal payments are required.	[Yes / No]	[Yes / No]
Therefore, risk to the entity is	[High / Low]	[High / Low]
But its cost is relatively	[High / Low]	[High / Low]

12. Corcoran Company has the following permanent capital:

Debt capital .... $ 80,000

Equity capital 20,000

      Total $100,000

  (a) Its debt ratio is _____ %.

  (b) The company is said to be highly

    _____ .

13. Able Company owns 51 percent of the stock of Charlie Company, 50 percent of the stock of David Company, and 49 percent of the stock of Eastern Company. Able Company is the _____ company. The accounts of _____ Company and _____ Company would be consolidated in consolidated financial statements. The equity of the shareholders who own 49 percent of the stock of Charlie Company would be reported as the item _____ on the consolidated balance sheet.

14. Able Company's income statement reported revenue of $1,000,000, of which $10,000 was sales to Charlie Company. Charlie Company's income statement reported revenue of $500,000, of which $20,000 was sales to Able Company. Revenue on the consolidated income statement would be reported as $_____.

Answers for Post Test 9 are on pages 36–37.

POST TEST 10

1. The preparation of a statement of cash flows is . . . [recommended / required] by U.S. accounting rules.

2. The income statement reports net income on a(n) _____ basis. The statement of cash flows adjusts net income to a(n) _____ basis.

3. There are two methods that may be used to prepare the statement of cash flows. What are they? The _____ method and the _____ method.

4. For purposes of the statement of cash flows, "cash" includes not only money, but also cash equivalents. Examples of these equivalents are ....

5. The three sections of the statement of cash flows are:

cash flow from ....

cash flow from ....

cash flow from ....

6. At December 31, 19x1, XYZ Corp. had accounts receivable of $70,000. At December 31, 19x2, the company's accounts receivable balance was $65,000. This $5,000 decrease of accounts receivable . . . [decreased / had no effect on / increased] net income adjusted to a cash basis.

7. Accounts payable for XYZ Corp. decreased by $3,000 between December 31, 19x1 and December 31, 19x2. This change . . . [decreased / had no effect on / increased] net income adjusted to a cash basis.

8. The change in XYZ Corp.'s cash balance from the end of 19x1 to the end of 19x2 . . . [is / is not] part of the changes in current assets used to calculate "cash flow from operating activities."

9. XYZ Corp. had $2,000 in depreciation expense in 19x2. This . . . [was / was not] a cash outflow during that year.

10. To adjust XYZ Corp.'s net income to a cash basis, the $2,000 in depreciation expense should be . . . [added to net income / subtracted from net income / ignored].

11. Complete the "cash flow from operating activities" section of XYZ Corp.'s statement of cash flows. Assume accounts receivable decreased by $5,000, accounts payable decreased by $3,000, and depreciation expense was $2,000. There were no other changes in current assets.

Net income	$50,000
....	_____
....	_____
....	_____
Total cash flow from operations	$_____

Answers for Post Test 10 are on page 37.

POST TEST 11

The following financial statements are to be used in answering questions 1 through 9.

KAY COMPANY

Balance Sheet as of December 31, 19x1

Assets		Liabilities and Equity	
Current assets			
Cash	10	Current liabilities	40
Accounts receivable	30	Noncurrent liabilities ..	80
Inventory	20	Equity	100
Other	40		
Subtotal	100		
Noncurrent assets	120	Total liabilities	
Total assets	220	and equity	220

KAY COMPANY

Income Statement for 19x1

Sales revenue	100
Cost of sales	60
Gross margin	40
Operating expenses	10
Earnings before interest and taxes	30
Interest and income taxes	20
Net income	10

1. The current ratio was:

_____ = ____

2. The inventory turnover was:

_____ = _____ times

3. The profit margin percentage was:

_____ = _____ %

4. The debt ratio (to the nearest percent) was:

_____ = _____ %

5. The return on equity investment was:

_____ = _____ %

6. The EBIT margin was:

_____ = _____ %

7. The capital turnover (to one decimal place) was:

_____ = _____ times

8. The pretax return on permanent capital (to the nearest percent) was

_____ = _____ %

9. The pretax return on permanent capital can also be calculated as:

_____ x _____ = _____ %

Note: This does not exactly check with Question 8 because of rounding.

10. A company can decrease its equity by:

(a) . . . [increasing / decreasing] its assets.

(b) . . . [increasing / decreasing] its liabilities.

11. Liquidity means ....

....

....

....

12. Solvency means ....

....

....

....

13. Give three reasons why accounting cannot provide a complete picture of the status or performance of an entity.

(a) ....

....

(b) ....

....

(c) ....

....

14. Three bases (i.e., standards) that are used in judging an entity's performance are comparisons with

(a) ....

....

(b) ....

....

(c) ....

....

Answers for Post Test 11 are on page 38.

Answers for Post Tests

ANSWERS FOR POST TEST 1

1. (a) assets
   (b) cash
   (c) liabilities
   (d) equity

2. liabilities
   equity

3. at a point in time

4. Assets = Liabilities + Equity

5. Dual-aspect concept

6. This is necessary so that amounts can be added together or subtracted from one another.

7. money-measurement concept

8. no better or worse off; less; entity

9. Accounts are kept for entities as distinguished from the persons who own these entities.

10.   LEWIS CORPORATION

        Balance Sheet as of December 31, 19x1

Assets		Liabilities and Equity	
Cash	$12,000	Liabilities	$10,000
Other assets	25,000	Equity	27,000
Total	$37,000	Total	$37,000

ANSWERS FOR POST TEST 2

1. Accounting assumes that an entity will continue to operate indefinitely.

2. Accounting focuses on the cost of assets, rather than on their market value.

3. (a) Market values are subjective.
   (b) Many assets are not likely to be sold, so there is no need to know their market value.

4. Yes: (a), (e), (f)
   No: (b), (c), (d)

5. A favorable name or reputation purchased by the entity.

6. one year

7. current; noncurrent

8. shoes in a shoe store, groceries in a grocery store

9. prepaid insurance, prepaid rent

10. a building, an item of equipment, automobiles

11. (b)

12. inventory; property and plant

13. All the statements are false. Assets must have been acquired at a measurable cost. Neither the amount reported as paid-in capital nor the amount of total equity has any necessary relation to market value or what the entity is worth. Retained earnings is not cash; cash is an asset on the left-hand side of the balance sheet. Land is reported at its cost, which is not necessarily the same as what it is now worth.

14. $$\frac{\text{Current assets}}{\text{Current liabilities}}$$

ANSWERS FOR POST TEST 3

1.

BROWN COMPANY
Balance Sheet as of January 31

Assets		Liabilities and Equity	
Cash	$11,500	Notes payable	$15,000
Accounts receivable	2,500		
		Paid-in capital	5,000
Inventory	2,000	Retained earnings	3,000
Automobile	7,000		
Total	$23,000	Total	$23,000

BROWN COMPANY
Income Statement for January

Revenue	$6,000
Expense	2,000
Income	$4,000

2. The difference is the $1,000 that Brown withdrew.

3. No. The balance sheet should not be changed because assets are reported at their cost, not their "worth" or market value.

1.

JOURNAL

19x1	Transactions	Dr.	Cr.
March 5	Inventory	6,000	
	Cash		6,000
10	Cash	6,000	
	Accounts receivable	9,000	
	Revenues		15,000
10	Expenses	8,000	
	Inventory		8,000
31	Revenues	15,000	
	Retained earnings		15,000
31	Retained earnings	8,000	
	Expenses		8,000

2. and 3. (The numbers in parentheses refer to the question that the posting answers.)

Cash			Accounts Payable		
Bal. 25,000	6,000(2)			16,000 Bal.	
6,000(2)					
Bal. 25,000			**Paid-in Capital**		
				60,000 Bal.	
Accounts Receivable					
Bal. 11,000			**Retained Earnings**		
9,000(2)			8,000(3)	30,000 Bal.	
Bal. 20,000				15,000 (3)	
				37,000	
Inventory					
Bal. 40,000	8,000 (2)		**Revenues**		
6,000(2)			15,000(3)	15,000(2)	
Bal. 38,000					
			Expenses		
Property and Plant			8,000(2)	8,000 (3)	
Bal. 30,000					

4.

KAY COMPANY

Balance Sheet as of March 31

Assets		Liabilities and Equity	
Cash	$25,000	Accounts payable	$16,000
Accounts receivable	20,000	Paid-in capital ..	60,000
Inventory	38,000	Retained earnings	37,000
Property and Plant	30,000		
Total	$113,000	Total	$113,000

KAY COMPANY

Income Statement for March

Revenues	$15,000
Expenses	8,000
Income	$7,000

5.

	Debits	Credits
Increases in asset accounts are	X	
Decreases in asset accounts are		X
Increases in liability accounts are		X
Decreases in liability accounts are	X	
Increases in equity accounts are		X
Decreases in equity accounts are	X	
Increases in revenue accounts are		X
Increases in expense accounts are	X	

6. Income is an increase in retained earnings, not necessarily in cash. For example, the sales revenue of Kay Company in March was $15,000 and its income was $7,000 even though $9,000 was received in cash.

ANSWERS FOR POST TEST 5

1. (a) Recognize increases in equity only when they are reasonably certain.
   (b) Recognize decreases as soon as they are reasonably possible.

2. (a) Disregard trivial matters.
   (b) Disclose all important matters.

3. one year; interim

4. equity (or retained earnings)

5. revenues; expenses; income

6. delivered

7. November

8. (a) Advances from customers (a liability)
   (b) Revenue
   (c) Accounts receivable

9. (a) Accounts receivable
   (b) Cash
   (c) Advances from customers

10.
February	Cash	100	
	Advances from customers		100
March	Accounts receivable	500	
	Advances from customers	100	
	Revenue		600
March	Expenses	400	
	Inventory		400
April	Cash	500	
	Accounts receivable		500

11. (a) Bad debt expense or Revenue
    (b) Allowance for doubtful accounts
    (c) $198,000
    (d) $598,000

12. (a) Allowance for doubtful accounts
    (b) Accounts receivable

ANSWERS FOR POST TEST 6

1. acquired; consumed

2. (a) March   May
   (b) February   February
   (c) February   April
   (d) February   March

3. expenditure; asset; expense

4. unexpired; expired

5. Costs associated with the revenues of a period are expenses of that period.

6. (a) costs of the goods or services delivered during the period;
   (b) other expenditures that benefit operations of the period;
   (c) losses.

7. Prepaid; asset

Accrued; liability

8. $10,000

9. The difference between sales revenue and cost of sales.

10. Gross margin
Sales revenue

11. The difference between revenues and expenses in an accounting period (*or* the amount by which equity [i.e., retained earnings] increased from operating activities during the period).

12. A distribution of earnings to shareholders.

13. (d) = (c) + (a) – (b)

ANSWERS FOR POST TEST 7

1.

Dr. Cash	800	
Cr. Revenue		800
Dr. Cost of Sales	600	
Cr. Inventory		600

2. A record is kept for each item, showing receipts, issues, and the amount on hand.

3. Cost of sales = beginning inventory + purchases – ending inventory.

4. (a) by taking a physical inventory

(b) same as the ending inventory of the prior period.

5.

	Cost of Sales	Inventory July 31
(a) FIFO	$300	$340
(b) LIFO	340	300
(c) Average cost	320	320

6. It gives a higher cost of sales and hence a lower taxable income.

7.

Dr. Cost of Sales	1,000	
Cr. Inventory		1,000

8. Direct materials, direct labor, and overhead.

9. In the period in which they were incurred.

10. In the period in which the products were sold.

11. $110 [= $50 + $40 + $20]

12. Better. It indicates that less capital is tied up in inventory, and there is less risk that the inventory will become obsolete.

ANSWERS FOR POST TEST 8

1. All costs incurred to make the asset ready for its intended use (such as transportation and installation).

2. five

3. Its service life is indefinitely long.

4. (a) $18,000
(b) 10 percent
(c) $1,800
(d) Dr. Depreciation expense
Cr. Accumulated depreciation
(e) (1) Plant $20,000
(2) Less accumulated
depreciation 9,000
(3) Book value $11,000

5. (a) zero
(b) Machine (or plant) $20,000
Accumulated depreciation 20,000
Book value 0

6. (a) gain; $3,000
(b) Dr. Cash
Cr. Gain on disposition of plant

7.

	Example	Write-off process
Plant asset	machine, building	Depreciation
Wasting asset	coal, oil, minerals	Depletion
Intangible asset	goodwill, trademark	Amortization

8. $400,000 (40,000 barrels @ $10 per barrel)

9. Wasting assets and intangible assets are reported at the net amount only. Plant assets' cost, accumulated depreciation, and net amount (i.e., book value) are reported.

10. low; fairly

11. more; less; the same

12. It reduces taxable income and hence income tax in the early years, so the company has the use of more money in these years.

13. $2,400,000

14. Deferred income tax; liability

ANSWERS FOR POST TEST 9

1. the difference between current assets and current liabilities

2. debt (noncurrent liabilities); equity (shareholder equity)

3. make regular interest payments; repay principal when due;
sometimes (i.e., when due date is within the next year)

4. paid-in capital from shareholders; retained earnings (income not paid out as dividends)

5.

Cash	10,000	
Common stock		1,000
Other paid-in capital		9,000

6. (a) $10

(b) $30,000

(c) can't tell (equity does not represent "worth")

(d) can't tell (equity has no relation to cash)

(e) at least $40,000 (it exceeds $40,000 by the amount of dividends)

(f) can't tell (equity does not show liquidation value)

7. issued; outstanding

8. treasury; 140,000

9. dividends; par value in the event of liquidation

10. decreases; does not change; increases

11.

Yes	No
Yes	No
High	Low
Low	High

12. (a) 80 percent

(b) leveraged

13. parent;

Able Company, Charlie Company (not David Company);

minority interest

14. $1,470,000 (= $1,000,000 − 10,000 + 500,000 − 20,000)

ANSWERS FOR POST TEST 10

1. required

2. accrual; cash (or, cash flow)

3. direct, indirect (*either order*)

4. certificates of deposit; money market accounts

5. operating activities; investing activities; financing activities

6. increased

7. decreased

8. is not

9. was not

10. added to

11.

net income	$50,000
depreciation expense	2,000
decrease in accounts receivable	5,000
decrease in accounts payable	(3,000)
Total cash flow from operations	$54,000

1. $\dfrac{100}{40} = 2.5$

2. $\dfrac{60}{20} = 3$ times

3. $\dfrac{10}{100} = 10\%$

4. $\dfrac{80}{180} = 44\%$

5. $\dfrac{10}{100} = 10\%$

6. $\dfrac{30}{100} = 30\%$

7. $\dfrac{100}{180} = 0.6$ times

8. $\dfrac{30}{180} = 17\%$

9. $0.3 \times 0.6 = 18\%$

10. (a) decreasing
    (b) increasing

11. a company's ability to meet its current obligations

12. a company's ability to meet its long-term obligations

13. Any three of the following.
    - Accounting deals only with events that can be reported in monetary terms.
    - Financial statements report only past events.
    - Balance sheets do not show the market value of certain assets.
    - The accountant and management have some latitude in choosing among alternative ways of recording an event (e.g., LIFO, FIFO, or average cost).
    - Accounting amounts are affected by estimates.

14. (a) its own performance in a previous period(s) (historical)
    (b) other companies in the same industry (external)
    (c) a judgmental standard
    (*any order*)

Glossary and Index

Note: The definitions here are brief. For a fuller discussion and examples, see the frames indicated. References are to parts and frames; e.g. 1:13–17 means part 1, frames 13–17.

Accelerated depreciation A method of depreciation that charges off more of the original cost of a plant asset in the earlier years than in the later years of the asset's service life. Used mainly in calculating taxable income. **(8:36–38, 62–77)**

Account A record in which the changes for a balance sheet or income statement item are recorded. **(4:1–2)**

Account payable The amount that the entity owes to a supplier, not evidenced by a note. **(2:60–61)**

Account receivable An amount that is owed to the business, usually as a result of the ordinary extension of credit to one of its customers. **(2:40)**

Accounting income Income measured according to accounting principles. Contrast with **Taxable income**. **(8:63–65, 72)**

Accounting period The period of time over which an income statement summarizes the changes in equity. Usually the *official* period is one year, but income statements are also prepared for a shorter, or *interim*, period. **(5:3–7)**

Accrual accounting Accounting for revenues in the period in which they are earned and for expenses in the period in which they are incurred. This is normal accounting practice. Cash accounting, which accounts only for cash receipts and payments, is usually not acceptable. **(5:8–19)**

Accrued expense Another term for **Accrued liability**. Note that this is a liability account, not an expense account. **(6:35–39)**

Accrued liability A liability that arises because an expense occurs in a period prior to the related cash payment. Example: accrued wages payable. **(6:37–39)**

Accrued pensions The amount a company owes its employees for the benefits they accumulated under a pension plan. The liability is measured as the benefits accumulate. **(6:40–42)**

Accumulated depreciation An account showing the total amount of an asset's depreciation that has been accumulated to date. It is subtracted from the cost of the asset; the difference is the asset's **Book value**. **(8:43–54)**

Additional paid-in capital The amount paid by investors in excess of the par or stated value of the stock. **(9:26)**

Advances from customers A liability account showing the amount due customers who have paid for goods or services in advance of their delivery. Sometimes called **Deferred revenue**, **Precollected revenue**, or **Unearned revenue**. **(5:46–53)**

Allowance for doubtful accounts The amount of estimated bad debts that is included in accounts receivable. This amount is subtracted from accounts receivable on the balance sheet. **(5:67–73)**

Amortization The process of writing off the cost of intangible assets. Sometimes used as a name for expensing the cost of all assets. **(8:83–84)**

Asset A valuable item that is owned or controlled by the entity and that was acquired at a measurable cost. **(2:26–33)**

Auditing An examination of accounting records by independent, outside public accountants. **(11:6–10)**

Authorized stock The total number of shares of stock that a corporation is permitted to issue. (The total number actually issued is usually a smaller amount.) **(9:29)**

Available for sale The sum of beginning inventory and purchases during the period. **(7:13–15)**

Average-cost method Finding cost of sales by taking the average cost per unit of the beginning inventory plus purchases. **(7:36–37)**

Bad debt An account receivable that never will be collected. **(5:61–64)**

Bad debt expense The estimated amount of bad debts applicable to an accounting period. **(5:60–72)**

Balance The difference between the totals of the two sides of an account. An account has either a debit balance or a credit balance. (See **4:8, 63** for procedure for balancing an account.)

Balance sheet A financial statement that reports the assets, liabilities, and equity of a company at one point in time. Assets are listed on the left and liabilities and equity on the right. (For balance sheet items, *see* **2:22–80**.)

Benchmarking Comparing an entity's performance against the performance of the company thought to be the best managed in the industry. **(11:15)**

Bond A written promise to repay money furnished the business, with interest, at some future date, usually more than one year hence. **(9:8–16)**

Book value The difference between the cost and the accumulated depreciation of a depreciable asset. **(8:46)**

Calendar year The year that ends on the last day of the calendar, December 31. The accounting period for many entities is the calendar year, but some use the **Natural business year**. **(5:5–6)**

Capital In general, the amount of funds supplied to an entity. **(9:1–6)** Also used as the name for **Paid-in capital** in a proprietorship or partnership.

Capital-intensive Characterizes a company that has a large capital investment in relation to its sales revenue. **(11:66)**

Capital lease An item the entity controls by a lease agreement that extends over almost the whole life of the item. A capital lease is an asset. **(8:9–12)**

Capital stock A balance sheet account showing the amount that the **shareholders** contributed in exchange for stock. This plus retained earnings equals equity in a corporation. **(9:17–39)**

Capital turnover A ratio obtained by dividing annual sales by the amount of **permanent capital.** **(11:65–66)**

Capital utilization, tests of **(11:29–50)**

Cash The name for money, whether in currency or in a bank account. **(2:36–37)**

Cash flow statement A financial statement reporting the sources and uses of cash during an accounting period. **(Part 10)**

Cash-basis accounting An accounting system that does not use the accrual basis; it records only cash receipts and payments. Usually not an acceptable basis for accounting. **(5:16–19)**

Charge (verb) To debit an account.

Claim Amount owed to creditors or others who have provided money or have extended credit to a business. **(1:13,14)**

Closing entries Journal entries that transfer the balances in revenue and expense accounts for a period to retained earnings. **(4:52–61)**

Common stock Stock whose owners are not entitled to preferential treatment with regard to dividends or to the distribution of assets in the event of liquidation. **(9:25–32)** Its book value is not related to its market value. **(9:33–35)**

Comparisons, bases of Performance can be compared with past performance, with performance of other entities, or with a judgmental standard. (*See* **11:14–17**)

Concepts *See* **6:90–98** for a summary of accounting concepts.

Conservatism concept Recognize increases in equity only when they are reasonably certain; recognize decreases as soon as they are reasonably possible. **(5:20–24)**

Consolidated statements Financial statements prepared for a whole corporate family as an entity. The family consists of a **Parent** and its **Subsidiaries.** **(9:75–88)**

Contra-asset account An account whose balance is subtracted from that of the corresponding asset account. **(5:67)**

Conversion cost The labor and overhead costs of converting raw material into finished products. **(7:49)**

Cost A monetary measure of the amount of resources used for some purpose. (For product cost, *see* **7:55–63**. For acquisition cost, *see* **8:5–8**. *See also* **Period costs.**)

Cost accounting The process of identifying and accumulating manufacturing costs and assigning them to goods in the manufacturing process. **(7:54)**

Cost concept Accounting focuses on the cost of assets, rather than on their market value. **(2:6–15)**

Cost of goods sold Same as **Cost of sales.**

Cost of sales Cost of the same products whose revenues are included in sales revenue. **(Part 7)**

Credit (noun) The right-hand side of an account or an amount entered on the right-hand side of an account. Abbreviated as Cr. **(4:26–31)**

Credit (verb) To make an entry on the right-hand side of an account. Rules for debit and credit are summarized in **4:42.**

Creditor A person who lends money or extends credit to an entity. **(1:12–14)**

Current assets Cash and assets that are expected to be converted into cash or used up in the near future, usually within one year. **(2:35–48)**

Current liabilities Obligations that become due within a short period of time, usually one year. **(2:58–65)**

Current ratio The ratio obtained by dividing the total of the current assets by the total of the current liabilities. **(2:66–67; 11:41–42)**

Days' sales uncollected The number of days of sales that are tied up in accounts receivable as of the end of the accounting period. Sales per day is found by dividing annual credit sales by 365, and accounts receivable is divided by sales per days to find the days' receivables. **(5:76–79; 11:36)**

Debit (noun) The left-hand side of an account or an amount entered on the left-hand side of an account. Abbreviated as Dr. **(4:26–31)**

Debit (verb) To make an entry on the left-hand side of an account. Rules for debit and credit are summarized in **4:42.**

Debt capital The capital raised by the issuance of debt securities, usually bonds. **(9:7–9)** For differences between debt capital and equity capital, *see* **9:60–74.**

Debt ratio The ratio of debt capital to total permanent capital. **(9:76–78; 11:45–48)**

Deduction method Finding cost of sales by adding the beginning inventory and purchases and subtracting the ending inventory. **(7:9–18)**

Deferred income taxes The difference between the actual income tax for the period and income tax expense. **(8:73–77)**

Deferred revenue *See* **Advances from customers.**

Depletion The process of writing off the cost of a wasting asset, such as natural gas, coal, oil, or other minerals. **(8:78–82)**

Depreciable cost The difference between the cost of a plant asset and its estimated residual value. **(8:28)**

Depreciation expense The portion of the estimated net cost of plant assets (e.g., buildings, equipment) that becomes an expense in a given accounting period. **(6:34; 8:13–54)** (For accounting entries, *see* **8:39–54**. For depreciation in calculating taxable income, *see* **8:62–77**.)

Depreciation rate The percentage of the cost of an asset that is an expense each year. In the straight-line method, the rate is 1 divided by the service life. **(8:33–34)**

Direct labor or materials The labor or material that is used directly on a product. **(7:51–53)**

Disposition of plant, gain or loss on The difference between book value and the amount actually realized from a sale of a plant asset. **(8:55–57)**

Dividend The funds generated by profitable operations that are distributed to shareholders. Dividends are *not* an expense. **(6:76; 9:40–59)**

Double-entry system A characteristic of accounting in which each transaction recorded causes at least two changes in the accounts.

Dual-aspect concept The total assets of an entity always are equal to its total liabilities and equity. **(1:27–30)**

Earnings Another term for **Net income**. **(3:54)**

Earnings before interest and taxes (EBIT) An amount used in calculating return on permanent capital. **(11:61–63)**

Earnings per share A ratio obtained by dividing the total earnings for a given period by the number of shares of common stock outstanding. **(11:53)**

EBIT margin Earnings before interest and income taxes as a percentage of sales revenue. **(11:62)**

Entity A business or other organization for which a set of accounts is kept. **(1:2, 3)**

Entity concept Accounts are kept for entities, rather than for the persons who own, operate, or are otherwise associated with those entities. **(1:50–55)**

Entry The accounting record made for a single transaction. **(4:43, 44)**

Equation, fundamental accounting Assets = Liabilities + Equity. **(1:27–30)**

Equity Capital supplied by (1) equity investors and (2) the entity's retained earnings. Also, claims against the entity by equity investors. **(2:71–80; 9:17–46)**

Equity capital The capital supplied by owners, who are called equity investors. **(9:17–22)** For differences between debt capital and equity capital, *see* **9:60–74**.

Expenditure The decrease in an asset or increase in a liability associated with the acquisition of goods or services. Do not confuse with **Expense**, which represents the use of goods and services and which may occur after the expenditure. **(6:3–14)**

Expense A decrease in equity resulting from operations during an accounting period; that is, resources used up or consumed during an accounting period. **(3:46)** Example: wage expense. **(6:3–14)** For assets that will become expenses, *see* **6:17, 24–34**; for expenses that create liabilities, *see* **6:35–39**.

Expensing The process of charging the cost of an asset to expense.

Expired cost Another name for **Expense**. **(6:15–18)**

External basis of comparison Comparing an entity's performance with the performance of other entities. **(11:15)**

Face amount The total amount of a loan that must be repaid, specified on the face of a bond. **(9:9)**

FIFO (first-in, first-out) method Finding cost of sales on the assumption that the oldest goods (those first in) were the first to be sold (first out). **(7:28–32)**

Financial accounting income Income as measured according to accounting principles. **(8:63, 72)**

Financial statements *See* the three required financial statements: balance sheet, income statement, cash flow statement.

Fiscal year *See* **Natural business year**.

Fixed assets Tangible, **noncurrent assets (8:3)**

Free cash flow The amount remaining after special needs for cash in the coming period is subtracted from the cash flow expected from operating activities. (See note after 10-67)

Fringe benefits Benefits, principally monetary, beyond wages; owed to an employee because of his or her service to the company. **(6:40–44)**

Gain (or loss) on disposition of plant *See* 8:55–57.

Going-concern concept Accounting assumes that an entity will continue to operate indefinitely. **(2:1–5)**

Goods available for sale The sum of the beginning inventory plus purchases during the period. **(7:13–15)**

Goodwill An intangible asset; the amount paid in excess of the value of a company's identifiable net assets, representing an amount paid for a favorable location or reputation. Goodwill is an asset only if it was purchased. **(2:56)**

Gross margin The difference between sales revenue and cost of sales. **(6:71)**

Gross margin percentage Gross margin as a percentage of sales revenue. **(6:87–88; 11:22–25)**

Historic cost concept *See* **Cost concept**.

Historical basis of comparison Comparing an entity's performance with its own performance in the past. **(11:14)**

Income The amount by which equity increased as a result of operations during a period of time. **(3:37–41, 3:54)**

Income statement A statement of revenues and expenses, and the difference between them, for an accounting period; a flow report. It explains the changes in equity associated with operations of the period. **(3:41–56; 6:67–78)**

Income summary A temporary ledger account used to calculate net income.

Income tax A tax levied as a percentage of taxable income. *See* **Taxable income**.

Intangible asset An asset that has no physical substance, such as **goodwill** or the protection provided by an insurance policy. **(2:45–46, 54; 6:26–31; 8:83–85)**

Interest The amount paid for the use of money. A loan requires payment of both interest and **Principal**. **(9:12–16)**

Interest expense The entity's cost of using borrowed funds during an accounting period. **(9:12–16)**

Interest revenue Revenue earned from permitting someone to use the entity's money. Revenue from the "rental" of money. Often but erroneously called interest income. **(5:56–57)**

Interim statements Financial statements prepared for a period shorter than one year, such as a month or a quarter. **(5:4)**

Intrafamily transactions Transactions between the corporations in a consolidated family. These transactions are eliminated in preparing consolidated financial statements. **(9:79–82)**

Inventory (noun) Goods being held for sale, and material and partially finished products that will be sold upon completion. (**2:42**) For inventory valuation methods, *see* **Part 7**.

Inventory (verb) To conduct a physical observation and count of inventory. (**7:16–17**)

Inventory turnover A ratio that shows how many times inventory was totally replaced during the year; calculated by dividing the average inventory into cost of sales. (**7:67–71; 11:38**)

Investments Securities that are held for a relatively long period of time and are purchased for reasons other than the temporary use of excess cash. They are noncurrent assets.

Issued stock The shares of stock that have been issued. Issued stock less **Treasury stock** equals **Outstanding stock**. (**9:29**) Contrast with **Authorized stock**.

Journal A record in which transactions are recorded in chronological order. It shows the accounts to be debited or credited and the amount of each debit and credit. Transactions are **Posted** to the **ledger**. (**4:44–45**)

Judgmental basis of comparison Comparing an entity's performance with our personal judgment. (**11:16**)

Land, life of *See* **8:13**.

Lease An agreement under which the owner of property permits someone else to use it. The owner is the *lessor*. The user is the *lessee*. (**8:9–12**)

Ledger A group of accounts. Entries are posted to the ledger from the **journal**. (**4:43**)

Leverage The proportion of **debt capital** to total **permanent capital**. A company that obtains a high proportion of its permanent capital from debt is said to be *highly leveraged*. (**9:70–71**)

Liability The equity or claim of a **creditor**. (**1:12; 2:58–70**)

LIFO (last-in, first-out) method Finding cost of sales on the assumption that the goods most recently purchased (last in) were the first to be sold (first out). (**7:33–35**)

Limitations on financial statement analysis (**11:1–5**)

Liquidity An entity's ability to meet its current obligations. Often measured by the **current ratio**. (**11:74**)

Losses Expenses resulting from assets whose future benefit has expired during a period, for example, from fire or theft, and liabilities occurring in a period, for example, from lawsuits. (**6:50–52**) *See also* **Gain (or loss)**.

Manufacturing company A company that converts raw materials into finished, salable products and then sells these products. (**7:47–50**) For accounting for inventory in a manufacturing company, *see* **7:47–66**.

Manufacturing overhead *See* **Production overhead cost**.

Market value The amount for which an asset can be sold in the marketplace. (**2:7–9**)

Marketable securities Securities that are expected to be converted into cash within a year; a current asset. (**2:39, 2:54**)

Matching concept Costs that are associated with the revenues of a period are expenses of that period. (**6:19–23**) For matching of income tax expense, *see* **8:73–77**.

Materiality concept Disregard trivial matters, but disclose all important matters. (**5:25–32**)

Measurable cost An item whose amount is known, usually because the item was acquired from an outside party. (**2:30**)

Merchandising company A company that sells goods that it has acquired from other businesses; for example, a retail store or a wholesaler. (**7:47–49**)

Minority interest The equity of those shareholders in a subsidiary other than the equity of the parent. Reported as an equity item on the consolidated balance sheet. (**9:85**)

Modified Accelerated Cost Recovery System A method of accelerated depreciation used for income tax calculations. (**8:66–72**)

Monetary assets Cash and promises by an outside party to pay the entity a specified amount of money. (**5:74–75**)

Money-measurement concept Accounting records report only facts that can be expressed in monetary amounts. Accounting therefore does not give a complete record of an entity. (**1:44–47**)

Mortgage A pledge of real estate as security for a loan. (**3:30**)

Mortgage payable The liability for a loan that is secured by a mortgage. (**3:30**)

Natural business year A year that ends on the day that activities are at a relatively low level. For some entities, the accounting period is the natural business year, rather than the calendar year. (**5:6**) Also called the **fiscal year**.

Net The amount remaining after something has been subtracted from a gross amount. Example: accounts receivable, net. (**5:70**)

Net income The amount by which total revenues exceed total expenses for an account period; the "bottom line." (**6:75**)

Net income percentage Net income expressed as a percentage of sales revenue. (**6:89**)

Net loss The amount by which total expenses exceed total revenues in an accounting period; negative net income. (**6:75**)

Net worth Another (but misleading) name for equity. (**9:45**)

Nonbusiness organizations Municipalities, hospitals, religious organizations, and other organizations that are not operated for the purpose of earning a profit. (**1:56**)

Noncurrent asset An asset that is expected to be of use to the entity for longer than one year. (**2:49–57**)

Noncurrent liability A claim that does not fall due within one year. Similar to **Debt capital**. (**2:68–70**)

No-par-value stock   Common stock that does not have a par value. It is recorded at its **Stated value**. (9:28)

Note   A written promise to pay. (3:10)

Note payable   A liability evidenced by a written promise to pay. (3:10)

Note receivable   An amount owed to the entity that is evidenced by a **promissory note**. (2:41)

Obsolescence   A loss in the usefulness of an asset because of the development of improved equipment, changes in style, or other causes not related to the physical condition of the asset. It is one cause of depreciation; the other cause is wearing out. (8:20)

Opinion or **Opinion letter**   The report in which the auditor gives his or her opinion as to the fairness of the financial statements. (11:7–10)

Other post-employment benefits (OPEB)   Health care or other fringe benefits, besides pensions, owed to an employee after his or her employment ends. (6:43–44)

Outstanding stock   Shares of stock held by investors. Consists of **Issued stock** less **Treasury stock**. (9:30)

Overhead   *See* **Production overhead cost**.

Overhead rate   A rate used to allocate overhead costs to products. (7:64–66)

Owners' equity   The claims of owners against the assets of a business. In a corporation, owners' equity consists of capital stock plus retained earnings. (2:71–76)

Package of accounting reports   *See* **Report package**.

Paid-in capital   The amount paid by investors in exchange for stock. The amount in excess of the stock's par or stated value is called **Additional paid–in capital**. (2:72–73; 9:26)

Par value   The specific amount printed on the face of some stock certificates. No longer significant in accounting. (9:25)

Parent   A corporation that controls one or more other corporations because it owns more than 50 percent of their stock. The controlled corporations are its **Subsidiaries**. (9:75)

Partnership   An unincorporated business with two or more owners. (1:55)

Patent   A grant that gives an inventor the exclusive right, for 17 years, to produce and sell an invention. (2:55)

Percentage   A number obtained by dividing one number by another (which is the base, or 100 percent), and multiplying by 100. Income statement items are often expressed as percentages of sales revenue.

Performance, measures of   For overall measures of performance, *see* **11:11–20**; for tests of capital utilization, *see* **11:29–52**; for other measures, see **11:53–68**.

Period costs   Costs associated with general sales and administrative activities. Contrast with **Product costs**. (7:55–63)

Permanent account   An account for a balance sheet item, so called because it is not closed at the end of the accounting period. Contrast with **Temporary account**. (4:62)

Permanent capital   The sum of noncurrent liabilities and equity. (9:6–9,17–24)

Perpetual inventory   A record of the cost of each item in inventory showing the quantity and the cost of receipts, issues, and the amount on hand, updated nearly simultaneously for each day's activity. (7:5–6)

Physical inventory   The amount of inventory currently on hand, obtained by making a physical count. (7:16–17)

Plant assets   All tangible, noncurrent assets except land. (2:52; 8:4) For acquisition of plant assets, *see* 8:5–8. For sale of plant assets, *see* 8:55–57.

Posting   The process of transferring transactions from the **journal** to the **ledger**. (4:49, 50)

Precollected revenue   See **Advances from customers**.

Preferred stock   Stock whose owners have a preferential claim over common stockholders for dividends and for assets in the event of liquidation. (9:36–39)

Prepaid expenses   The general name for intangible assets that will become expenses in future periods when the services they represent are used up. Example: prepaid insurance. (2:47; 6:27–31)

Price-earnings ratio   A ratio obtained by dividing the average market price of the stock by the earnings per share. (11:56–58)

Principal   The amount that must be repaid on a loan. The total repayment consists of principal plus **Interest**. (9:12)

Product   Goods or services sold or to be sold. (Sometimes refers only to tangible goods.)

Product costs   The direct materials, direct labor, and production overhead costs of a product. Contrast with **Period costs**. (7:55–63)

Production overhead cost   Product costs other than direct materials and direct labor. Includes, for example, supervision, building maintenance, and power. (7:52–53) *See also* **Overhead rate**.

Profit   Another name for **Income**. (3:54)

Profit and loss statement   Another name for **Income statement**. (6:65)

Profit margin percentage   Net income divided by sales revenue. (11:26)

Promissory note   A written acknowledgement of the amount that a borrower owes a creditor. A note receivable on the books of the lender and a note payable on the books of the borrower. (2:41)

Proprietorship   An unincorporated business with a single owner. (1:55; 3:5)

Ratio The result of dividing one number by another. *See*, for example, **Current ratio**.

Realization concept Revenue is recognized when goods or services are delivered, in an amount that is reasonably certain to be realized. **(5:33–40)**

Reasonably certain A criterion for deciding on the amount to be entered for an asset or liability account. **(5:61)**

Recognition The act of recording a revenue or expense item as being applicable to a given accounting period. Revenue recognition is governed by the **realization concept**. **(5:33–59)**

Rental revenue Revenue earned from permitting someone to use a building or other property. **(5:55–57)**

Report, Auditors' *See* **Opinion**.

Report package Consists of a balance sheet for the beginning and end of the accounting period and an income statement for the accounting period. **(6:79–82)**

Residual claim The claim of equity investors. **(1:18)**

Residual value The amount for which a company expects to be able to sell a plant asset for at the end of its service life. **(8:25–26)**

Retained earnings The increase in equity that has resulted from the operations of the entity. It is an equity item, not an asset. **(2:77–79; 6:80–84; 9:40–46)**

Return on equity (ROE) A ratio obtained by dividing net income by the amount of equity. **(11:12–28)**

Return on investment (ROI) Earnings before interest and taxes divided by noncurrent liabilities plus equity. (Some people calculate it in other ways.) **(11:59–63)**

Return on permanent capital Another name for **return on investment**. **(11:59–63)**

Revenue The increase in owners' equity resulting from operations during a period of time, usually from the sale of goods or services. **(3:45, 47)** For measuring the amount of revenue, *see* **5:60–73**.

Sales income Sometimes used to mean **Sales revenue**; a misleading term because income is the difference between sales revenue and expenses.

Sales revenue Revenue from the delivery of goods or services. **(5:39)**

Security An instrument such as a stock or bond. Securities give the entity that owns them valuable rights from the entity that issued them. **(2:38–39)**

Service An intangible product. Examples are personal services, rent, and insurance protection. **(5:54–57)**

Service life The period of time over which an asset is estimated to be of service to the entity. **(8:16–17, 21)**

Service revenue Revenue from the performance of services. **(5:54–57)**

Shareholder equity The equity section of a corporation's balance sheet. **(9:23)** Also called stockholder equity. *See also* **Equity**.

Shareholders The owners of a corporation. Also referred to as **stockholders**. **(9:23)**

Shrinkages Goods that have been stolen or spoiled and hence are no longer in inventory. **(7:19)**

Sole proprietorship *See* **Proprietorship**.

Solvency An entity's ability to meet its long-term obligations. Often measured by the **Debt ratio**. **(11:75)**

Specific identification method A way of calculating cost of sales by keeping track of the specific item (e.g., an automobile) sold. **(7:2)**

Stated value The amount at which **no-par-value stock** is reported on the balance sheet, as voted by the directors. **(9:28)**

Statement of financial position Another name for a **Balance sheet**.

Stock *See* **Capital stock**, **common stock**, **preferred stock**.

Stock dividend A dividend consisting of shares of stock in the corporation. **(9:49–54)**

Stock split An exchange of the number of shares of stock outstanding for a substantially larger number. **(9:55–59)**

Stockholders *See* **Shareholders**.

Straight-line depreciation A depreciation method that charges off an equal fraction of the estimated **depreciable cost** of a plant asset over each year of its service life. **(8:31–35)**

Subsidiary A corporation that is controlled by another corporation, the **parent**, which owns more than 50 percent of its stock. **(9:75–76)**

T-account The simplest version of an account. **(4:2–6)**

Tangible assets Assets that can be touched; they have physical substance. Noncurrent tangible assets are often referred to as property, plant, and equipment. **(2:50–53)**

Tax accounting principles (See **8:62–72**).

Tax depreciation The depreciation used in calculating taxable income. **(8:62–77)**

Taxable income The amount of income subject to income tax, computed according to the rules of the Internal Revenue Service. For difference between taxable income and accounting income and the treatment of depreciation, *see* **8:62–77**.

Temporary account A revenue or expense account. A temporary account is closed at the end of each accounting period. Contrast with **Permanent account**. **(4:62)**

Trademark A distinctive name for a manufactured good or a service. **(2:55)**

Transaction An event that is recorded in the accounting records; it always has at least two elements. **(3:15–18)**

Treasury stock Previously issued stock that has been bought back by the corporation. **(9:30)**

Unearned revenue   *See* **Advances from customers**.

Unexpired cost   The cost of assets on hand now that will be consumed in future accounting periods. **(6:15–18)**

Units-of-production method   A depreciation method. A cost per unit of production is calculated, and depreciation expense for a year is found by multiplying this unit cost by the number of units that the asset produced in that year. **(8:30)**

Wasting assets   Natural resources, such as coal, oil, and other minerals. The process of charging wasting assets to expense is called **depletion**. **(8:78)**

Working capital   The difference between current assets and current liabilities. **(9:4)**

Write down   To reduce the cost of an item, especially inventory, to its market value. **(7:43–46)**

Write-off of bad debt   To remove a bad debt from Accounts Receivable. **(5:71–73)**

Zero coupon bonds   Bonds that do not pay interest. Buyers purchase these for less than their **principal** amount; the issuer promises to pay the full principal amount on the due date. **(9:16)**